JIM CROW NETWORKS

A VOLUME IN THE SERIES
Studies in Print Culture and the History of the Book

EDITED BY
Greg Barnhisel, Robert A. Gross, Joan Shelley Rubin,
and Michael Winship

JIM CROW NETWORKS

African American Periodical Cultures

EURIE DAHN

University of Massachusetts Press
Amherst and Boston

Printed in the United States of America

ISBN 978-1-62534-526-4 (paper); 525-7 (hardcover)

Designed by Deste Roosa
Set in Fairfield and Bodoni
Printed and bound by Books International, Inc.

Cover design by Cheryl Carrington
Cover art: Tree Concept Illustration, iStock.com/filo

Library of Congress Cataloging-in-Publication Data
Names: Dahn, Eurie, author.
Title: Jim Crow networks : African American periodical cultures / Eurie Dahn.
Identifiers: LCCN 2020019221 | ISBN 9781625345257 (hardcover) | ISBN 9781625345264 (paperback) | ISBN 9781613767757 (ebook) | ISBN 9781613767764 (ebook)
Subjects: LCSH: African American periodicals—History—20th century. | African American newspapers—History—20th century. | American literature—African American authors—Publishing—History. | African Americans and mass media. | African Americans—Legal status, laws, etc. | Racism—United States.
Classification: LCC PN4882.5 .D35 2021 | DDC 071/.308996073—dc23
LC record available at https://lccn.loc.gov/2020019221

British Library Cataloguing-in-Publication Data
A catalog record for this book is available from the British Library.

An earlier version of chapter two was previously published as "'Unashamedly Black': Jim Crow Aesthetics and the Visual Logic of Shame," *MELUS* 39, no. 2 (2014): 93–114. This article is used by permission of Oxford University Press. A briefer version of chapter four appeared as "*Cane* in the Magazines: Race, Form, and Global Periodical Networks," *Journal of Modern Periodical Studies* 3, no. 2 (December 2012): 119–35, copyright © 2012 Pennsylvania State University Press. This article is used by permission of The Pennsylvania State University Press.

FOR HIEP

CONTENTS

PREFACE

As I was completing the writing of this book, the *Chicago Defender* newspaper ceased existing as a print publication. At the same time, *Ebony* magazine, which was facing an uncertain future after experiencing the turmoil of bankruptcy proceedings in recent years, sold its photography archive, though happily to a consortium dedicated to keeping the archive available to the public. Other periodicals discussed in *Jim Crow Networks: African American Periodical Cultures* have been confronted with the various pressures on print journalism that have marked the opening of the twenty-first century, pressures that are magnified for the African American press, which has always faced challenges in terms of circulation and longevity. Historically significant publications such as the *Crisis* and the *New York Amsterdam News* have had to make significant budget cuts and have held on largely through shifting their focus toward their digital editions and websites.

When the news about the *Defender* broke, multiple friends and colleagues sent me links to articles. They know my scholarly obsessions too well. That newspaper, which I first encountered on microfilm in a library basement one summer, was the spark that led to my deep and abiding interest in periodical studies, particularly in relation to the Black press. *Jim Crow Networks* tracks the interracial and intraracial periodical and literary networks that endeavored to resist racial violence during the first half of the twentieth century. The gradual deaths of these vestiges of Jim Crow networks mark the end of an era and certainly highlight the precarity of the Black press. However, as I discuss in my conclusion, these networks extend forward into the future, into the twenty-first-century's media networks of activism. My concern then, ultimately, is not to eulogize the Black press but to draw out its living legacy and to trace its transformations and adaptations.

It is perhaps predictable to say that a book on networks could not have been written without my own networks of support, but it is no less true. I could not have written this book without the conversations I have had with Jeannie Britton, Lori Cole, Susan Cumings, Lisa Kannenberg, Sean Latham, Angela Ledford, Silvia Mejía, David Morrow, Gayle Rogers, Rone Shavers, Ryane Straus, Brian Sweeney, Kenneth Warren, and Bridgett Williams-Searle. Their support, various kindnesses, and intellects have sustained me and made this book possible. Mark Gaipa, Tim Ryan, Jay Watson, Robert Weems, Jr., and Teresa Zackodnik have been exceedingly helpful at different moments. At a critical point, Gerry Lorentz, the dean of the School of Arts and Humanities at the College of Saint Rose, provided generous support for this project—thank you. My work has benefited from the discussions I have had at the National Endowment for the Humanities (NEH) Magazine Modernisms summer seminar, at numerous conferences and presentations, with my colleagues, and, finally, with my lovely students. Thank you all.

My materials—the periodicals—came to me as a hodgepodge—as hard copies tracked down on eBay and at flea markets, bound volumes found in library stacks, reprints, unbound issues in archives, full-color issues from digital archives, and even microfilm. The study of periodicals requires these multiple approaches because the archives have many gaps; the archive of Black print in particular has been historically undervalued and confronted with preservation challenges. Ultimately, this is a book that could not have been written without the work of librarians and archivists, past and present, with physical and digital resources. In particular, I thank the Beinecke Rare Book and Manuscript Library at Yale University, the Joseph Regenstein Library at the University of Chicago, the New York Public Library, the Modernist Journals Project, the Blue Mountain Project, the McFarlin Library at the University of Tulsa, the Howard Gotlieb Archival Research Center at Boston University, the Tamiment Library and Robert F. Wagner Labor Archives at the New York University Library, the HathiTrust Digital Library, the Vivian G. Harsh Research Collection at the Chicago Public Library, and the Neil Hellman Library at the College of Saint Rose (particularly the excellent Interlibrary Loan Services).

Aside from the NEH summer seminar, my work has been supported by a Short-Term Fellowship in African American Studies from the Black Metropolis Research Consortium, a travel award from the Eastern New

York chapter of the Association of College and Research Libraries, and various forms of professional development at the College of Saint Rose (particularly the School of Arts and Humanities and the Office of the Provost), including a Center for Citizenship, Race, and Ethnicity Studies fellowship, a professional development grant, and a sabbatical leave that occurred at a pivotal moment in the project. An earlier version of chapter two was published as "'Unashamedly Black': Jim Crow Aesthetics and the Visual Logic of Shame," *MELUS* 39, no. 2 (2014): 93–114, while a briefer version of chapter four appeared as "*Cane* in the Magazines: Race, Form, and Global Periodical Networks," *Journal of Modern Periodical Studies* 3, no. 2 (December 2012): 119–35. My thanks to the editors and anonymous readers of these journals and to Oxford University Press and Penn State University Press.

The anonymous readers of my manuscript have helped sharpen my claims, and I very much appreciate their generous and keen-eyed comments. I am also grateful for the University of Massachusetts Press and the way various people shepherded my manuscript through the publishing process. My thanks go first to Brian Halley, who is a clear, rigorous, and supportive editor. I also appreciate the thoughtful comments from the series editors of the Studies in Print Culture and the History of the Book. Thank you also to Rachael DeShano for her guidance in the production process and to Julie Shilling for her detailed copyediting.

My love and thanks to my family: my mother, Molly Dahn, and my late father, Kevin Dahn; Junie Dahn and Seojin Kang; and Yumie Dahn and Ryan Rominger. Much thanks also to my husband's family—Lan Thai, Hogan Hoang, the Bievenues, and the Buddendecks. This book is dedicated to my husband, Hiep Hoang. He has been my best supporter—full of intelligence, good humor, generosity, and love. He is more than I have ever expected. Our lives have been made infinitely more joyful by our brilliant and wildly imaginative daughter, Hana, and, now, our sweet son, Nico, whose timing is impeccable.

JIM CROW NETWORKS

INTRODUCTION

In 1892, Thomas Moss, Calvin McDowell, and Will Stewart, owners of the People's Grocery Company, were lynched in Memphis, Tennessee, for, in part, daring to compete with a white-owned grocery store that had previously maintained a monopoly. In her autobiography *Crusade for Justice* (1970), Ida B. Wells (also known as Wells-Barnett) wrote that this lynching "changed the whole course of my life."[1] It eventually led to a chain of events that would transform Wells into an influential anti-lynching activist who wielded the press as a weapon against racial injustices.

In her pamphlet *Southern Horrors: Lynch Law in All Its Phases* (1892), Wells declared, "The press contains unreliable and doctored reports of lynchings, and one of the most necessary things for the race to do is to get these facts before the public. The people must know before they can act and there is no educator to compare with the press."[2] She continued, "The Afro-American papers are the only ones which will print the truth, and they lack means to employ agents and detectives to get at the facts. The race must rally a mighty host to the support of their journals, and thus enable them to do much in the way of investigation."[3] The support of the Black press is, in other words, the responsibility of the race. Here Wells highlighted the fact that the African American press exists in a dialogic relationship with its readers for sociopolitical justice.

This relationship in which the press influences its readers, who, in turn, influence the press, I argue, is a central trait of African American periodicals of the Jim Crow era. An understanding of the work of this dialogic relationship reveals the extent to which authorship and meaning-making is a public interaction rather than solely a private act. Meaning and, specifically, the drive toward sociopolitical justice are generated through the interactions among author, periodical, reader, advertiser, editor, and more; these interactions make up the networks of the Jim Crow period.

In their seminal essay on periodical studies, Sean Latham and Robert Scholes write in *PMLA* that periodicals "create and occupy typically complex and often unstable positions in sometimes collaborative and sometimes competitive cultural networks."[4] In *Jim Crow Networks: African American Periodical Cultures,* I examine the networks in which African American periodicals of the first half of the twentieth century were embedded. Through the examination of these networks, I work to fill gaps in our understanding about dialogic relationships between periodicals, between periodicals and literary texts, and between periodicals and readers in American literary studies, African American studies, and the increasingly influential field of periodical studies. Writers like James Weldon Johnson, Nella Larsen, William Faulkner, and Jean Toomer were active in interracial and intraracial periodical networks that shaped their literature and concerns about racial inequality. Examining these networks reveals that moves toward sociopolitical change were negotiated and produced by dialogic relationships within, between, and around periodicals and literary texts during a period of legalized segregation.

Print culture networks, certainly, are not solely a twentieth-century or Jim Crow phenomenon. The Black print culture networks of the eighteenth and nineteenth centuries in the United States, for example, have been an area of focus by scholars such as Eric Gardner and Benjamin Fagan. The volume *Early African American Print Culture* (2012), edited by Lara Langer Cohen and Jordan Alexander Stein, has drawn particular attention to the importance of examining print culture in the eighteenth and nineteenth centuries.[5] In their introduction, Cohen and Stein note that "the late eighteenth and nineteenth centuries witnessed the consolidation of what historians have come to know as 'print culture' in the United States. Spurred by technological improvements to the printing press, innovations in papermaking and binding, increasing divisions of labor and automation, and the expansion of distribution networks enabled by railroad and steamship, print shops turned out a huge variety of printed goods in unprecedented quantities . . . Printed matter became a part of everyday life, mediating and reshaping the already fluctuating social relations of the early United States."[6] This consolidation of print culture, as Cohen and Stein argue, coincided with and enabled in part the "inauguration of what scholars have identified as an African American literary tradition."[7] Parts of this tradition are examined by

Gardner and Fagan in their respective studies on the communities that are formed through periodicals. In examining newspapers such as the *Colored American* and *Freedom's Journal*, Fagan writes, "Membership in a certain race or class, or adherence to a particular revolutionary ideology, could (dis)qualify one as a member of a particular newspaper's community."[8] While networks are not necessarily communities, communities are certainly networks. These communities in the eighteenth and nineteenth centuries were focused on slavery, its abolition, and its immediate aftermath. What I am arguing here is that dialogic Jim Crow networks are distinguished by their turn from focusing on slavery—although, of course, this is still a significant influence—to a focus on racial violence and resistance in response to the conditions of legalized segregation.

In naming these network relationships as "dialogic," I highlight them as specifically dynamic interactions that shape one another; these interactions contain elements of contingency as they often lead to unexpected collisions and encounters. The use of "dialogic" in the network context, of course, owes a debt to M. M. Bakhtin's use of the term in connection with language. The constitutive relationality of the term is integral to networks, and Bakhtinian dialogism itself as a concept is a kind of network. For Bakhtin, "the word is born in a dialogue as a living rejoinder within it; the word is shaped in dialogic interaction with an alien world that is already in the object. A word forms a concept of its own object in a dialogic way."[9] In a basic sense then, language exists within an interactive and dynamic network. Adapting this interplay to periodical studies allows us to see how individual nodes within Jim Crow networks are themselves "shaped in dialogic interaction" and must be discussed in the context of these interactions. The newspapers and magazines of the Jim Crow era, both Black and white, were, I argue, key sites where readers and writers worked toward bottom-up sociopolitical changes, sometimes in addition to and sometimes in opposition to top-down legislative transformations. The very decentralized nature of power in networks is another constitutive characteristic that makes possible the sociopolitical work of questioning the racial and class hierarchies of the Jim Crow era. In other words, the dialogic affordance of networks—the ability of nodes to "speak" back to one another, which is, in fact, one of their essential qualities—provides a counter to vertical hierarchies of power by offering alternatives.

Despite some excellent scholarship on African American periodicals, there is still a marked gap in the literary criticism. While critics like Anne Elizabeth Carroll and Russ Castronovo have focused on highbrow African American periodicals, there has been less attention paid to the popular and middlebrow periodicals that regular African Americans—and elite leaders, thinkers, and artists—read regularly during the Jim Crow period.[10] The highbrow little magazines, associated with an intellectually elite audience with interests in art, particularly in relation to the avant-garde, are objects of a great deal of deserved scholarly attention due to the influential aesthetic works and now-canonical authors published in them.[11] An obvious example is the *Little Review,* the cosmopolitan little magazine (with a mostly white audience) that serialized parts of James Joyce's *Ulysses* from 1918 to 1920. Definitions of little magazines highlight the relatively small size of their readerships along with their concern with avant-garde literature and art. While I do examine the work of little magazines, including the *Little Review,* I expand our view of the periodical landscape by emphasizing middlebrow and more popular magazines and newspapers—in other words, the periodicals that the vast majority of people read, such as the *Chicago Defender* newspaper. My aim is to provide new perspectives on well-known (and lesser known) literary texts and periodicals by examining their original contexts and juxtapositions.

In mapping the ways in which periodicals can be grouped, Robert Scholes and Clifford Wulfman point out that "the crucial categories required to unpack the concept of little magazine, then, would seem to be duration, circulation, and textual content, to which we might add the amount of advertising (relatively low) and the sort of contributors (usually, though not always, relatively new and unrecognized)."[12] They then state that "at the other end of the scale from what have been called little magazines lie what have been called mass magazines."[13] They emphasize that "terms like little and mass magazines are in fact modernist notions, designed to make an invidious division into version of 'high' and 'low,' . . . and therefore very much in need of deconstruction, if we are to see modernism from outside its own perspectives."[14] In my analysis of the periodical networks that connect magazines and newspapers that fit into elite and non-elite categories, I show their dialogic relationships and demonstrate the work that these periodicals engaged in to position themselves within particular cultural categories, like highbrow or middlebrow. These categories shifted and were used by periodicals and authors to market themselves; as a result, the magazines and newspapers that are seen as belonging to certain categories cannot be discussed in isolation, as they exist within networks of dialogic relationships, connecting categories, and connections between the periodical players, such as the editor, reader, author, and advertiser.

In looking at these expansive periodical networks, I highlight the ways that these categorizations of highbrow, middlebrow, and lowbrow were used by the periodicals and authors to position themselves within the periodical marketplace; cultural categorizations rest on contested grounds, after all. Even rarer than scholarship that focuses on non-elite periodicals are studies that examine the connections between these different periodicals—high, middle, and low—with intersecting and differing audiences; most critical works isolate a single periodical as an object of study. My goal is to trace the relationships between these periodicals and between the periodicals and elite modernist and Harlem Renaissance writers. This tracing brings to light the way these networks worked to respond to racial injustices, even as they were shaped by market pressures.

In particular, I argue that writers like Johnson, Larsen, Faulkner, and Toomer existed in periodical networks made up of magazines and newspapers like the *Half-Century Magazine,* the *Chicago Defender, Ebony,* the *Crisis,* the *Double Dealer, Broom,* and more. In focusing on networks, my argument encompasses both the networks internal to the periodical—the intranets—with the relationships between advertisements, editorials, letters to the editor, art, and so forth, as well as the networks within which the periodicals were embedded—the internets—in which a magazine, for example, exists in a dialogic relationship with other magazines, literary culture, and marketing demands. *Jim Crow Networks,* in other words, helps us understand the dialogic relationships between periodical components, between periodicals, between periodicals and literary texts, and between periodicals and readers.

The metaphor of the network is an emerging influence on literary studies and periodical studies in particular, as it has been in sociology, mathematics, computational studies, biology, and other disciplines.[15] Sociologist Manuel Castells is well known for his formulation of the concept of the "network society," and he has expanded his interest in networks with his discussion of social movements, particularly those such as the Arab Spring and the Occupy movement that have been fueled by social media.[16] In the field of literary studies, Jonathan H. Grossman has discussed transportation and communications networks in analyzing the complexities of Charles Dickens's plots, while Richard Jean So has examined transpacific networks in the twentieth century, and Patrick Jagoda's *Network Aesthetics* has identified networks across multiple media forms, including novels, television series, films, and video games.[17] Eric Bulson and Wesley Beal have traced global periodical networks and American networks of literary modernism, respectively.[18] In describing networks across multiple disciplines, M. E. J. Newman has defined them as "a general yet powerful means of representing patterns of connections or interactions between the parts of a system," while Alexander R. Galloway has similarly emphasized networks as "systems of interconnectivity" that "assume a certain level of complexity."[19] Recently, Caroline Levine has observed that networks are forms with "defined patterns of interconnection and exchange that organize social and aesthetic experience."[20]

Jim Crow Networks is part of this conversation but, at the same time, it takes a different approach in at least two key ways. First, it emphasizes the networks within the text—specifically, the periodical—along with those external to it, such as the connections to other texts. My argument relies on multiple networks that exist intratextually within a magazine or newspaper and intertextually between periodicals, literary texts, readers, authors, advertisers, editors, and publishers. Due to the affordances of the periodical as a network and those of the network within which the periodical exists, meanings are produced in interactions, exchanges, and juxtapositions. Second, *Jim Crow Networks* provides an intervention into network studies by focusing on race. Periodical studies scholars often rely on the metaphor of the network to explain the interactions within and between periodicals, yet there has been little study of African American periodicals in relation to other African American periodicals and in relation to white mainstream ones. I call these "Jim Crow networks" not simply because of the temporal scope of this project but because of the shared concerns of the literature and periodicals—even for white writers and white-focused texts—in responding to the pressures of de jure and de facto segregation. These concerns connect these texts and writers into interracial and intraracial networks that were used and tested for the possibilities of transformation in the Jim Crow era.

Talking about networks is a tricky business due to the slipperiness of a concept that is both easily graspable and yet sometimes overly capacious. "Networks" can seem empty and voracious as a concept; they seem to mean nothing because they can be used to describe so much. I offer strategies for reading Jim Crow networks grounded in periodicals and literary texts. The theoretical underpinnings necessary for examining networks are made up of myriad influences, necessarily so. In other words, networks of theoretical concepts are essential for defining and using networks. This network brings together theories about networks (naturally), African American studies, and periodical studies to develop a picture of the workings of Jim Crow networks. In this introduction, I aim to sketch this network of theoretical concepts in order to provide the foundation for discussing Jim Crow networks, even as I recognize the futility of completely mapping this particular network (and, really, any network).

Networks have held and continue to hold a great deal of power in providing an explanatory model for relationships of various kinds. *Actor-network theory* (ANT) as outlined by Bruno Latour has had a surge of interest within the field of literary studies due to the work of Rita Felski. Latour's work has illuminated the distributed nature of agency in networks and, as a result, it has provided a deeper understanding of the dialogic interactions between human actors and non-human actors.[21] In discussing the possibilities of ANT, as it is commonly called, Felski observes that it "is thus a matter of tracing out the paths by which entities of all kinds—from scallops to subway trains, from springboks to boxsprings—are constituted by their relations"; it is a descriptive approach to relationality rather than an attempt to provide an overarching theory of the workings of those relations.[22] Significantly, her reading of Latour emphasizes that actors—also called "actants" to emphasize that they are not necessarily human beings but are rather "any and all phenomena whose existence makes a difference," do "exist not in themselves but only through their networks of association."[23] In other words, writers, readers, editors, and publishers of a given periodical are not the only actors within the network, but are joined by the advertisements, illustrations, and even paper quality, to name a few. Relationality lends meaning to these actants.

In speaking of the role of politics in these networks of association, Latour points out that "it's worth noting at this point that ANT has been accused of two symmetric and contradictory sins: the first is that it extends politics everywhere, including the inner sanctum of science and technology; the second is that it is so indifferent to inequalities and power struggles that it offers no critical leverage—being content only to connive with those in power.[24] Latour asks the rhetorical question: "So in the end, what is ANT's political project?"[25] In responding to these criticisms in *The Limits of Critique*, Felski declares, "What is needed, in short, is a politics of relation rather than negation, of mediation rather than co-option, of alliance and assembly rather than alienated critique."[26] She further defines this project: "Politics, in the sense developed by actor-network theory, is no longer a matter of gesturing toward the hidden forces that explain everything; it is the process of tracing the interconnections, attachments, and conflicts among actors and mediators as they come into view."[27] In their respective accounts of their descriptive approaches, Latour and Felski both refrain, for the most part, from providing specifics about the workings of the political in networks. During the Jim Crow era, these networks, tied to periodicals, were constituted and driven by their political orientations. Levine's interest in hierarchy and networks as two separate forms that can interact is relevant here to my focus on how hierarchies of race, class, and aesthetics intersect with the networks of periodicals and literary texts. Networks affirm these hierarchies, yet also call them into question. In other words, networks offer the possibility of countering hierarchies.

The relationality that is important to Latour's work is integral to Gilles Deleuze and Félix Guattari's discussion of a particular kind of network—the rhizome: "Unlike trees or their roots, the rhizome connects any point to any other point, and its traits are not necessarily linked to traits of the same nature."[28] In presenting the rhizome as a contrast to the figure of the tree, Deleuze and Guattari emphasize that its points "can be connected to anything other, and must be"; and that "in contrast to centered (even polycentric) systems with hierarchical modes of communication and preestablished paths, the rhizome is an acentered, nonhierarchical, nonsignifying system without a General and without an organizing memory or central automaton, defined solely by a circulation of states."[29] The sprawling nonhierarchical connectivity of the rhizome is a key characteristic: "A rhizome has no beginning or end; it is always in the middle, between things, interbeing, *intermezzo*. The tree is filiation, but the rhizome is alliance, unique alliance. The tree imposes the verb 'to be,' but the fabric of the rhizome is the conjunction, 'and . . . and . . . and . . .'"[30] This conjunctive quality is also important to Pierre Bourdieu's concept of the field, which, as I will discuss in greater detail in chapter one, is itself a network: "In analytic terms, a field may be defined as a network, or a configuration, of objective relations between positions." The field as a network, for Bourdieu—and unlike for Deleuze and Guattari—can lead to hierarchical positioning.[31] A network's relationship to hierarchical structures is important to my examination of the way networks can both allow for the destabilization of authority, as in the case of *Ebony* readers' responses to Faulkner's essay, and also for the construction of hierarchies, as in the case of the *Half-Century*'s strategic use of the cultural category of the middlebrow. Ultimately, both the rhizome and the field are kinds of networks, defined by their connectivity and interactivity.

These characteristics of networks—connectivity and interactivity—are what Levine and other scholars who are influenced by design theory have identified as "affordances." Donald A. Norman, who is credited with popularizing the concept in design theory, defines *affordance* as "the relationship between a physical object and a person (or for that matter, any interacting agent, whether animal or human, or even machines and robots). An affordance is a relationship between the properties of an object and the capabilities of the agent that determine just how the object could possibly be used."[32] In the revised edition to his volume *The Design of Everyday Things*, Norman makes a point of emphasizing that affordances are relationships and not properties inherent in the object. The relational nature of affordance is essential to periodical studies because it highlights the interactions between reader and periodical. In speaking of forms, a category that includes networks, Levine points to the usefulness of the concept of affordance, calling it "a term used to describe the potential uses or actions latent in materials and designs."[33] She describes affordances as the "limited range of potentialities" of a form, while Latham in the context of periodical studies describes affordance as the "'action possibilities' in an object: the physical, material, and conceptual properties that both make possible and limit what an agent can do with it."[34] Latham compares the affordances of magazines to those of the codex book by stating that books "afford agents very few possibilities for action beyond reading the text in a linear, serial order," in contrast to magazines with their affordance of the potential for non-linear reading.[35]

Certainly, books can be approached from a number of different angles and they have their own contingencies in terms of juxtapositions of, for example, what Jerome J. McGann has influentially called the *bibliographic codes* and the *linguistic codes*.[36] As Leah Price has demonstrated, readers do not necessarily perceive novelistic linearity as a mandate. She observes: "Sheer scale helps define the novel. So do the pace and duration of reading which that scale elicits. But the novel depends just as much on readers' resistance to those demands. Skipping (or anthologizing) and skimming (or abridging) have never been separable from a genre that cracks under its own weight."[37] Readerly engagement with novels is often fluid and non-linear and, at the same time, there are many novels that play with linearity, especially in the field of modernist literature, but, with these caveats, it is important to emphasize that periodicals overall are meant to be read in a less linear way than are novels presented in book form. (Of course, a novel that has been serialized within the pages of magazine is bound up in the periodical's own affordance of readerly fluidity.) As Margaret Beetham points out, "It is an unusual reader of any periodical who reads every word from cover to cover let alone in the order in which they are printed. . . . The periodical . . . is a form which openly offers readers the chance to construct their own texts."[38] Periodicals by their very form explicitly—"openly," as Beetham puts it—afford this non-linear mode of reading and overall fluidity via tables of contents that offer the option to pick and choose what the reader might read and in what order. The Modernist Journals Project, a digital humanities site that provides an archive of magazines from the early twentieth century, even includes hyperlinks in the table of contents to re-create, in part, the non-linear magazine reading experience.[39] Periodicals also afford non-linearity through the incorporation of calls to turn to certain pages to read the endings of various articles and insertions of advertisements that often interrupt articles, both visually and narratively.

The concept of affordance is essential to my argument about the workings of the networks of periodicals and literary texts and the mechanisms by which meaning is produced. As Latham has pointed out, another affordance of periodicals is that of *emergence*:

> N. Katherine Hayles concisely defines this idea in *My Mother Was a Computer*, writing that it "is any behavior or property that cannot be found in either a system's individual components or their additive properties, but that arises, often unpredictably, from the *interaction* of a system's components." I hope this sounds as tantalizing to you as it does to me since it offers a very useful way to conceptualize magazines as something more than the mere additive sum of their parts. Understanding them as complex systems capable of producing meaning through the unplanned and even unexpected interaction of their components helps us free them from the dominant metaphors of the book. Put another way, the wide affordances of the magazine produce

> the conditions for emergence—for the creation of interconnected networks of meaning that are not only difficult to map or anticipate, but that elude stabilizing concepts like author, intention, and even textuality.[40]

One significant ramification of the workings of emergence in periodicals and, more broadly, among networks is that the agency behind meaning-making is dispersed beyond single agents to the overall interactions between the components of the system. The intertwined notions of affordance and emergence are central to my argument about the meanings created by the internal networks of periodicals and also by the networks in which periodicals and literary texts are produced and are embedded. Levine points out that "literary and cultural studies scholars who have been interested in networks have typically focused on one at a time: the slave trade, the print marketplace, the telegraph, global capital."[41] In contrast, she emphasizes the "overlapping of multiple networks."[42]

I take Levine's criticism about the misleading nature of isolated studies of networks seriously; indeed, my argument relies on multiple networks that exist intratextually within a magazine or newspaper and intertextually between magazines, literary texts, readers, authors, advertisers, editors, and publishers. A periodical is both a kind of a network (in which its parts, including the features, advertisements, editorials, letters to the editor, and images, interact and produce the emergence of meanings) and a node within a sprawling network comprised of nodes that may include readers, advertisers, other periodicals, and literary texts (which themselves are nodes in other networks). These overlapping networks can only be mapped partially. In discussing Charles Dickens's treatment of networks in *Bleak House,* Levine compellingly argues that the novel gestures toward a universal truth about networks: "We cannot ever apprehend the totality of the networks that organize us."[43]

George Bornstein, influenced by McGann's editorial theory, has argued for a way of reading that "recognize[s] that the literary text consists not only of words (its linguistic code) but also of the semantic features of its material instantiations (its bibliographic code). Such bibliographic codes might include cover design, page layout, or spacing, among other factors."[44] The bibliographic code can also include "broader issues which D. F. McKenzie might call 'the sociology of texts,' like publisher, print run, price, or audience."[45] McGann has argued for "the text as a laced network of linguistic and bibliographical codes."[46] In discussing this network of codes in relation to magazines, Peter Brooker and Andrew Thacker have usefully coined the phrase "the periodical code," a subset of the bibliographic code; periodical codes can be "internal to the design of a magazine (paper, typeface, layout, etc.)" and also "constitute its external relations (distribution in a bookshop, support from patrons)."[47] Notably, they emphasize that "it is often the *relationship* between internal and external periodical codes that is most significant."[48] One of the claims of this book overall is that these internal and external periodical codes are part of the internet and intranet of the periodical. Due to the affordances of the periodical as a network and the network within which the periodical exists, meanings are produced in interactions, exchanges, and juxtapositions—through emergence, in other words. As Latham and Scholes have observed, "Periodicals . . . are by their nature collaborative objects, assembled in complex interactions between editors, authors, advertisers, sales agents, and even readers."[49] The nodes in these periodical networks exist in a dialogic relationship that influences their positions.

Latour has wryly declared, "The word network is so ambiguous that we should have abandoned it long ago."[50] In referring to this quotation, Jagoda states, "The word network is thus a keyword of the historical present, but at the same time, given its relentless usage, it increasingly lacks descriptive edge."[51] It is precisely this ambiguity and edgelessness that makes the concept of networks useful in discussing periodical intranets and internets, as it captures the weak connections within and without periodicals that spring from the contingency that marks the periodical's form. The nodes of a network are linked by connections of varying strengths. When there are fluctuations or shifts in a node, these changes ripple out to the rest of the nodes in the network in varying strengths. In this way, the nodes are like tectonic plates, shifting and being shifted by each other. These nodes are diverse in nature and can be made up of authors, editors, readers, advertisers, and others, as the periodical form is constituted by the multiple actors and actants who shape it.

Any discussion of a periodical must include an acknowledgment of the role of contingency in these networks. Part of the pleasure and overall experience of reading a periodical is in reading the juxtapositions present in periodical intranets—for example, the placement of a cosmetics advertisement next to an editorial extoling Black beauty. However, a periodical—with some exceptions—is not a single-authored text. Periodical juxtapositions can be coincidental or the result of various publishing exigencies, such as the need to fill blank space on the page. Thinking about periodicals as networks and as existing in networks allows us to consider the place of contingency by recognizing the dispersal of agency in these networks. An affordance of networks is this distributed agency. There is no single author who acts as the sole meaning-maker in a periodical. As in the case of novels, the periodical author, reader, and editor construct meaning together, but, unlike novels, periodicals not only offer multiple texts (authored by multiple individuals) that sometimes contradict one another but also specifically encourage "radial reading," to use McGann's phrase, over linear reading.[52] For McGann, radial reading, which as a concept owes a debt to Barthesian and Foucauldian claims about the death of the author, "involves decoding one or more of the contexts that interpenetrate the scripted and physical text."[53] Texts are radial, not simply linguistic: "To see that books function in a radial field, that they interact with their contexts, carries important consequences for the way we will read them."[54] McGann applies this concept to books in particular, but periodicals explicitly afford radial reading due to the multiple reading contexts that are offered within issues and the juxtapositions within the periodical intranets and internets. An individual reader, who exists within the periodical network, encounters these juxtapositions and develops meanings from them.

This concept of radial reading is useful for periodical studies because it places authorial intention and agency in a subordinate role. Its debts to Roland Barthes and Michel Foucault are clear. Barthes famously announced that "the birth of the reader must be at the cost of the death of the Author."[55] He asserted that "a text is made of multiple writings, drawn from many cultures and entering into mutual relations of dialogue, parody, contestation, but there is one place where this multiplicity is focused and that place is the reader, not, as was hitherto said, the author."[56] Similarly, Foucault has asked, "What difference does it make who is speaking?"[57] Yet, this is a question that only the privileged can ask with what he calls "the stirring of an indifference."[58] Along the lines of Foucault's question, Barthes suggests that "a text's unity lies not in its origin but in its destination. Yet this destination cannot any longer be personal: the reader is without history, biography, psychology; he is simply that *someone* who holds together in a single field all the traces by which the written text is constituted."[59] Barthes's comment that the reader is "simply that *someone*" erases the central role of identity and inequality from the equation.

While Jim Crow networks, which contain authors and readers, disperse meaning-making from an individual to the juxtapositions and interactions of all the network nodes, they cannot be denuded of the who that is speaking and the "history, biography, psychology" of the someone, the reader. In fact, authors and readers, as seen in the case of letters to the editor, often insisted on the relevance of their autobiographies to their claims. Langston Hughes criticized the possibility of the omitting the "who" of the author in "The Negro Artist and the Racial Mountain" (1926) in his opening anecdote about "one of the most promising of the young Negro poets," presumably a reference to Countée Cullen.[60] This poet, Hughes writes, "said to me once, 'I want to be a poet—not a Negro poet,' meaning, I believe, 'I want to write like a white poet'; meaning subconsciously, 'I would like to be a white poet'; meaning behind that, 'I would like to be white.' And I was sorry the young man said that, for no great poet has ever been afraid of being himself."[61] This "desire to pour racial individuality into the mold of American standardization, and to be as little Negro and as much American possible" is what Hughes calls the racial mountain for the Negro artist.[62] His overall claim here is about the worth of Black lives, particularly those of what he calls "the low-down folks," for the purposes of artistic representation, but he is also suggesting that the erasure of racial identity is not politically and aesthetically viable for a Black artist.[63] To put it another way, the privilege of erasing personal history is not available to African American readers and writers of the Jim Crow period. At the same time, these readers and writers recognize the importance of these histories and often deploy them in their refutation of de jure and de facto segregation.

As Noliwe M. Rooks has noted, the archive of African American periodicals is relatively small and, at times, difficult to access.[64] In weaving together a diverse set of archival materials, I map the terrain of Jim Crow periodical networks to reconfigure our perspectives on some well-known periodicals, such as the *Chicago Defender* and the *Crisis*, and argue for the importance of lesser-known periodicals, such as the *Half-Century*. It is important to note that these Jim Crow networks are not solely made up of African American periodicals, readers, and writers; rather, these networks are interracial and defined by a shared concern with the conditions of inequality of the era, although this shared concern was not matched by shared strategies in responding to Jim Crow. Scholes and Wulfman in *Modernism in the Magazines* (2010), a text that marks the rising interest in periodical studies in the field of twentieth-century literary studies, argue convincingly that modernism was born in the magazines. However, in their field-defining work, Scholes and Wulfman devote very little space to African American periodicals and African Americans in periodicals, even though, as critics like Michael North have noted, white modernist writers often used Blackness to proclaim their modernity.[65]

In Jim Crow Networks I unearth the overlooked intersections of the Black press to modernist and Harlem Renaissance texts by not merely re-contextualizing literary works within their original publication contexts but by also emphasizing the networks in which they existed. In doing so, the book's argument expands our knowledge of how periodical and literary texts were shaped in opposition to and in affiliation with one another. I not only focus on the connections between periodicals through their shared writers and concerns but I also emphasize the networks as sites of dynamic interactions that linked writers (who were often readers), readers (who were sometimes writers), editors, and advertisers. At the same time, the content was shaped by the periodicals' positions relative to one another in the public and counterpublic spheres. Examining the periodical ecology, made up of these networks, creates a clearer picture of how the literature and periodicals interacted with one another; it provides a deeper understanding of the dialogues, debates, and jockeying for position between the literature and the various newspapers and magazines within their Jim Crow networks.

In *Southern Horrors,* which was written after her friends were lynched and the offices of the newspaper she co-owned, the *Memphis Free Speech and Headlight,* were destroyed as a result of her anti-lynching editorial, Wells relied upon excerpts from newspapers to expose the truths about lynching; at the same time, she proposed periodicals as essential tools in African American activism. In arguing that "nobody in this section of the country believes the old thread bare lie that Negro men rape white women," Wells cited and refuted white-run newspapers like the *Daily Commercial* and the *Evening Scimitar.*[66] At the same time, she quoted from other white-run newspapers, such as the *Cleveland Gazette* and the *Memphis Ledger,* to prove that white women were not being raped by Black men, who were thus being unjustly lynched. By providing an excess of examples containing journalistic details and written in an objective style, Wells forcefully argued against what she called "lynch law." Toward the end of her pamphlet, Wells offered some solutions—what she defines as "self help"—to the threat of racial violence.[67] Along with arguing that African Americans should engage in boycotts, migrate, and carry guns for self-defense, she cited periodicals as a mode of self-help.

Wells's imbrication in the newspaper culture of the period and her insistence on the power of Black periodicals to combat lynching make her an early theorist of race and periodicals. In her involvement with the *Free Speech* and, later, the *New York Age,* the Chicago *Inter-Ocean,* and other periodicals and her use of the white and Black press in her anti-lynching work, Wells is, I argue, a precursor to later figures central to early-twentieth-century periodical culture; her emphasis on the press's role in combating racial injustice is a defining trait of the African American periodicals of the Jim Crow period, although each periodical approached the task with differing strategies.

In her discussion of different white-run newspapers, Wells plays the newspapers off one another by using quotations from some newspapers to contradict quotations from other newspapers. This dialogic use of newspapers displays Wells's understanding of these periodicals as existing within a network. Her deployment of this network is an essential component of what Teresa Zackodnik has called her "pedagogy of American lynching."[68] In inserting herself into this network—a network that, for the most part, did not include someone like her due to her position as a Black woman in the Jim Crow United States—Wells makes the argument for the place of her newspaper, the *Free Speech*, in it; her Black-owned newspaper speaks to and through these white newspapers to criticize the culture of lynching.

In responding to the lynchings of the early years of the Jim Crow era, Wells turned to periodicals as a vehicle for responding to accounts of Black men being lynched for allegedly assaulting white women; her work is a precursor to W. E. B. Du Bois's *Crisis* magazine, the official organ of the National Association for the Advancement of Colored People (NAACP), which worked to stop lynching a couple decades later. Throughout her writings, Wells used newspapers to provide authority to her claims while undermining the authority of other newspapers through her analyses of their stories. Relying upon her deep understanding of Jim Crow networks, she wielded periodical citations as weapons, using intertextual references upon references to place a variety of periodicals, white and Black, in conversation with one another. This technique lent support to her claim that lynching was a grave injustice that had very little to do with the publicly stated reasons and everything to do with racial terrorism meant to keep African Americans in their "places."

Wells opened the preface to *Southern Horrors* by stating, "The greater part of what is contained in these pages was published in the *New York Age* June 25, 1892, in explanation of the editorial which the Memphis whites considered sufficiently infamous to justify the destruction of my paper, *The Free Speech*."[69] Jacqueline Goldsby has noted that this opening establishes the pamphlet "as an autobiographical-eyewitness narrative, but one whose authority proceeds from the writer's vulnerability to the violence of lynching."[70] At the same time, Wells acknowledged and called attention to the genealogy of her anti-lynching pamphlet by emphasizing the material's original publication in an influential Black newspaper; she also created a link between her Southern newspaper and that Northern newspaper with its wider reach and influence. The pamphlet then, from its outset, must be read in the context of a periodical network that stretches from the North to the South, emphasizing the national scope of Wells's anti-lynching campaign. This campaign would go on to have a transatlantic reach, as particularly evident in her second pamphlet, *A Red Record* (1895), which emerged from her speaking tours in England, Scotland, and Wales. *A Red Record* relies on "the compilation of statistics touching upon lynching" from the *Chicago Tribune* newspaper.[71] Wells listed in her pamphlet those statistics with names, dates, locations, and the stated offenses that led to the lynchings and then provided more narrative details along with a few images. In using the statistics of a white mainstream periodical alongside her narrative accounts and commentary, Wells bolstered her case against lynch law to her transatlantic audiences.

On May 21, 1892, Wells published the editorial that led to her exile from Memphis and launched her anti-lynching campaign. Her editorial emphatically pushed back against the notion that lynching is justified because it punishes Black men who assault white women. Wells instead argued, through a meticulous analysis of newspaper accounts coupled with an abundance of evidence, that, in many of those cases, there had in fact been a consensual relationship between the Black man and the white woman and, often, the white women had been the instigators of the sexual relationships. In using these accounts, mostly from white newspapers, she emphasized the hypocrisy of the mainstream periodicals by juxtaposing these accounts with their lies about the bestiality of African Americans. Wells, as Zackodnik has argued, condemned the white press's complicity in lynching through its "active incitement of the mob."[72] In other words, Wells's actions were twofold: she bolstered her authority through her citations of the white press while simultaneously demolishing the white press's authority through her strategic work with the periodical network that discusses lynching. She highlighted the structure of this network by incorporating quotations and excerpts from white and Black periodicals. Her juxtapositions teach the reader to see beyond the surface meanings to what is really being said. In effect, her pamphlet teaches the reader how to read periodicals.

Wells also worked to destabilize white authority through her strategic use of question marks in parentheses throughout her writings. For example, in *Southern Horrors,* she wrote, "So great is Southern hate and prejudice, they legally (?) hung poor little thirteen year old Mildrey Brown at Columbia, S. C., Oct. 7th, on the circumstantial evidence that she poisoned a white infant."[73] Wells strategically places question marks next to certain words to cause the reader to question the truth value of those words. Here, she questions the official account that claims that Mildrey Brown was executed within the bounds of the law; through this move, along with her exposure of the press's lies, Wells argues for the destabilization of official and mainstream accounts that legitimize extralegal acts of terrorism and instructs her readers to become authorities themselves in reading periodicals. In effect, periodicals create the potential for the dispersion of authority.

Her technique, as mentioned, relies on quotations and, at times, quotations of quotations; these embedded quotations reveal the periodical network that is coalesced around the topic of lynching. For example, she begins chapter one of her pamphlet with two quotations: the first is directly from her 1892 *Free Speech* editorial, and the second is from the mainstream Memphis press writing about that same *Free Speech* editorial: "The negroes may as well understand that there is no mercy for the negro rapist and little patience with his defenders. A negro organ printed in this city, in a recent issue publishes the following atrocious paragraph: 'Nobody in this section of the country believes the old thread-bare lie that negro men rape white women.'"[74] By presenting her editorial above that of the mainstream press, Wells asked the reader to read the *Daily Commercial*'s comments about her editorial through her lens. She then continued by quoting from a Black editor named J. C. Duke, who in his newspaper, the *Herald,* stated claims that were similar to those in the *Free Speech:* "We greatly suspect it is the growing appreciation of white Juliets for colored Romeos."[75] Wells emphasizes that Duke "was forced to leave the city," just as she had been forced to; in doing so, she places herself in a network that includes the white press.[76] Although Wells claims authority for herself by placing the original *Free Speech* quotation first in the pamphlet, she also shores up this authority by using the white press in opposition to other white-owned periodicals. In another example, she presents excerpts from the *Cleveland Gazette* to show how William Offett, an African American man, was unjustly imprisoned for raping Mrs. J. S. Underwood, a white minister's wife. Eventually, Mrs. Underwood confessed that she had had consensual sexual relations with Offett.[77] Over and over in her pamphlet Wells presents one piece of evidence after another from the white press proving the existence of "white Juliets" and making a compelling case for the horrors of lynching by demonstrating that charges of assault on white women were simply pretexts to engage in mob violence to terrorize African Americans.

In her discussion of how African Americans must defend themselves from this terrorism, Wells stated that "a Winchester rifle should have a place of honor in every black home, and it should be used for that protection which the law refuses to give."[78] Directly after this advice, Wells insisted on the importance of the Black press exposing the deceptions of the white press to provide "that protection which the law refuses to give." In other words, rifle and periodical are both weapons of self-defense in a nation where the government has abdicated its own responsibility in defending its people; the rifle is meant to be used to protect the domestic space, while the press protects the race overall. Ultimately, she stated that "nothing is more definitely settled than [that the Afro American] must act for himself."[79] She argued, "The assertion has been substantiated throughout these pages that the press contains unreliable and doctored reports of lynchings, and one of the most necessary things for the race to do is to get these facts before the public. The people must know before they can act, and there is no educator to compare with the press."[80] Her argument depends on the identification and use of interracial periodical networks in which unreliable press accounts of lynchings are juxtaposed with truthful accounts; this awareness of these juxtapositions allows the reader to understand the enormity of the problem of racial violence and the true reasons behind it.

These late nineteenth-century discussions of the periodical as educator, the periodical as a tool of self-help for the race, and the periodical as embedded within a larger network of periodicals are precursors to early twentieth-century conversations about the role of the press during the Jim Crow period. Wells's journalistic activism is part of a long line of periodical figures, ranging from those before Wells who were involved with abolitionist newspapers in the antebellum period to those figures after Wells like Robert S. Abbott of the *Chicago Defender* and Du Bois of the *Crisis*. In 2020, Wells herself was awarded a posthumous special Pulitzer Prize citation "for her outstanding and courageous reporting on the horrific and vicious violence against African Americans during the era of lynching."[81] Wells's activism relies on portraying African Americans as victims of racial violence while also arming them with the tools to fight back, particularly in terms of teaching them how to read newspapers. Many later magazines and newspapers emphasized the aesthetic and social achievements of African Americans and highlighted their artistic productions throughout their pages to counter the dehumanizing narratives in the mainstream press. These strategies are a mix of what Kenneth W. Warren has described as "instrumental"—using these texts to "achieve a social end"—and "indexical"—using artistic creation as evidence of Black humanity.[82] These strategies of instrumentality and indexicality are important to the periodicals of the Jim Crow era and reveal yet another dimension to the role of the periodical as educator. During these decades, African American magazines and newspapers relied to varying degrees on these strategies to act in opposition to racial injustices and, in so doing, formed counterpublic spheres.

Michael Warner defines a *counterpublic* as a public that exists in a subordinate position to a dominant public: "A counterpublic maintains at some level, conscious or not, an awareness of its subordinate status. The cultural horizon against which it marks itself off is not just a general or wider public but a dominant one."[83] African American periodicals of the Jim Crow era always existed with a consciousness of the subordinate status of their readers, writers, and, consequently, the periodicals themselves; in fact, it is safe to say that African Americans founded (and read) these periodicals as an alternative and antidote to the dominant public. Warner continues, "Dominant publics are by definition those that can take their discourse pragmatics and their lifeworlds for granted, misrecognizing the indefinite scope of their expansive address as universality or normalcy. Counterpublics are spaces of circulation in which it is hoped that the poesis of scene making will be transformative, not replicative merely."[84] Wells's conception of the periodical as educator and mode for self-help, a conception that extends into the twentieth century for her periodical descendants, reveals the transformative potential, hope, and power of the counterpublics of Jim Crow periodical cultures.

Jim Crow Networks argues that these counterpublics were embedded in networks that included the dominant publics of mainstream periodicals. Spanning the years of the Jim Crow era, from the height of the Great Migration and the Harlem Renaissance to the *Brown v. Board of Education* era, *Jim Crow Networks* traces how a diverse set of periodicals and also literary texts respond to racial violence. The interactions between periodical and literature in the Jim Crow networks I examine are varied. James Weldon Johnson's republication and serialization of his novel *The Autobiography of an Ex-Colored Man* in the *Half-Century Magazine,* as I discuss in the first chapter, provides insight to the magazine's self-positioning in cultural categories through the seeming misalignment of a novel about lynching and racial passing with a middlebrow publication venue that focuses on domesticity. Similarly, I explore this question of fit between a work of literature and its magazine publication venues in the fourth chapter through an analysis of the diverse set of periodicals in which Jean Toomer chose to publish the various components that would eventually make up his Harlem Renaissance masterpiece, *Cane;* this analysis exposes the spatial—regional, national, and global—and temporal networks in which the text should be read, along with the racial, cultural, and aesthetic identities that it explores.

In thinking about these interactions between periodical and literary works, I do not simply focus on literature that is found in periodical contexts. For example, in juxtaposing the *Chicago Defender* letters to the editor with Nella Larsen's *Quicksand* in chapter two, I focus on the shared rhetoric around the visual dynamic of shame in relation to race and class in these texts, rather than arguing for any direct historical links between the two (although, due to the *Defender*'s popularity and her own biographical connections to Chicago, it would not be a stretch to say that

Larsen would likely have read it). This chapter in particular argues that the respective work of periodicals and novels is distinctive but linked; both the letters to the editor and Larsen's novel share not simply themes but also formal characteristics that argue for the abuses and uses of the affect of shame. The newspaper and the novel, in effect, exist in a media network that in part is held together through a shared concern with affect. By looking at *Ebony* magazine readers' responses to Faulkner's gradualist advice in the days following the *Brown v. Board of Education* decision, I extend my analysis of the letters to the editor to chapter three, arguing for possibilities of the periodical in affirming or destabilizing authorial authority. Unlike a novel, the magazine allows the readers to speak back to the author, creating a heterogeneous network of author and readers. Taken together, chapters two and three offer an approach to reading letters to the editor, a genre that poses interpretive challenges.

This book's overall argument is organized around the tactics of activism that these networks afford. What I mean by activism ranges from the radical literary experimentation of Toomer to the more conservative respectability politics of the *Half-Century* and *Defender* to the widely reviled gradualist politics of Faulkner; these were all responses to the hierarchies of the Jim Crow era that relied upon and/or were combated by networks grounded in periodicals and literature. These tactics were themselves connected within Jim Crow networks. There are many ways to talk about networks in general, as suggested by my discussions of literary critics, such as Levine and Jagoda, and theorists, such as Latour, Bourdieu, and Deleuze and Guattari; it is a metaphor that causes the proliferation of other metaphors due to its capaciousness and usefulness. However, in *Jim Crow Networks,* I will highlight networks in terms of cultural hierarchies, affective language, readers, and space and time in order to analyze the workings of the Jim Crow activism and resistance that were at play in periodicals and literary texts. To discuss networks in this way means to reject the tyranny of chronology in tracing out the connections between different nodes that span the years within the period. It also demands chapters that are organized around these tactics with linkages that could be made between chapters in non-linear ways. One of the affordances of a network is to open the way to thinking beyond the linear or hierarchical. The argument of *Jim Crow Networks* is not driven by linearity or chronology; through an investigation of network affordances, it traces the aesthetic, political, and cultural tactics used in response to Jim Crow racial violence and systems of inequality and the relations between those tactics. In other words, this argument is itself networked and must marshal its forces from a range of sources—theoretical, periodical, and literary. To talk about networks, we must use networks.

Chapter one, titled "Middlebrow Networks: James Weldon Johnson and the *Half-Century Magazine*," lays the groundwork for discussing aesthetic positioning between Black periodicals. Using Bourdieu's notion of the cultural field, I trace the work the *Half-Century* magazine engaged in to carve out its market position within the networks of African American magazines and newspapers. As a middlebrow magazine concerned with issues of respectability, fashion, and homemaking, it situated its approach to racial politics as being distinctive from that of the powerhouses of the *Crisis* magazine and the *Chicago Defender* newspaper by claiming the middle's value. While much of the fiction is forgettable, Johnson's *The Autobiography of an Ex-Colored Man* was serialized in its pages after its initial 1912 publication but before its Harlem Renaissance republication. The seemingly incongruous appearance of this novel—with its affiliation to Harlem Renaissance networks of activism and political and aesthetic risk-taking—in a middlebrow magazine highlights and complicates this picture of Black networks and cultural categories, and is a fact often overlooked in accounts of the novel's publication history. Too often African American periodicals are discussed individually and in isolation from one another—or they are discussed only in relation to magazines, with obvious resemblances as seen in the oft-discussed coupling of the *Crisis* and *Opportunity* magazines. However, all these periodicals existed in a rich context of different audiences and alliances that were marked by hierarchies of taste and the language of cultural "brows." In chapter one, I bring to light the work of the *Half-Century* in positioning itself in the middle of the increasingly crowded marketplace of these networks.

While periodicals jostled one another to strategically position themselves, their readers also spoke to one another through letters to the editor. Chapter two, "Affective Networks: Nella Larsen and the *Chicago Defender*," highlights the language of shame in the letters page of the *Defender* and in Larsen's Harlem Renaissance novel *Quicksand* (1928) during the 1920s. This attention to shame reveals the affective network that connects these texts. While the Harlem Renaissance is generally thought of as a period of great racial pride, it also contained hidden narratives of racial shame. However, shame acts as something more than a toxic affect that renders one passive. It was not only an engine in shaping the content of the public discourse about race, but, in the *Defender* letters-to-the-editor page and Larsen's modernist novel, its visual logic is used to reject the passivity that often is the result of shame. In this chapter, both novel and letters page share the affordance of containing multiple perspectives, and in this multiplicity lies a potential antidote to the toxicity of shame.

As an examination of the *Defender*'s letters to the editor demonstrates, periodicals were sites of dialogue, and, in some cases, they allowed for the readers to speak back to authors. For example, while Faulkner's influence on and intersections with African American writers have been discussed before, his relationship with his Black magazine-reading publics has been overlooked. Although his readership certainly included elite writers, it was also composed of ordinary readers of middlebrow periodicals like *Ebony* and *Life* magazines. In chapter three, "Readerly Networks: William Faulkner's Magazine Publics," I argue that *Ebony* magazine's letters page offers insight into the interactions between the author and his publics, and constructs the networks formed by the readers in relation to and, sometimes, in opposition to the celebrity author. In September 1956, *Ebony* published Faulkner's "If I Were a Negro," an essay that calls for gradualism as a solution to the race problem by repeating the striking phrase "If I were a Negro." Faulkner's assumption of authority through the act of imagining himself as Black was not left unchallenged in this post-*Brown v. Board of Education* moment; in the letters to the editor, the magazine's readers countered Faulkner's essay by arguing for the authority that comes through Black lived experience rather than the aesthetic imagination of a white author. Unlike a novel, the magazine affords readers the possibility of speaking to the author and to one another. Ultimately, the letters page works as a site where the author's authority risks destabilization and the ties between the readers of the magazine are affirmed; at the same time, the letters page also calls to attention the editors' agency in invisibly shaping the community of letter writers through the page's advocacy for an implicit editorial platform.

Much of this book focuses on so-called lowbrow and middlebrow periodicals, like *Ebony* and the *Half-Century*, as they have been under-studied, but highbrow magazines were also part of the Black periodical networks of the time; these networks included not only magazines aimed at Black audiences but also those that were directed at a majority white readership, even at times outside of the United States. Chapter four, "Global Networks: *Cane* in the Magazines," traces these relationships through *Cane*'s publication in a diverse set of magazines, such as *Broom*, the *Double Dealer*, the *Little Review*, and the *Crisis*. I argue that, in thinking about *Cane*'s form, we must consider its pre-book publication history in the magazines; the affordances of the magazines highlight the global and temporal contexts in which the book is invested. *Cane* (1923) is a heterogeneous literary work that lies at the intersection of different aesthetic, political, and social projects and, consequently, the intersection of different reading audiences. Reading *Cane* through the lens of periodical studies reanimates our understanding of the text and its readership—and of the periodicals themselves. In looking at the roads between *Cane* in the magazines and *Cane* as a book, I highlight the potential of periodical studies in illuminating the invisible global and temporal networks that magazines and individual works of literature construct and engage with.

Finally, *Jim Crow Networks* closes by moving beyond the Jim Crow period to the opening decades of the twenty-first century, with its media networks of Black activism, particularly in the context of the activism of the Black Lives Matter movement. The networks of the Jim Crow era extend forward into the twenty-first century; the network affordances of today, despite significant differences, produce a counterpublic that shares a kinship with those found in the magazines and newspapers of the first half of the twentieth century. Throughout these pages, I make the argument that reimagining the Jim Crow period as significantly constituted by a diverse set of networks coalesced around but not limited to periodicals unveils the multiple pathways by which injustices were challenged and tactics in questioning dehumanizing norms and laws were formulated and tested.

CHAPTER ONE
Middlebrow Networks
James Weldon Johnson and the Half-Century Magazine

In its opening editorial published in August 1916, the *Half-Century Magazine* declared, "We shall refrain from publishing such articles as 'Sister Smith of Bastrop gave a chicken dinner last Sunday for Brother Jones of Monroe,' as we believe that of all our readers only four persons would be interested in seeing such an item."[1] Chicken dinners seem like trivial things to highlight, even disparagingly, in an opening editorial, but the *Half-Century*'s disdain for notices about chicken dinners argues for the distinctive qualities of the new magazine. It is, of course, no accident that this editorial concentrates on chicken dinners in particular. As Psyche A. Williams-Forson has written, "Foods like chicken were imbued with class tensions as African Americans struggled for citizenship and acceptance in American society. Consequently, many middle-class members of black society sought to separate migrant communities from their traditional southern mores."[2] During the period of the Great Migration, racial uplift efforts in the cities were often directed at the working-class Southern migrants, who were perceived by Black Northerners to be insufficiently socialized for the urban North and, thus, detriments to the upward trajectory of the race; the *Half-Century*'s rejection of these chicken dinners reveals its part in this project.

The early twentieth century is marked by the births of many important African American periodicals as the Great Migration sharpened the hunger for more news about African Americans by African Americans. An increased literacy rate was also a factor: as Patrick S. Washburn notes, "black illiteracy had dropped from 44.5 percent in 1900 to 30.4 percent just ten years later, black incomes were rising, and black newspapers now rivaled black churches in influence . . . Thus, by 1910 a survey showed there were 288 black newspapers in the country, with a combined circulation of about 500,000, and at least one paper was published in every city with a sizable black population."[3] The *Half-Century* was one of a group of lesser-known periodicals that had to carve out places for themselves in the preexisting counterpublic networks, which were dominated by other more popular and established periodicals. Throughout its pages, the *Half-Century Magazine* (1916–25), with its focus on fashion and housekeeping, continually worked to make the argument for why readers should purchase and read its issues. In this way, although it certainly relied on more conventional advertisements, the magazine also incorporated advertising for itself in its very content, linking the consumption of the periodical—and certain advertised products—to racial uplift. This marketing strategy was a necessary move during a period that saw the rise of several influential periodicals, most notably W. E. B. Du Bois's *Crisis* (1910–34) and the *Half-Century*'s hometown competitor, the *Chicago Defender* (1905–2019, and then online only). In effect, the *Half-Century* made the case for its inclusion in the same periodical networks as these other publications, which themselves existed in other overlapping networks. The *Crisis*, for example, is often discussed alongside *Opportunity* magazine (1923–49), the official publication of the National Urban League, and the *Messenger* (1917–28), whereas the *Chicago Defender* existed within a network of other weekly Black newspapers, such as the *New York Amsterdam News* (1909–present, largely online) and the *Pittsburgh Courier* (1907–66). The *Half-Century* was particularly and clearly focused on the *Defender* and the *Crisis* due to their enormous influence and, in the former's case, its geographical proximity.

Since the *Crisis* and the *Defender*, like the *Half-Century*, made it clear that reading their pages was essential to racial uplift, the *Half-Century* had to create a niche for itself; the "middle" became a strategic position by which this magazine distinguished itself. While critics such as Anne Elizabeth Carroll have identified interactions between African American periodicals during this period, they often overlook the less elite magazines and newspapers.[4] My focus on the magazine's positional work in relation to its more influential rivals highlights the middle, specifically the middlebrow, as a strategic position, and provides a deeper understanding of Black periodical networks and cultural categories. In effect, the insistence on the middle makes explicit the periodical's acknowledgement of and investment in its audience's radial reading of the magazine. The readers did not read each issue's article in isolation from the others and they did not read the *Half-Century* in isolation from its competitors. They made connections between the different components of the magazine and between the magazine and other publications; through the integration of advertising in its content and its claiming of the middle, the magazine both acknowledged and strategically used the inevitability of radial reading practices.

The magazine itself contained a mix of household tips, health tips, legal advice, editorials, fashion advice, and fiction with photographs and advertisements; the opening editorial of the July 1917 issue states that the publisher's purpose is "to make the HALF-CENTURY the greatest *home journal* of the race—one that will be a real service and credit."[5] While much of the fiction is forgettable, James Weldon Johnson's *The Autobiography of an Ex-Colored Man* was serialized in its pages, after the volume's initial 1912 publication and before its Harlem Renaissance republication, a fact that critics often overlook in recounting the novel's publication history (see figure 1). Johnson is an important figure here as he himself was part of multiple networks—political and aesthetic—in his roles as editor, author, and political activist. The publication of his novel with its affiliation with Harlem Renaissance networks of activism and political and aesthetic risk-taking in a middlebrow periodical highlights and complicates this picture of Black networks and cultural categories. In this chapter, as I focus on internal and external periodical codes, I will first discuss the *Half-Century*'s strategic uses of the middle before turning to Johnson's novel's seemingly incongruous appearance in the magazine's pages to draw attention to the process by which positions in networks are often strategically chosen or made rather than simply emerging organically. This active work of position-taking reveals investments that Black magazines made in the political, aesthetic, and economic realms (and the corresponding entanglements between the three). In particular, the fiction in these magazines, both the short domestic fiction and the longer fiction of Johnson, exposes the tensions between these realms and also their affinities.

FIGURE 1. Cover of *Half-Century Magazine* 9, no. 3 (October 1920). Courtesy of the General Research Division, the New York Public Library.

THE MIDDLEBROW'S INSTABILITY

The *Half-Century*'s title explicitly refers to the period of time since Emancipation; an internal advertisement for the magazine states that it "takes its name from Freedom's fiftieth anniversary" and "marks a new epoch in the development and growth of the Negro magazine."[6] Yet, it does not seem coincidental that it brings to mind the influential white genteel periodical, the *Century Illustrated Monthly Magazine* (1881–1930). Mark Noonan has described the *Century* as "a self-proclaimed 'democratic' periodical brimming with historical and biographical essays, serialized novels, updates on science and technology, and manifold discussions of contemporary events and issues that both instructed and entertained its predominantly middle-class readership."[7] Noonan continues by emphasizing that it "was part of what John Tomisch has called the 'genteel endeavor'—the attempt by northeastern elites to guide and improve the taste, manners, and behavior of America's middle, and sometimes, lower classes"; editors believed that "art and literature could symbolize national greatness, guide the public taste, and help unify the nation."[8] The *Half-Century* was interested in improving the taste and behavior of its readers, but it did not see art and literature as the main paths to that goal. Instead, as I demonstrate, the magazine's drive toward racial—rather than national—improvement coupled fiction with consumerism that was aimed particularly at women in the domestic sphere.

The *Half-Century*'s subtitle was "A Colored Monthly for the Business Man and the Home Maker," and it announced itself as containing "General Race News, Classy Fiction, Business, Fashion, Sports, Music, Fun." The magazine itself contained a mixture of fiction, practical essays, helpful tips, photo spreads of the latest fashions, and editorials; its advertisements with their emphasis on cosmetics and domestic products were, for the most part, aimed at women readers. Its first issue in August 1916 cost ten cents, while a year-long subscription was advertised at seventy-five cents. More than a year later, in the March 1917 issue, the magazine also began advertising foreign and Canadian subscription fees, demonstrating its success and expanded reach. In November 1919, costs were raised to fifteen cents for an issue and $1.50 for the year.[9] Noliwe Rooks comments, "While reliable circulation figures are impossible to obtain, some scholars have estimated that they reached as high as sixteen thousand copies per month (though the magazine itself put this number closer to forty-two thousand)."[10] An internal advertisement for the magazine states that its circulation was 47,000 in the May 1919 issue, although the time period for that circulation figure was not specified.[11] At their heights, the *Crisis* and the *Defender* had circulation figures of approximately 100,000 and 280,000, respectively.[12] The *Crisis* was based in New York City and the *Defender*'s and *Half-Century*'s editorial offices were located in Chicago, but all three periodicals had national reaches; however, it is important to note that, as the official organ of the NAACP, the *Crisis* most likely had a more racially mixed audience than did the other two. Clearly, assuming these figures are correct, the *Half-Century*'s tactics were successful in garnering a respectable share of the periodical audience, landing it squarely in the middle of the three periodicals in terms of peak circulation figures.

A November 1917 legal statement of ownership, as well as the statements of ownership in other issues, in the magazine states that Katherine E. Williams was the owner of the magazine.[13] However, as Robert Weems, Jr., has argued, it seems likely that Anthony Overton, an African American businessman who was involved in various ventures including the cosmetics industry and banking, backed Williams's endeavor in some way. The first issue of the magazine—and all subsequent issues—is filled with advertising for Overton's ventures, both in advertisements and articles. Overton founded the Overton Hygienic Manufacturing Company in 1898 to sell cosmetics aimed at Black women (see figure 2). This company led Overton to new business ventures in the banking, insurance, and periodical industries, and, as Weems has demonstrated, all these ventures were intertwined. The *Half-Century* promoted Overton's business concerns in its pages, and one way it did so was through marketing to a female audience. Weems claims that "the evidence strongly suggests that Overton utilized Williams as a 'front' for this female-oriented publication."[14] This strategy was part of Overton's long history of putting women at the center of his product marketing in order to sell to women while also relying on the rhetoric of racial uplift and Black pride to sell products. Regardless of Overton's role, two women were the public face of the magazine. Williams, later Williams-Irvin, was the editor in chief, while Kathryn M. Johnson acted as associate editor beginning in the November 1916 issue.

(There were other associate editors, including Howard A. Phelps, but Johnson was the constant.) This strategy brought commercial success to Overton and his Overton Hygienic Manufacturing Company, as seen in an increase in cosmetics sales after the founding of the magazine.[15]

The Versailles Treaty and the White Race

THE following article from one of the white dailies in Chicago shows the fear that is ever lurking near the white race that they will not always occupy their present positon. The great loss of whites in the world war and the rapid rise of the darker races keeps ever before them the unwelcome fact that "racial supremacy is merely a matter of dates in history. One race comes to the fore, plays its little part for a few years or a few centuries and leaves the center of the stage while its successor reigns supreme.

The publication of the official inquiry into the war losses reveals the shocking fact that the white race has lost more than forty million lives on account of the world war.

This is as if the entire population of France a nd Belgium had been wiped out by a deluge or as if the entire population of Great Britain had been destroyed or half the population of America.

But the worst of the story is not told when the number of lives lost is told. Those who fell in battle or died of military service were at the most productive and creative period of life and represent a loss of two or three times as great as those who die at any other period in life.

In Asia there are about nine hundred million people slumbering, with the exception of the Japanese. The Japanese are awake, are imperialistic, militaristic and internationally unscrupulous; they are capable in their own good time of awakening the sleeping hundreds of millions on their own continent.

They have within the last ten years doubled their resources and doubled their population. By the acquisition of Korea they have taken military control of twenty-three million Christians, whose religion, history, language and institutions they are slowly but ruthlessly destroying for the purpose of making the next generation wholly Japanese.

We had a treaty with the Koreans by which we promised to assist them under such circumstances, but among the traditions we have now temporarily abandoned is that of helping the weak against the stronger tyrant.

Under the provisions of the infamous treaty of Versailles, with its league of nations appendage, Japan was given Shantung aginst all decency and in rank betrayal of President Wilson of our ally China. Shantung adds forty millions of people to Japan's military resources. In twenty years, when these dominions have been thoroughly amalgamated with Japan, she will have a population greatly exceeding our own and will be in a position so dominating Asia that she will add the eight hundred millions of Asiatic peoples to her potential military strength.

Aiding and abetting Japan to gather this dangerous strength and destroying each other in internecine war is the method the white race has apparently adopted for commiting suicide.

Not contented with the lives already lost in the world war, the international bankers and militarists of France, England and the United States seem determined to destroy the two hundred million white men in Russia whom fate has placed on the map to be the pioneer defenders of the white race against the future awakening of the Asiatic hordes.

SYNOPSIS OF THE AUTOBIOGRAPHY OF AN EX-COLORED MAN.

The Ex-colored man, born in Georgia, is raised in Connecticut. His mother supports herself and son by sewing and gets a little financial help from the father. When he is ten, the boy is told that he is colored and that he is illegitimate because intermarriage between the races is prohibited in the South.

The father marries a white woman and the boy and his mother never hear from him again. After graduation from high school, the boy's mother dies and he decides to go South in accordance with her wishes and enter Atlanta University.

He is directed by a young Colored man to a cheap lodging house where all of his money, $400 is stolen. A colored railroad porter takes him in his soiled clothes hamper to Jacksonville, Fla., where he finds work in a Cuban cigar factory. Later when the factory closes he goes to New York with some Cuban friends in search of employment. He finds it impossible to work and gamble all night, so he decides in favor of gambling as a means of livlihood. He falls completely under the spell of this night life and finds it almost impossible to break away from it. He learns to play ragtime and becomes acquainted with a beautiful and wealthy white woman, known in the underworld as "the rich widow."

He also becomes acquainted ith a middle aged man, known as the "millionaire" who hires him to play for parties and thus gives him an opportunity to earn considerable money honestly. The "rich widow" and her escort, a little black man whom she supports, and who is very jealous of her, quarrel and the widow invites the ex-colored man to join her at a champagne party in order to excite the little black man's jealousy. The black man shoots the widow, killing her instantly. The ex-colored man makes his escape during the excitement and is picked up several hours later by the "millionaire." The millionaire decides to take him to Europe next day. While in Paris, during a performance at the theatre the ex-colored man sees his father for the second time in his life, and also his little sister whom he has never seen before. So strong was his desire to talk to his sister that he is forced to leave the theatre and drown his sorrows in drink.

Leaving Paris, they go to Holland, England and Germany. Just as they are packing for a tour of the orient, the ex-colored man decides that he will return to the United States and begin his work among the Colored people. In spite of the millionaire's protests, he sails for America. On board he meets a Colored doctor from Washington, D. C., who discusses the Negro question with him on voyage and invites him to visit his home. After his visit with the doctor he goes into the heart of the South and visits camp meetings, and other gatherings where he can study the Colored people closely. During this tour of the black belt he witnesses a lynching and burning of a man at stake. He becomes so disgusted he decided to pass for white, change his name, and accordingly he goes to New York to make friends and find work among white people. He loses himself entirely

EVER HEAR OF KINCAID ROW?

The Tales of Kincaid Row Will Begin in an Early Issue of "The Half-Century."

DON'T MISS THEM!

AIDA HAIR POMADE
(Aida Overton Walker)
CREATED FOR UTILITY AND FASHION
A perfect Hair Dressing, especially prepared for usage with the irons. Gives the hair a natural soft and silken lustre. Keeps the hair in the desired position in the warmest weather. If you are not one of its users, buy a can today and you will say: "It is just what I need." Aida Pomade is also used as a daily Hair Dressing, making rough hair soft and pliable.
MANUFACTURED BY
THE OVERTON-HYGIENIC MFG. CO.
DEPT. H. C. CHICAGO, ILL.

HIGH-BROWN SOAP
As much care should be exercised in the selection and use of a good toilet soap as with one's food.
OUR HIGH-BROWN SAVON DE LUXE represents the Acme of Perfection in scientific soap-making—it is daintily scented and is fragrance you will find delightful and pleasing.
Put up in a handsome Brown and Gold package.
Manufactured by
OVERTON-HYGIENIC MFG. CO.
Dept. H. C.
CHICAGO, ILL.

FIGURE 2. Overton-Hygienic cosmetics advertisements, *Half-Century Magazine* 9, no. 4 (November 1920): 11. Courtesy of the General Research Division, the New York Public Library.

In 1925, Overton and Williams-Irvin transformed the *Half-Century* into a weekly newspaper, the *Chicago Bee,* which lasted until 1946. Christopher Robert Reed describes the *Bee* as a "major weekly newspaper that presented a more middle-class conservative tone and content aimed at a sedate Sunday's reading."[16] In publishing the *Bee,* Overton and Williams-Irvin continued working to distinguish the periodical from Robert Abbott's *Defender:* "The *Bee* envisioned itself as taking an evolutionary step beyond Abbott's sensationalism, acceptance of fraudulent advertising, and promotion of superstitious, exploitative gimmicks."[17] The newspaper form, as opposed to the magazine, afforded a greater audience and provided the opportunity to compete more directly with the *Defender,* which was also a weekly; the newspaper form also allowed for the immediacy that a weekly provides with the focus on current events, rather than on fiction and features. Significantly, while Overton was frequently discussed in the pages of the *Defender* as a notable Chicago businessman and a credit to the race, particularly in relation to the Overton Hygienic Manufacturing Company, the frequency of mentions seems to decline after the founding of his magazine, suggesting that the *Defender* may have begun to see him as a competitor.

By rejecting chicken dinners, the *Half-Century* distances itself from a specific rural Southern aspiration that, the magazine implies, the *Defender* traffics in with its focus on recent Southern migrants. For example, in *The Autobiography of an Ex-Colored Man,* Johnson's nameless narrator travels to the rural South and discusses the Black churches he finds there: "Food, in the form of those two Southern luxuries, fried chicken and roast pork, is plentiful, and no one need go hungry. On the opening Sunday the women are immaculate in starched stiff white dresses adorned with ribbons either red or blue. Even a great many of the men wear streamers of vari-colored ribbons in the buttonholes of their coats."[18] The humble chicken dinner is here described as a luxury that is accompanied by respectable, non-ordinary, and aspirational fashions. The *Half-Century,* in rejecting the news of chicken dinners, refuses an affiliation with the rural South. It argues for an urban (and urbane) Northern respectability that is distinct from a rural Southern respectability.

In contrast to a focus on chicken dinners, the domestic columns of the *Half-Century* discuss vaguely exotic yet accessible dishes like oatmeal croquettes, French toast, and peas and egg compote,[19] while letters to the magazine describe embarrassment over working-class and rural Southern migrant dinners of neckbones and cabbages.[20] These "domestic surprises" are in effect aspirational leftovers, gussied up with words associated with French cuisine. Although French cuisine holds cultural connotations of elevated taste, it is important to note that these dishes were still accessible to readers; this accessible aspiration defines the middlebrow and places these foods in opposition to the lowbrow meals associated with the rural South. In speaking about those chicken dinners, the opening editorial continues by saying, "As such news items are fully covered by our leading Colored weeklies, we leave the field to their complete monopolistic control."[21] The rejection of lowbrow articles about lower-class chicken dinners—likely a reference to the *Defender,* which aimed to rehabilitate the manners and customs of Southern migrants—was one tool in the magazine's strategy for carving out a space for itself in an increasingly crowded periodical marketplace.

At the same time, the magazine aligned itself with the people. In a 1917 editorial, the magazine states, "The HALF-CENTURY is a popular magazine—that is to say, the people's magazine. The people we aim to please—the PEOPLE we must please—that is to say, the people and nobody else."[22] With this statement, the magazine situates itself in a class-based and taste-based hierarchy. It rejects highbrows and aligns itself with the masses, positioning itself as resolutely middlebrow; the news items about chicken dinners belong in the undiscriminating weeklies that were open to all kinds of news and, therefore, all kinds of readers. However, "the people and nobody else" do not equal the lowbrow for the magazine; like the *Defender,* the *Half-Century* was both explicitly and implicitly interested in questions of respectability. The magazine ran an etiquette column, and, like the *Defender*'s "What the People Say" page of letters to the editor, the *Half-Century*'s "The People's Forum," which made its debut in the February 1919 issue, was a lively place for discussing what it meant to be in public.

Notably, the *Half-Century* worked to argue against the *Defender*'s sensationalistic reporting style, positioning itself as a more respectable alternative. Ethan Michaeli notes that, early in its life, the *Defender* hit upon a winning formula, led by managing editor J. Hockley Smith, that relied on "using modern design concepts borrowed from the Hearst- and Pulitzer-owned dailies, separating the news and sports sections and spreading out headlines, with giant red letters across multiple columns to grab readers' attention. As with any other newspaper in the country, there were plenty of crime stories laced with salacious details, but the articles that really built circulation were those focusing on the atrocities committed in the South."[23] While the *Half-Century* predictably condemned the white press for portraying African Americans in a negative light, it also criticized the Black press, particularly the *Defender:* "Many of the Colored papers, following the beaten path of the white journals are filling their columns full to overflowing with scandals of every kind."[24] In making this criticism, the magazine sought to differentiate itself by carving out a place in the preexisting counterpublic networks, dominated by other more popular and established periodicals. Examining the Black press reveals the extent to which the counterpublic sphere of the newspapers and magazines was a site for discussing what it meant to be in public. The public realm was seen to be politically charged, and the periodicals' focus on respectability worked to take control of the political meanings of being in public, whether in print or in society.

Even as the magazine's rejection of chicken dinner news is a rejection of the *Defender* and other weekly newspapers, the emphasis on "the people" in the *Half-Century*'s editorial is a dig at the *Crisis* and its like. Abby Arthur Johnson and Ronald Maberry Johnson have noted that "more of the *Crisis* audience was probably middle rather than working class, and some readers were lured away by competing periodicals."[25] As one of these "competing periodicals," the *Half-Century* lured away readers through its explicit focus on the people. While Ann Ardis has analyzed the *Crisis* in relation to the middlebrow—a relationship, it should be noted, that does not seem particularly controversial—the magazine was not seen as middlebrow by some of its contemporaries.[26] In situating itself in an aesthetic hierarchy by rejecting the "highbrows" of Du Bois's *Crisis,* the *Half-Century* declares, "It will not be our sole ambition to make this magazine a 'literary gem' either for our own gratification or to suit the fancy of the 'highbrows,' but to present facts in plain, commonsense language, so that the masses may read and understand."[27] The magazine then worked to distinguish itself from its more famous competitor by arguing for its place with the masses; however, the "masses" that made up the magazine's ideal readership were not just anyone, since the magazine not only had the task of distinguishing itself from Du Bois's magazine but also from the more "lowbrow" *Chicago Defender.* The rhetoric of middleness acted as a strategy to prove the magazine's worth within its periodical network, instead of condemning the magazine as mediocre or average. Through, in part, the technique of explicitly defining itself in opposition to the *Crisis* and the *Defender,* the *Half-Century* constructed its middleness and took ownership of it for strategic reasons that were political, aesthetic, and, most of all, economic.

Clearly, the question of intellectual and aesthetic "brows," terminology that originates in racist phrenological hierarchies, is a tricky one, but I propose a mode of reading that provides a deeper understanding of the relationships between African American periodicals during the early twentieth century.[28] A deeper engagement with periodical networks and their marketing pressures and strategies offers insight into the aesthetic classifications of the time. The positional work of the *Half-Century* in relation to the *Crisis* and the *Defender* acted as a market strategy, grounded in the ideology of uplift, to carve out a niche in the world of the Black press. Rooks's compelling examination of the *Half-Century* foregrounds its emphasis on fashion as a means to uplift within the context of migration; she observes, "The chance to view African American women occupying public spaces, to read about African American female heroines as they negotiated an urban environment that was new to many of the fictional characters, as well as to the stories' readers, quickly made the magazine a project different from those undertaken by previous publications."[29] Since all three periodicals highlighted respectability to varying degrees, they had to frame these discussions in distinctive ways to maintain their positions within a competitive market, and the *Half-Century* continually engaged in fashioning itself as an alternative to other periodicals.

Through this kind of position-taking and competition, the magazine asserted itself in a network of other African American magazines, not to mention the networks of mainstream white magazines. For example, the first issue of the magazine contains a section titled "With Our Exchanges" with excerpts from the *Louisville News*, the *Amsterdam News*, and the *Chicago Defender*.[30] These networks are what Pierre Bourdieu has called *fields*: "In analytic terms, a field may be defined as a network, or a configuration, of objective relations between positions."[31] In his discussion of these networks, Bourdieu describes the relationality of positions in the arts world as a field of cultural production in which a shift in the position of one literary genre, for example, changes the position of another. The field contains positions that range from the commercial to the aesthetic and everything in between, and the field of cultural production itself has varying relations to the social and economic fields, according to Bourdieu. The field acts as a network, although the specific use of the term "field" here emphasizes the relativity of the positions in the particular network of which the Black periodicals are a part. While the concept of the field can be seen to leave out human agency due to the characterization of the field as being composed of forces that interact with one another, my reading of Bourdieu emphasizes the agency of the actors in the field; cultural institutions, like the magazine, actively choose to position themselves in particular ways based on the relative positions of other institutions in that field. Bourdieu states, "Participants in a field, say, economic firms, high fashion designers, or novelists, constantly work to differentiate themselves from their closest rivals in order to reduce competition and to establish a monopoly over a particular subsector of the field."[32] Thus, the *Half-Century's* taking of the middle position is about competing through differentiation, even though the middle is often linked to the mediocre. The position of the middle within a field is particularly relational as genres or, as in this case, cultural institutions in the middle negotiate their distance from the high and the low to define themselves.

Due to the middlebrow's instability as a category, it is often defined only in relation to other categories, as the middle between the high and the low—not one or the other but both and none. Melissa Sullivan and

Sophie Blanch identify this constitutive characteristic as the middlebrow's "cultural variability," what Bourdieu has identified as the relationality of the field.[33] The *Half-Century* played with the very slipperiness of the middle to shape itself within the periodical marketplace by allowing the magazine to affiliate itself with the aims of its competitors, even as it disavowed those periodicals' methods: "A person subscribing for the HALF-CENTURY will always feel satisfied that he is getting a magazine that doesn't contain the same things that some other magazine he is subscribing for already contains; and will feel that the two, while different in principle and policy, are yet complementary in aim and purpose."[34]

John Guillory has pointed out that claiming the middle can often be a way of disavowing political engagement: "Middlebrow culture is very much characterized by this antipathy to the political, as it sees culture wholly as a means to individual self-improvement and has long since divorced such improvement from the arena of political citizenship."[35] In their pioneering study of twentieth-century African American magazines, Johnson and Johnson describe the *Half-Century* as a "black popular journal," a genre that "tried to entertain rather than to instruct or lead the larger Afro-American reading public."[36] Through its very name, the *Half-Century* chose to present itself as being less explicitly political than its competitors, with the names of the *Defender* and the *Crisis*, the latter taking its name from James Russell Lowell's nineteenth-century abolitionist poem "The Present Crisis."

Yet an African American magazine during the Jim Crow period could not completely divorce itself from the political realm, and so the magazine began incorporating politics into its middlebrow concerns. In its early days, the magazine was made up of sections titled "Pin Money Frocks," "What They Are Wearing," "Musical and Dramatic," "Etiquette," "Beauty Hints," "If It's Funny—Laugh!," and "Domestic Science," along with fiction, poetry, and "General Race News." Over time, it gradually began including more political content, particularly beginning around the time of the First World War. Kathryn Johnson, the associate editor, seems responsible for the push toward discussing racial injustices, as her bylines were often associated with the articles on racial violence. The magnitude of the events of the day during the war and the juxtapositions of Black patriotism and Jim Crow injustices seemed to lead the magazine to a deeper engagement with politics, even as it maintained its focus on the home and so-called feminine concerns. This gradual shift also indicates the readers' demand for coverage of both types of topics and, consequently, the absence of any sense that either readers or the magazine's staff perceived these foci as contradictory. This sometimes led to some unusual juxtapositions, such as when the magazine covered the 1922 "Who Is the Prettiest Colored Girl in the United States?" contest, which was judged by such luminaries as Anthony Overton, Mrs. Robert Abbott (wife of the publisher of the *Chicago Defender*), and Ida Wells-Barnett.[37] The most overtly political sections were the unsigned opening editorials, presumably written by Williams-Irvin, and essays penned by a figure called "the Investigator," who may have been Williams-Irvin or Johnson.

Despite its focus on respectability, the magazine did not shy away from pointing out the very real biases, threats, and grievances that led to the race riots of the period. In an editorial titled "East St. Louis," which was accompanied by her portrait, Johnson delves into the reasons for the "riot": "That ninety million whites should take such a mean and vicious advantage of ten million Colored people as has been taken in this country through numerous riots and lynchings, seems preposterous. And yet they do so, and then have no hesitation in asking them to fight to preserve and defend the same government that permits such atrocities."[38] She closes the editorial by discussing "1200 Negro men, splendid in physique, masterly in intellect, and sober and clean in their lives, preparing themselves to lead troops of their own color into the great world carnage."[39] In making the connection between racial terrorism and the patriotism of African American troops, Johnson highlights the hypocrisy of the Jim Crow nation. In the strongly worded editorial "Race Riots in Chicago," the Investigator explains the race riots that rocked the Red Summer of 1919. Throughout the piece, the author describes the white perpetrators as "ruffians" and the Black people who died as a result of the violence as "heroes": "Such Colored men and women who protected their own lives and homes and the lives and homes of hundreds of Colored men, widows and children were not hoodlums. Not that we approve of rioting, but the blood which these Colored men spilled *was a holy libation poured on the altar for race liberty.*"[40] In redefining the people involved in the riots, the Investigator labels the riots as not just self-defense, but specifically as protests and acts of resistance to racial violence and inequality—acts that she describes in religious terms. She uses vivid language that seems out of place amid the magazine's discussions of etiquette and shopping: "What occurred in Chicago may occur in a greater or lesser degree in other places. The same agony and hell must go abroad before some white people learn that the Negro has retreated his last time and that we will choke up the streets with our dead before we will stand for the brutalisms which we have been too long subjected to."[41] The implicit overall argument of the magazine is that domestic concerns and individual self-improvement on the one hand, and political engagement with the racial issues of the day on the other hand are not contradictory. Consumerism and homemaking are part of fighting against those "brutalisms."

At the same time, the magazine's politics were fashioned as oppositional not only to Jim Crow practices but to the politics of its rival periodicals. While the three periodicals shared the goal of Black uplift, they—or, rather the *Half-Century*—professed serious differences in the best strategies for progress. Despite its concern with political issues of the day, the *Half-Century* resisted conceiving of itself as a tool for propaganda, which would then create an overlap with the *Crisis.* A 1917 editorial declares, "The HALF-CENTURY is different from any other magazine published for the benefit of Colored people . . . To begin with—the HALF-CENTURY is not the organ of any cause, religion, sect or propaganda . . . The field of propaganda is thoroughly and creditably covered by, at least, one other monthly publication; and we are glad to tell our readers and friends that it is no part of our desires to divide the field with this well-known organ. Our policy calls for specialization, not 'Along The Color Line,' but along other and equally essential lines."[42] The reference to Du Bois's "Along the Color Line" column makes it clear that the editorial refers to the propaganda of the *Crisis,* the official organ of the NAACP. The *Half-Century,* thus, walked a delicate line between condemning the racial sensationalism of the *Defender* as being harmful to the race and refusing to emphasize propaganda of the kind that the *Crisis* engaged in. The opening editorial of the April 1917 issue, titled "Reciprocity and Co-operation," made the magazine's political positioning within the middle explicit: "In its temperament, the HALF-CENTURY is neither staid nor sensational—neither conservative nor radical. Happy is that organ 'of the people, by the people, for the people' that can find the middle ground and not be diverted to either extreme."[43]

A focus on domestic concerns allowed the *Half-Century Magazine* to claim the middle and provided it with a position on uplift that was different from the *Defender*'s emphasis on public spaces like city streets, and from the *Crisis*'s national and global perspective. (Of course, the *Half-Century* believed that those domestic spaces were ultimately public since the clothing made at home from the patterns offered by the magazine would eventually be worn on the streets.) In her study of the twentieth-century British novel, Nicola Humble defined the middlebrow as having "a particular concentration on feminine aspects of life, a fascination with domestic space, a concern with courtship and marriage, a preoccupation with aspects of class and manners."[44] The *Half-Century*'s focus on the homemaker suggests that the responsibility for Black respectability was firmly the domain of Black women in the domestic sphere; women, in other words, had the obligation to cultivate respectability, as it was perceived as being birthed in the home before being put on display in the public arena. This obligation also reinforced the consumer status of women, to whom advertisements concerning domesticity and, consequently, respectability were aimed.

Like the *Half-Century*, the *Defender*'s pages were filled with discussions of racial uplift through respectability from a variety of genres, such as photographs, cartoons, letters to the editor, columns, and articles; however, though domesticity was important to the newspaper's vision of respectability, it was overshadowed by an emphasis on being seen in public, particularly on urban streets, during the period of the Great Migration. While the *Crisis* engaged in what Evelyn Brooks Higginbotham has called "the politics of respectability" through its depictions of the Talented Tenth and its lack of depictions of those African Americans who did not fit the mold of elite professionalism that was central to uplift, it was far from a Booker T. Washington model of uplift wherein African American respectability was the main path toward rights.[45] Du Bois's vision of political engagement confronted lynchings and other forms of racial injustice by criticizing the structural conditions that allowed them to flourish in the Jim Crow United States. It is fair to say that the *Half-Century* contained far less in the way of explicit discussions of politics in comparison to the *Defender* and, especially, the *Crisis,* which called itself a "record of the darker races" and saw its main concern to be the fight against racial violence and the unjust structures of Jim Crow. But, as previously discussed, the *Half-Century* did not completely shy away from talking about the political issues of the day, such as debates around the vote, war, Race Riot Commission, and concerns about white philanthropy.

Those discussions seem to conflict with the placid domestic fiction published in its pages, but, again, the domestic fiction and concerns of the magazine cannot be dismissed as completely apolitical. In fact, in their July 1917 opening editorial, the editors presented a guide for reading the fiction in relation to the goal of racial uplift: "The fiction in this magazine is intended to combine with the other features so as always to accentuate this predominant endeavor of its publishers and editors."[46] In juxtaposing sections on racial injustices with stories about marriage and fashion, the magazine revealed the connections between the domestic sphere and the larger world; these juxtapositions make the argument for prioritizing the private space of the home to push back against racism, segregation, and violence.

At the same time, the magazine in its editorials and readers' letters became a space where the discussion of what constituted a respectable Black press took place. What, in other words, is the role of the Black press? The *Defender* defined the newspaper's responsibility to provide guidance to its readers with a staff editorial that states, "If people have not yet learned how to conduct themselves in a city, they should be taught—and no agency is better fitted to teach them than a newspaper."[47] The *Half-Century,* however, argued that newspapers like the *Defender* undo their good work through their seemingly sensationalistic reporting. In a 1921 editorial titled "Bombing Your Own Home," by the

Investigator, the importance of the press and the potential for its abuse are highlighted.[48] The Investigator asks, "What we should like to know, however, is just why colored publications insist on printing every bit of damaging information possible, true or alleged, about members of the race in every issue of the paper?" Eventually, the writer points out, "No sane man would bomb his house just because a white man had bombed it, but publishing such articles is just as damaging as bomb throwing." In linking the *Defender*'s tactics to bomb-throwing, the Investigator argues that the Black newspaper has committed an act that is as harmful to the race as racial violence is.

This editorial from the *Half-Century* suggests that the *Defender* and its ilk were not respectable, despite their obvious concern with respectability. Indeed, in so arguing, the magazine takes part in what Joan Shelley Rubin has called the "terrain of middlebrow culture" that "proved solid ground on which the genteel outlook [of the nineteenth century] could be reconstituted" within the first half of the twentieth century.[49] A 1923 *Half-Century* editorial states, "The average white person, reading one of our journals would get the impression that we are a race of thieves and murderers, that all of our women are disreputable and that scandal is the very breath of life to us. Why not clean up a bit and seek some news that is cleaner and uplifting."[50] This language about press hygiene resembles the language commonly used to discuss cleaning up the ill-mannered people and unpleasant homes that were seen as dragging down the race; the press's respectability shared a kinship with individual and group respectability, and all these kinds of respectability were located in relation to actual and imagined white surveillance.

In "The People's Forum" section of the June 1920 issue of the magazine, for example, a Mrs. W. M. Newman complains about a woman who "ran out of a nearby house clad only in her kimono and bedroom slippers. Her hair was not combed and she wore no stockings . . . I don't believe that there would be half as much friction between the races if every [Colored person] made an effort to keep himself and his premises immaculately clean and tidy."[51] Similarly, an "immaculately clean and tidy" press is important to reducing the "friction between the races." It is no accident that the "Scandal" editorial from 1923 mentioned the perception that "all of our women are disreputable," and the 1920 letter complained about a woman's apparent lack of cleanliness; this emphasis on uplift is gendered, and the magazine connects women to the important task of cultivating cleanliness within the context of white surveillance that is refracted through a discourse of intraracial surveillance. According to this uplift ideology, women and a press that is aimed at women are both responsible for producing respectability.

These concerns with the politics of respectability are linked to middle-class ideals. Yet it would be a mistake to simply equate the middlebrow with the middle class, as aesthetic brows are informed by class considerations but not determined by them. Writing during the 1920s, E. Franklin Frazier observed, "Class differentiation among Negroes is reflected in their church organizations, educational institutions, private clubs, and the whole range of social life. Although these class distinctions may rest upon what would seem to outsiders flimsy and inconsequential matters, they are the social realities of Negro life, and no amount of reasoning can rid his mind of them."[52] While Reed claims that "a highly discernible, multitiered middle class existed as well by 1920," it seems clear that, based on the insistence of continually differentiating the middle class from the working class in the pages of the *Half-Century*, the Black middle class displayed anxiety about its position and boundaries.[53] The Black middle class's position during Jim Crow and the Great Migration was more unstable than that of its white counterpart's, so the counterpublic sphere was continually occupied with defining itself and its difference from others.

The *Half-Century* explicitly and implicitly worked to provide a more defined shape to the middle class, and it acted as a mirror by which its members could see themselves and, even more likely, as an aspirational ideal for those in the working class. The periodical then was both constructive and reflexive in its relation to the Black middle class. One element of Black middle class self-definition lies in the creation of reading material that reflected and constructed what it meant to be part of this group. As Bourdieu has noted, taste is central to class definitions. While the label of "middlebrow" has most often been used by those who sneer at the purveyors and consumers of middlebrow art, the label was claimed with pride by the *Half-Century* because of its very associations with the middle-class public. The middle class acted as an aspirational category for African Americans reading the magazine; the promise of the middlebrow is the promise that reading its art identifies the reader with the middle class or, at the very least, can allow him or her to perform middle class identity (with its attendant tastes, as Bourdieu has suggested).

READING THE MIDDLE: SHORT FICTION IN THE MAGAZINE

The *Half-Century* magazine did not simply exist within a field of Black periodicals. Its entanglements in class politics were deeply embedded in white middle-class status; it was in dialogue with white middle-class ideologies, and, correspondingly, with middlebrow periodicals aimed at a white audience at the time. Although defined by its difference from the larger public, the counterpublic of the *Half-Century* was in many ways invested in the norms that defined the larger public of the dominant social group. A February 1917 internal advertisement declares, "The HALF-CENTURY is primarily a Colored Ladies' Home Journal. We aim to please the women and make it popular."[54] In a July 1917 discussion about the magazine expanding its focus on fiction, the magazine links itself with mainstream, white-focused magazines like the "*American, Ladies' Home Journal, Everybody's, Hearst*'s, [and] *Woman's Home Companion.*"[55] These mainstream magazines emphasized fiction, and some of them, particularly the extraordinarily popular *Ladies' Home Journal* (1883–present) and *Woman's Home Companion* (1873–1957), were aimed mainly at white women and included articles related to domestic concerns.[56]

Helen Damon-Moore in her comparative study of *Ladies' Home Journal* and the *Saturday Evening Post* has argued that these magazines were part of a turn-of-the-century shift that "helped to promote a relationship between gender and commerce that has been complicated, long-lasting, and powerful."[57] Jennifer Scanlon points out that the *Ladies' Home Journal* was particularly successful in providing "a balance between the fostering of anxiety that draws readers to seek out advice and the offering of positive messages that encourage them to return the following month."[58] This strategy was essential to marketing the periodical and shaping women as consumers. Scanlon claims that "the *Journal* suggested that democracy for women meant little more than the choice between one brand of soap and another, one flavor of soup and another."[59] With its focus on Black women as consumers and consumption as a form of activism, the *Half-Century* parallels the *Ladies' Home Journal*'s emphasis on "women as the culture's primary consumers and women as primarily consumers."[60] As I will demonstrate, the construction and portrayal of Black women as consumers serves to link consumption to the overall progress of the race. The *Half-Century*'s relative positionality to these white magazines reveals the pushes and pulls between hegemonic white ideals and Black pride within the periodical field.

In its efforts to promote itself as a news source and better alternative to its competition, the *Half-Century* often displayed a concern with reading that was both self-promoting and racially uplifting. This emphasis on advertising the magazine by extoling the virtues of specific reading practices is seen most clearly in an April 1922 editorial titled "Read More": "Colored people should read Colored publications regularly. That is the surest means of learning the truth about themselves. White papers seldom print anything about us except that which is funny, ridiculous, or the misdemeanors of the miscreants of the race."[61] This editorial ends by saying, "The surest way to keep well informed and abreast of the times is to read *The Half-Century Magazine* each month. Fifty cents in stamps or coin pays for a year's subscription."[62] The magazine makes explicit the link between reading and behavior, which is then linked to perceptions of the race. In fact, the private activity of reading is described as having public consequences for the race. The *Half-Century* went so far as to portray reading as a public activity in its advertising strategy, which asked its readers to pass on sample issues to others, who should then wish to subscribe to the magazine; almost every issue of the magazine contains a box in the opening editorial page with a note saying, "We ask that each person receiving a sample copy, and also all regular subscribers, show the Magazine to others, hoping that they too will like our Magazine."[63]

The magazine's connections between self-promotion, uplift, and reading were extended in a July–August 1922 editorial titled "What Do Your Children Read?," which warns: "A deplorably large number of stories found in the popular magazines of the day, feature heroines who smoke incessantly and appear in public with dresses remarkable for their fabulous cost, their scantiness and transparency."[64] It continues, "Young people must read, but it is well to see that they are supplied with good books and with magazines that will not taint the mind."[65] Several issues of the magazine contain Progressive Book Publishing Company advertisements, which asked the question, "Why Don't You Get Acquainted with Your Race?" and gave the suggestion of buying a collection of songs and spirituals, or a book on Paul Laurence Dunbar or the *Encyclopedia of Colored People*.[66] This emphasis on uplifting books is grounded in the notion that reading could teach a person how to be a respectable member of the race; this, of course, aligned with the *Half-Century*'s overall marketing strategy by emphasizing the importance of also reading a magazine that would not taint the mind. A March 1919 unsigned editorial, titled "Our Program," even declares, "The *Half-Century Magazine* set up an ideal of clean literature and clean advertising when it first came into being"; the language of cleanliness links the magazine's literature and advertisements to the previously discussed language of cleanliness that is essential to racial uplift.[67] This emphasis on reading is a deliberate move that reveals the tie between the magazine's editorials and its marketing. Ultimately, uplift is not simply a political strategy, but also a marketing one.

Indeed, the magazine places its helpful features on domestic issues alongside fiction that highlights these issues. For example, Evelyn Eastman's one-page short story "Bab Prepares Herself" reveals how a young woman can work to improve herself before marriage.[68] In this story, Bab, who is described as someone who doesn't "know the first thing about cooking or sewing" and "wouldn't even know what to do with a scrub brush," is schooled by her future mother-in-law in how to take care of the domestic space and "everything else a wife should know from one who really could teach [her] right."[69] At the end, Bab proudly says to Tom, "I can wash and iron and sew and make hats, too, and Mother Gray says I can clean up the house about as well and as quickly as she can."[70] However, before Bab turned to Mrs. Gray for domestic guidance, she had attended cooking school and worked at a millinery store to learn these valuable domestic skills but, as she says, "at the cooking school I only learned food values and so far haven't learned how prepare a single dish and at the millinery store I only learned how to make buckram shapes and they told me it would be a year or more before I learned really how to make a hat fit to wear."[71] These alternative education sources prove to be inadequate, whereas Mrs. Gray as a maternal figure successfully inculcates Bab in the ideology of domesticity to make her a worthy wife for Tom and, in fact, a second Mrs. Gray. The magazine's articles on etiquette, like Margaret Lyndon's "Serving the Dinner" and Mary Black's "The Duties of the Hostess," in effect, act as Mother Grays by providing practical domestic advice for readers who might not have their own knowledgeable mothers or mothers-in-law.[72] Similarly, advertisements for domestic products like Universal Metal Polish, which is associated with "Cleanliness and Good Cheer," teach readers what products to use to maintain an ideal domestic space.[73] The fiction, features, and advertising work together to teach the readers what they should desire, do, and be.

This technique of weaving together the different aspects of the magazine to create an integrated marketing message is extended further through the *Half-Century*'s emphasis on shopping, rather than maintaining a sole focus on racial injustice—unlike in the *Crisis,* in which consumerism is not as strongly tied to the task of crafting social change. The early twentieth century was marked by a rise in the number of advertisements in periodicals as magazines became more and more dependent on revenue from advertisements rather than on subscriptions alone. In discussing this shift, Ellen Gruber Garvey has written, "As advertisers increasingly defined women as their target audience, advertising-dependent magazines presented their women readers with fiction that encouraged them in their role as consumers."[74] She continues, "In a sense, the magazine itself, like the department store, exalted consumerist choice making. Both magazines and department stores were considered respectable spaces in which middle-class women could wander."[75]

The *Half-Century* itself was like a department store in that it offered goods for sale, not only in its advertisements, but also in its content, tying consumerism to racial uplift and race pride. The magazine, for example, offered shopping and pattern services, which made it possible for readers to write in and buy clothing or patterns that would then allow them to buy or make clothing that would align them with the fashionable women depicted in the magazine's pages and distinguish them from those who must make do with provincial fashions. Fashion, therefore, was not conceived of as frivolous within the magazine, as it supported women in looking their best and thus participating in the project of racial uplift. At the same time, sustaining the Black economy allowed the woman as consumer to be a central driver in racial uplift. In contrast to the populist *Defender* and the elite *Crisis,* the *Half-Century* oriented itself to a large degree toward women. While the other periodicals do acknowledge women's issues and concerns, the *Half-Century* magazine makes explicit claims for the feminine as its domain through its emphasis on a consumerist domesticity and, in more general terms, the middlebrow's associations with the feminine.

This is made abundantly clear in a short story by Jane Jones titled "The Awakening of Jim Gray"; this story works in concert with the advertisements and in particular the shopping service within the magazine to counter criticisms of shopping and to emphasize its non-materialistic benefits. The protagonist, Muriel Gray, hungers to buy clothing from the department store Condon's, but her husband, who makes a decent living, "would rather wear rags than to break into a certain sum of money and purchase a decent suit of clothes."[76] Eventually, Jim Gray comes around and realizes that Muriel is a "good wife, pure, quiet, self-denying" and, thus, deserves to have some money spent on her; the title of the story connects this realization to a spiritual "awakening" for Jim.[77] As a surprise, he purchases a "blue canton crepe dress" for his wife from a "catalog of New York styles," and all is well at the end. The marriage is strengthened through the recognition that shopping is not frivolous and, in fact, necessary at times.[78]

Throughout the story, materialism is consistently associated with the natural world. The story, for example, begins with a description of the store windows of Condon's: "Wax figures of beautiful women, clad in wonderful garments, smiled blankly at great jars of beautiful flowers and exotic birds posed on flower-laden trees."[79] Here, the department store is depicted as a site affiliated with the natural world with its flowers and birds. Muriel splurges on a dress at Condon's, but her previous "splurge" was planting flowers in her yard (as opposed to the more practical vegetables that Jim wanted).[80] Muriel desires the dress and the flowers for the same reason: she has a "beauty-hungry soul."[81] That clothing and flowers fulfill the same role of aesthetic pleasure for Muriel reveals the story's conjoining of material objects and the natural world. At the end of the story, Jim not only buys Muriel a dress but he allows her to have "all the front yard for flowers."[82] This story implicitly argues that shopping fulfills a natural spiritual longing for beauty; it sanctions and encourages readers' desires to spend money and shop. This valorization of consumerism corresponds to racial uplift in the pages of the *Half-Century,* in particular through Overton's emphasis on Black economy. In other words, the magazine continually encouraged and cajoled its readers to buy Black-made products, such as cosmetics, as a way of expressing race pride and working toward uplift. Black consumerism is a kind of activism according to the magazine's stories, editorials, and advertisements.

The link between condemning its competitors, such as the *Defender,* as not being respectable and, thus, detrimental to the race overall, and its marketing of itself is made explicit in the *Half-Century*'s criticisms of its rival's advertisements: "A single edition of a Colored newspaper recently contained twenty-one ads, mostly from fake white concerns who promise to bleach the skin, and forty ads that guarantee to make the hair long, straight and glossy."[83] This editorial, titled "Betrayers of the Race," makes it clear that advertising products made by white-owned companies are detrimental to racial uplift: "It is lamentable that these [Colored] editors will help a white man swindle the race solely because they are receiving good pay for printing their ads."[84] As Garvey has argued, "Magazines as a group constructed the reader as consumer," and, in so doing, the magazine also insisted on the link between consumption and racial uplift.[85]

This focus on advertising was an important part of the magazine, both in terms of promoting the magazine itself and in advertising the various ventures of Overton, the magazine's supposed publisher. Margaret Beetham has observed that magazines are "deeply involved in capitalist production and consumption as well as circulating in the cultural economy of collective meanings and constructing an identity for the individual reader as gendered and sexual being."[86] However, in mainstream magazines like the *Ladies' Home Journal,* African American readers were not the overt focus of the advertisements; as Scanlon observes, "When it came to race and ethnicity, advertisers could and generally did ignore potential consumers in spite of information that these women were in fact purchasing products, even their products."[87] In fact, during the 1910s and 1920s, in "the most popular women's magazine of the day," the *Ladies' Home Journal,* "the only African American presence . . . was an occasional servant and, more frequently, characters in advertisements for Aunt Jemima Pancake Syrup and Cream of Wheat, both of which featured prevalent cultural stereotypes."[88] Black women, who indeed read periodicals like the *Ladies' Home Journal,* would only have been able to see themselves in mainstream magazines in limited and often stereotypical roles, which cast them as adjacent to white consumers.

In contrast, the *Half-Century*'s advertisements positioned Black women specifically as consumers and offered mirrors in which their desires were reflected. The advertisements intertwined with the editorial content; consumerism was an integral component of the uplift mission within the internal network of the magazine. This synergy, as we may call it in modern advertising terms, is and was, as Scanlon notes, a common component of women's magazines in which "the line between the magazine's internal departments, the editorial material and fiction, and the advertising, which came from external agencies, was often less than clearly drawn."[89] In the case of the *Half-Century,* the extent of Overton's editorial involvement in the magazine is difficult to know, but the explicit and implicit advertising for Overton's business concerns seems to suggest that he had at least some involvement. Advertising for Overton cosmetics—such as Ro-Zol bleaching cream, Aida Pomade, and High-Brown Hair Grower—is intertwined with the magazine's content.

The magazine calls, for example, for readers to support skin bleaching cream companies owned by African Americans; these were accompanied by letters from readers testifying to the horrors of white-produced skin bleaching creams. The editorial pages laud the launch of the Douglass Bank, owned by Overton, in the editorial pages, even as the issues contained full-page advertisements for the bank that were, in fact, difficult to distinguish from regular magazine features.

JAMES WELDON JOHNSON IN THE *HALF-CENTURY*

Alongside the cosmetics and bank ads and the stories about marriage, mothers-in-law, and shopping, the *Half-Century* serialized a very different work of fiction from its other published pieces: James Weldon Johnson's *The Autobiography of an Ex-Colored Man*. Readers of the October 1920 issue would have been faced with three rather different pieces of fiction. First up was a short story by Leona Gray titled "Mammy Sue" that told the tale of a devoted Black servant, a "mammy," who, unlike the traitorous new white servants, faithfully nurses her white employers during an influenza crisis.[90] Also published in that issue was the first installment of "Identification for Two," a three-part story by W. Edward Davenport about a young man's marriage choices.[91] In this convoluted story, which is grounded in the ideals of respectability, a young man wishes, at first, to marry one woman who later rejects him. He then discovers that he has a sister, which causes him sadness because he is now in love with that woman. Fortunately, it turns out that she is, in fact, adopted, and thus not genetically related to him, allowing them to experience matrimonial bliss after all. The third piece of fiction was a particularly important installment of Johnson's *The Autobiography of an Ex-Colored Man*.[92] This installment portrayed the famous scene in which the narrator's horror over witnessing a lynching in the South catalyzes his decision to become an ex-colored man—to pass, in other words. In examining this selection from the novel in the context of the magazine, I aim, in part, to explain what it means for the harrowing lynching scene to be placed alongside these insipid works of fiction about "mammies" and marriage.

In a February 1917 request for fiction submissions, the magazine outlined its guiding principles in choosing appropriate short stories: "We do not want philosophy, science, sociology and eloquence—we editors have a plenty of that ourselves." It continued: "Our people—tired at the end of the day's work—have no time to consume [*sic*] reading solid literary stuff. They want diversion and recreation, and will read anything stimulating and refreshing." In particular, "they will read light, airy fiction—full of snap, pep and go."[93] While Johnson's novel can be described in a number of ways, it does not seem plausible to associate it with "light, airy fiction—full of snap, pep and go." Furthermore, the issue in which the lynching scene is published opens with an advertisement proclaiming, "The Secret of a Charming Personality Is In a Proper and Becoming Arrangement of the Hair"; the issue also included a feature on fall fashions—"What They Are Wearing"—and other columns titled "Domestic Science" and "Beauty Hints."[94]

The fact of the novel's serialization in the *Half-Century* has dropped out of its official publication history. What this means is that a full picture of the networks in which Johnson's novel was embedded is missing from the critical conversation. The generally accepted publication history of *The Autobiography of an Ex-Colored Man* is famous. Initially published anonymously in 1912, the novel was republished in 1927 under Johnson's name at the peak of the Harlem Renaissance.[95] This account suggests that the novel was mainly associated with two networks: the network associated with the initial anonymous edition and subsequent reviews and the network linked to the Harlem Renaissance elite. However, this publication history—and even Johnson's own autobiography—overlooks the novel's reprinting and serialization from November 1919 to December 1920 in the *Half-Century*. In other words, the novel is part of a middlebrow network that is in seeming tension with its later Harlem Renaissance affiliation.

Indeed, while the generally received history presents the novel's second publication as the introduction of Johnson as its author, an examination of the *Half-Century* reveals that Johnson's name was associated with the novel years before its second publication as a book by Alfred A. Knopf. In fact, the magazine began advertising the serialization of what it called "the great novel" in the July 1919 opening editorial; the

September 1919 issue presented a photograph of Johnson, along with photographs of Antoinette Garnes and Archibald J. Carey, in a section titled "Persons of Note" by Howard Phelps, an associate editor of the magazine.[96] Tellingly, no other work of fiction is given as much space in the magazine—the novel is serialized over thirteen issues from November 1919 through December 1920.

Most critics do not devote much time to analyzing the significance of this novel's appearance in this middlebrow magazine, though in her introduction to the 2015 edition Goldsby briefly alludes to the periodical serialization.[97] According to Goldsby, "In 1924, Johnson refused to issue serial rights to the *Pittsburgh Courier* because, he claimed, the novel had already been published by the black press twice."[98] In an endnote, Goldsby notes that "the second serialization was not identified or located."[99] The serialization of novels after their initial publication as standalone books was not unknown in the early twentieth century. *The Great Gatsby* is one famous example; as Matthew J. Bruccoli notes in a footnote, "After book publication the novel was serialized in *Famous Story Magazine* (April–August 1926); reprinted in a single issue of the British *Argosy* (August 1937); and condensed in the Sunday supplements of various American newspapers on 23 May 1937. Fitzgerald had nothing to do with these periodical texts."[100] Whereas Johnson's role in the serialization of his novel in the magazine is not clear (and he does not discuss it in his memoir, *Along This Way*), his refusal of the serial rights to the *Pittsburgh Courier* suggests that the *Half-Century* had his permission to serialize it. The magazine published it under his name and included a note stating that all rights were reserved by the author, which further suggests that he granted permission for the republication.

Johnson's political and aesthetic affiliations in his novel—what Goldsby has called an "early experiment in literary modernism"[101]—find a home in a magazine that is "betwixt and between," as Virginia Woolf disparagingly labeled the middlebrow.[102] Johnson's novel seems out of place in the pages of this middlebrow magazine as the book is generally associated with the aesthetic and political elite of the Harlem Renaissance. From 1920 to 1930, a period that overlaps with the serialization of his novel in the *Half-Century*, Johnson was the executive secretary—the chief operating officer—of the NAACP. This serialization seems to complicate the magazine's desire to distinguish itself from the *Crisis,* since Johnson's affiliation with the NAACP also creates a link to Du Bois's *Crisis*: Johnson's name was all over the pages of the *Crisis*. At the same time, the novel with its discussions of Black life in New York City, of music, cosmopolitan travel, passing, and lynching seems out of place in the context of the magazine's emphasis on the domestic space in its content, including its fiction.

The serialization and reprinting of Johnson's novel reveal the magazine's gesture to the cultural elite of the time. While the novel (and Johnson himself as a leader, editor, and artist) had not received the level of acclaim it would achieve with the Knopf printing, its 1912 publication generated multiple reviews in the press. Scholars such as Goldsby have argued for the novel having links to modernist literature, which is generally associated with the highbrow, due to what they see as Johnson's formal experimentation in the nonlinear use of time, reliance on stream of consciousness, emphasis on point of view, and the work's resemblance to proto-modernist and modernist texts.[103] On the surface, these factors make the reprinting and serialization of the novel in a middlebrow magazine a puzzle, although, as I will show, a closer examination of the ambivalences and contradictions in the novel reveals its fit with the ambivalences and contradictions of the *Half-Century*'s middleness.[104] The reprinting and serialization of the novel seems to suggest that the boundaries between the aesthetic and intellectual categories of high and low are, in fact, less stable than the magazine itself presents them to be. The middlebrow was, as it always is, a constructed identity for the magazine; the magazine itself defined the other periodicals as highbrow and lowbrow (emphasizing real differences and exaggerating others) in order to identify itself as in the middle. Of course, there was no essential middle; it was always shifting based on the needs of the magazine in its network. This instability is a constitutive characteristic of the middlebrow. Due to the aspirational quality of the magazine, it contained nods to the cultural elite even as it rejected the *Crisis* as being inaccessible to the people.

The novel itself, particularly in terms of racial politics, captures the same tensions that the magazine also grapples with. The novel is imbued with a concern with aspirationality, just as is the magazine (and the middlebrow as a cultural category). This aspirationality lies at the intersection of race and class. Johnson's famous description of a lynching that propels the narrator's decision to engage in racial passing reveals the aspirational drive at the heart of the novel: "Have you ever witnessed the transformation of human beings into savage beasts? Nothing can be more terrible . . . There he stood, a man only in form and stature, every sign of degeneracy stamped upon his countenance. His eyes were dull and vacant, indicating not a ray of thought. Evidently the realization of his fearful fate had robbed him of whatever reasoning power he had ever possessed."[105] While, initially, it seems as though this description of the "savage beasts" refers to the lynch mob and the spectators, it transitions into a description of the lynched victim as an unreasoning beast. Lynching seems to expose the liminal nature of being a Black man under Jim Crow and lynch law, as the lynching victim is described as both man, although "only in form and stature," and animal devoid of reason. Later, the narrator says, "All the while, I understood that it was not discouragement, or fear, or search for a larger field of action and opportunity, that was driving me out of the Negro race. I knew that it was shame, unbearable shame. Shame at being identified with a people that could with impunity be treated worse than animals."[106] The narrator's shame over being associated with the bestiality of the lynched man leads to him passing for white, leaving behind his race and, at the same time, his class (due to the fact that passing as white provides greater class mobility).[107] The narrator realizes that he does not wish to be associated with a man with "every sign of degeneracy stamped upon his countenance," and his fear and shame lead him away from his racial identification.

For Johnson's narrator, shame is not only a dynamic between self and the other but it is a triangulation between himself, the lynched man with whom he does not wish to identify in terms of both class and race, and the dominant white society. Du Bois identifies this shame when he points to the African American upper class's "secret shame of being identified with" the lower classes by the white gaze: "Because the upper colored group is desperately afraid of being represented before American whites by this lower group, or being mistaken for them, or being treated as though they were part of it, they are pushed to the extreme of effort to avoid contact with the poorest classes of Negroes."[108] Throughout the novel, the ex-colored man solidifies class divisions; for example, in discussing the lower classes, he states, "The unkempt appearance, the shambling, slouching gait and loud talk and laughter of these people aroused in me a feeling of almost repulsion," a feeling that is echoed when the narrator witnesses the lynching victim's loss of reason.[109] However, after the lynching, the narrator says that he was "as weak as a man who had lost blood," highlighting his inadvertent kinship with the murdered man, an identification that is related to his feelings of shame.[110] Becoming "ex-colored" allows him the freedom to move away from this identification, although it does, famously, leave him wondering if he has "chosen the lesser part."[111]

In the lynching installment of Johnson's novel reprinted in the *Half-Century,* there are some mostly minor changes from the 1912 version. Some of those changes seem to be typographical errors while others seem more substantive; it is not clear if Johnson himself or the editor made the changes to the magazine version. To take one example, toward the very end of the chapter in which the lynching takes place, the following sentence is included in the novel but not in the magazine: "For certainly the law would restrain and punish the malicious burning alive of animals."[112] The lines before this sentence include a discussion of the narrator's sense of shame after having witnessed the lynching, and this sentence points to the hypocrisy of a legal system that would condemn animal abuse but not the killing of a human being. The omission of this line in the *Half-Century*'s *Autobiography of an Ex-Colored Man,* whether intentional or not, and whether omitted by Johnson or someone associated with the magazine, softens the pointed criticism of the law with a focus on personal shame; in other words, it tempers the structural critique by shifting the focus to an individual's feelings about observing a lynching, and does so in the midst of debates on the Dyer

Anti-Lynching Bill during the aftermath of the Red Summer of 1919. This tempering is in line with the periodical's overall middlebrow politics, which highlight, for the most part, individual behaviors and choices in the project of racial uplift over the necessity for structural changes.

At the same time, it is important to acknowledge the magazine's increased explicitness about race politics—driven, in part, perhaps, by Kathryn Johnson. A closer look at the magazine's contents reveals discussions of passing and of racial violence, revealing its affiliation with the concerns of the novel. The July 1919 and August 1919 issues, for example, contain a two-part feature titled "The Confessions of an Ex-White Actress." These two anonymous epistolary essays consider the challenges facing Black actresses from the perspective of a biracial actress who has achieved success in her career by passing as white. She states, "I could and did 'pass' for white and today my mother and I are on 'easy street.' My friends could not 'pass' and today are fighting to keep up their front."[113] This feature, with its anonymous author, title, confessional style, narrator's emphasis on her commitment to her art, and thematic content of passing, seems strongly influenced by Johnson's *The Autobiography of an Ex-Colored Man,* even though it is presented as a nonfiction account.

Even the magazine's selection of fiction beyond Johnson's novel was, at times, explicitly focused on race politics. The June 1918 issue contains a short story titled "The Color Line" by William H. Scott. The story opens as a conventional romance about two people—Ashton, a wealthy businessman who has sworn off love, and Estelle Richardson, the best stenographer in his company—who fall in love. Estelle, however, tells him that love is not possible: "I love you but I am a Colored woman. You are a white man. There lies between you and me, not only wealth,—that can be bridged by love,—but the Color line which not even love dare step across."[114] After Estelle's confession, Ashton reveals that he, too, is Black: "I am white of skin; but according to the racial classification of this country which inexoribly [*sic*] decrees that one drop of black blood puts the possessor on the dark side of the Color-line, I am black, even as you are black, though your skin and mine are white. Now will you marry me?"[115] In an early issue from November 1916, the magazine dealt with passing along with racial violence; the story "The Black Brute," by William Louis Board, tells the story of Chauncey Monyay as he runs away from "a host of white savages" searching for a Black man who has committed a crime against a white woman.[116] Board sets up the narrative to appear to be a tragic tale—a type of story his readers would have been familiar with—of a Black man on the run from the lynch mob. At the end, after being badly injured, Chauncey discovers that the bloodhounds were not in fact on his trail, but on the trail of the true perpetrator, who had been in the vicinity. As his fiancée, Violet Bayard, explains to him, "The dying man made a full confession of his crime as streams of blood and perspiration washed hideous his white face from under its mask of black paint by which he hoped to conceal his crime, but the stupid blood-hounds had not learned from their masters the color of crime, and had tracked to his death the real 'Black Brute.'"[117] This short story takes the conventions of passing narratives, minstrelsy, accounts of lynchings, and even romance plots (with its discussion of Chauncey's love for Violet), and turns them around to show the truth behind racial violence. Taken together, "The Color Line" and "The Black Brute" play with generic conventions and expectations to expose the ramifications of Jim Crow on the private lives of American citizens. These stories are in the minority in comparison to the more conventional domestic tales that populate the pages of the magazine, but the juxtaposition between these fictional works focused on the color-line and the domestic fiction reveals the magazine's complex negotiation of race politics within its Jim Crow network.

Within Johnson's novel, despite his repulsed characterization of the lynching victim, the narrator also acknowledges that African Americans are not the source of the problem. After watching the lynching, the narrator feels "shame that I belonged to a race that could be so dealt with; and shame for my country, that it, the great example of democracy to the world, should be the only civilized, if not the only state on earth, where a human being would be burned alive."[118] This split sense of shame reveals the ambivalent racial political forces at work within the novel, which were also reflected in the *Half-Century* with its middlebrow emphasis on cosmetics and marriage and its concomitant concern with racial injustices. At the same time, Johnson's novel makes a more forceful critique of Jim Crow through its split voice, what some critics have identified as Johnson's use of irony[119]: the novel undercuts the narrator's voice with allusions to underlying sociopolitical ideals that Johnson himself held as a tireless activist for his race. The novel frames the "lesser part" that the narrator wonders if he has chosen as indeed being lesser, in that he is not part of those "making history and a race . . . in a work so glorious," work that Johnson himself was committed to.[120] In fact, in the very same issue of the *Half-Century* in which the novel's narrator flees from his race, a notice in the "General Race News" section states, "James Weldon Johnson, Field Secretary of the National Association for the Advancement of Colored People, has been appointed acting secretary to succeed John R. Shillady (white) who recently resigned."[121] This notice highlights the other path that the narrator could have taken—what is implicitly presented as the greater part; the characteristic juxtaposition of the magazine form provides an implicit rebuke of the narrator's path. In fact, directly following the announcement of the serialization of Johnson's novel, the July 1919 opening editorial includes an exhortation to join the NAACP, which is described as "a powerful and effective weapon to be used by Colored people in the interest of Colored people."[122] The publication of the novel in this middlebrow magazine is, in fact, Johnson's attempt to speak to a more diverse audience than the elite one that would follow the 1927 publication and engage in the structural critique that his narrator and the magazine often—especially in its early years—fall short of.

Goldsby points out that this technique is one that Johnson relied on later in his career too, as he "placed essays in the country's middlebrow magazines—*Century, Forum,* and *Current History*—in an effort to sway public opinion toward supporting the NAACP's agenda to criminalize lynching."[123] Johnson, due to his lifelong use of periodicals for activism, knew the power of the press: he worked for the Jacksonville *Times-Union* as a delivery boy when he was just thirteen, founded and edited the short-lived *Daily American* newspaper from 1895 until 1896, edited and wrote for the influential *New York Age* newspaper beginning in 1914, and was published in white and Black periodicals, including the *Century* and the *New York Times*. The reprinting of his novel in the pages of the *Half-Century* roughly correlated to his rise to the position of the NAACP's executive secretary and demonstrates Johnson's recognition that his activism needed to reach a wider audience, not simply the elite readers of the *Crisis*, in order to be fully effective. In looking at the internal and external periodical codes of the *Half-Century*, it is clear that Johnson used periodical networks to expand his activist and advocacy networks, and, in fact, as Ida B. Wells's discussion of the periodical as weapon suggests, these networks cannot be separated from one another.

CHAPTER TWO
Affective Networks
Nella Larsen and the Chicago Defender

In her autobiographical essay "How It Feels to Be Colored Me" (1928), Zora Neale Hurston famously positioned herself as a woman who is free of racial shame: "Sometimes, I feel discriminated against, but it does not make me angry. It merely astonishes me. How *can* any deny themselves the pleasure of my company? It's beyond me."[1] With this statement, Hurston rejects the notion that shame is an integral part of her experience as an African American woman during the Jim Crow period. However, just a few years later, in his essay "On Being Ashamed of Oneself: An Essay on Race Pride" (1933), W. E. B. Du Bois suggested that statements such as Hurston's are rare; despite political and social advances, African Americans "are still ashamed of ourselves and are thus estopped from valid objection when white folks are ashamed to call us human."[2] This racial shame is, Du Bois argues, toxic because it is more than an individual feeling; it has repercussions for the race as a whole due to its potential as a kind of "race suicide."[3]

Building on the work of the previous chapter, which focused on respectability as a marketing strategy in the *Half-Century*, this chapter shifts the focus to the *Half-Century*'s rival, the *Chicago Defender*. The *Defender*'s emphasis on respectability is part of a larger affective network that includes one of James Weldon Johnson's Harlem Renaissance contemporaries, Nella Larsen. Whereas the previous chapter dealt with the strategic market positioning of a magazine within a network, this chapter pays attention to how networks generate and are generated by affective bonds, particularly the bonds created by shame. Though shame might seem removed from marketing strategies, it is, as the previous chapter argues in relation to the language of the brows, part of a network engaged in resisting Jim Crow hierarchies. Both the use of the periodical field by the *Half-Century Magazine* and the emphasis on affect in the *Chicago Defender* rely on the rhizomatic qualities of the network to counter the era's governing hierarchies. One example of a network that was both produced by a discourse about shame and produced its own discourse about shame grew out of the letters to the editor section of the *Chicago Defender* newspaper. This network was grounded in power relations that worked to create intraracial class divisions through the language of a racial community centered on shame and shaming. I place this network in relation to Nella Larsen's Harlem Renaissance novel *Quicksand* to demonstrate the way that the newspaper and the novel existed in a broader affective network grounded in a shared concern with shame in relation to race, a network that is linked to larger Harlem Renaissance debates about art and politics. Though the novel does not have a direct connection with the newspaper—it was not serialized before its publication—and is not generally positioned in relation to the *Defender*, both publications were involved in the production of a discourse around shame in relation to race and class. In this chapter, my analysis serves as a model for understanding the distinctive but linked concerns of periodicals and novels, as both the *Defender*'s letters to the editor and Larsen's novel share not simply themes but also formal characteristics linked to the abuses and uses of shame. Reading periodicals and novels as existing in and constructing networks unfolds possibilities for periodical studies beyond simply reading texts in periodical contexts. In this case, I focus on affective networks that tie individual readers to a larger community of readers and also newspaper to novel within the Harlem Renaissance and, more generally, the Jim Crow period.

In writing about the relationship between shame and identity, Eve Kosofsky Sedgwick has stated that "the forms taken by shame are not distinct 'toxic' parts of a group or individual identity that can be excised; they are instead integral to and residual in the process by which identity itself is formed."[4] The affect's relational quality is key to its power since shaming and being ashamed depend on the presence of both a self and an other, imagined or real, who looks upon the self. According to Sedgwick, "shame, as opposed to guilt, is a bad feeling that does not attach to what one does, but to what one is."[5] In other words, this "bad feeling" says something about who an individual or group is. While the centrality of shame to identity—what one is—can be poisonous, it can also be transformative, as I will show in my analysis of Larsen's novel and the letters of the *Defender*. Thus, the defining quality of shame is double-edged. Intraracial shaming, on the one hand, becomes a tool by which readers with middle-class sensibilities and aspirations criticize aspects of Black working-class identity that they see as detrimental to overall racial identity. That shame speaks to individual and group identities means it can be used, on the other hand, to attempt to transform those identities to compel racial uplift, a strategy that has, at its heart, the goal of the sociopolitical recognition of Black equality.

Within African American periodicals and literature, shame has played a significant role. This is particularly true during the Harlem Renaissance, a period generally thought to be shaped by great racial pride. The flip side to racial pride is racial shame, and writings during the Harlem Renaissance (and more broadly during the Jim Crow era in the United States) worked to expose, grapple with, and represent the long history of racial shame for African Americans. Larsen's *Quicksand* (1928) and the letters page of the *Chicago Defender* are two such publications that unveil shame as a major force in shaping the content of public discourse concerning race during this period. These texts are driven by the perspective shifts inherent in shame. Ultimately, Larsen and the readers demonstrate how these shifts can also be used to loosen the grip of harmful affective narratives.

Quicksand and the *Defender* reveal the complex roles played by shame as both a toxic vehicle of race suicide and an affect with the potential for aesthetic and political transformation. The negative consequences of shame cannot be ignored: in Larsen's novel, shame over her sexual desires leads the protagonist to a physically and emotionally crushing marriage, while the intraracial shaming in the letters page of the newspaper reinforces and makes visible class divisions within a race that is often stereotyped as monolithic. However, Larsen's modernist experimentation with perspective and the use of shame by *Defender* readers for racial uplift reveal the means by which the shifts in perspective that are integral to shame can be deployed to reject racist classifications of

African Americans as second-class U.S. citizens. This chapter reveals shame to be embedded in a national network based on discussions of uplift ideology.

Shame can be understood as a form of what Du Bois has identified as double consciousness. His well-known claims about double consciousness are founded on the concept of the gaze, making him, as Shawn Michelle Smith has pointed out, "an early *visual* theorist of race and racism."[6] Du Bois proposed that an African American person has a "sense of always looking at one's self through the eyes of others, of measuring one's soul by the tape of a world that looks on in amused contempt and pity. One ever feels his two-ness,—an American, a Negro; two souls, two thoughts, two unreconciled strivings."[7] This sense of "two-ness" is also integral to the affect of shame with its internalizing of the imagined gaze of an other. At its core, shame is a dynamic of the act of looking, as the philosopher Bernard Williams has noted: "Even if shame and its motivations always involve in some way or other an idea of the gaze of another, it is important that for many of its operations the imagined gaze of an imagined other will do."[8]

I identify three different dynamics of looking, all of which spring from shame. First, the experience of shame is grounded in the internalization of the gaze of a powerful figure, often an authority figure. For example, Helga Crane in Larsen's novel feels shame over her sexual desires due to her internalization of the Black bourgeois norms of proper behavior. Second, shame is seen in the surveillance conducted by Black readers, which was often triangulated by the white gaze. *Defender* readers watched the Southern migrant working-class bodies in Northern cities and attempted to discipline them through shame by pointing out that they were being watched by whites. Essentially, these two dynamics were rooted in power relations since shame can be deployed to build and affirm hierarchies—in this case, intraracial class divisions that exploit broader U.S. racial hierarchies to maintain the power of the privileged urban Black middle class at the expense of Black Southern migrants and the working class. The third dynamic of looking is reflected in the perspectival shifts of the readers and of the novelistic form with its experiments with point of view. It is, as I will show, this dynamic that has the potential to question the pernicious influence of the first two. In other words, the affordances of the periodical, particularly its letters page, and of Larsen's novel provide a glimpse into shame's transformative potential. The networks between the readers and between the newspaper and novel reveal the multiplicity of perspectives to which shame gestures.

Studies concerning the visual work of race and racism, such as those by Elizabeth Abel, Anne Elizabeth Carroll, Caroline Goeser, W. J. T. Mitchell, Martha Jane Nadell, Shawn Michelle Smith, and Miriam Thaggert, have provided us with a deeper understanding of what Ralph Ellison called the "high visibility" of race that "actually rendered one *un*-visible."[9] Examining periodicals such as the *Crisis* and *Opportunity* as visual texts, Carroll argues compellingly for their "multi-media work," referring to the way visual elements, such as photographs, work in concert with the written word to represent the race.[10] However, I focus not on the juxtapositions between visual art and written text but on the way visuality is manifested in the written word. Rather than analyzing photography and/or illustrations, as Abel, Carroll, Goeser, Nadell, and Smith have done, this chapter draws attention to what Thaggert has called "the presence of the visual embedded in the literary."[11] At the same time, my analysis differs from Thaggert's because I emphasize visuality, particularly the dynamics of the gaze as reflected in perspectival shifts—as seen in the multiplicity of readers' views in the letters page and literary formal shifts in perspective—over corporeal appearances. Shame acts not only as an engine in shaping the content of the public discourse of race, but its visuality also shapes the periodical letters page and Larsen's modernist novel. These texts do not simply discuss the affect, but their very formal structures rely on shame's dynamics of the gaze. Shame's visuality, as I show, can be used as a tool in Jim Crow networks to fight against the very structures of inequality that led to the formation of double consciousness in Black citizens.

"WHAT NONSENSE IS THIS?"

Recognizing shame's power provides an understanding of the dynamics between art and politics during this period, a debate central to understanding the 1920s in general and the Harlem Renaissance in particular.

Du Bois's famous proclamation that "all Art is propaganda and ever must be" posits the political value of art and the responsibility of artists to work toward the goal of racial equality.[12] His claim was questioned by other Harlem Renaissance figures, such as Langston Hughes and Claude McKay. Shame, in social and aesthetic terms, is key to this debate. The Harlem Renaissance—with its narrative of a break from past ways of representing Black experiences in art—is often seen as distinct from, and at times a rejection of, the conservatism of the project of racial uplift that the *Defender* promoted. Although both rest on narratives of racial pride as strategies to repudiate the national narrative of African Americans as less than human, these narratives of pride simultaneously contain hidden narratives of shame. In *Quicksand*, Larsen exposes these narratives and demonstrates their power in the elite African American coteries and the project of racial uplift. In doing so, she advocates for an aesthetics that can represent the lived experience of shame without replicating it. For Larsen, both art and shame are varieties of imaginative looking that can compel social change because they articulate optimism about how the world could be.

Sedgwick's interpretations of the work of psychologist Silvan Tomkins are pivotal to the resurgence in critical interest in the role of shame in literature. Sedgwick and Tomkins follow a long history of theorists of the visual nature of shame. In *Being and Nothingness* (1943), Jean-Paul Sartre emphasizes that the affect "is in its primary structure shame *before somebody*. . . . By the mere appearance of the Other, I am put in the position of passing judgment on myself as on an object, for it is as an object that I appear to the Other."[13] The look of the other, in effect, shifts the self's universe: the self is forced to see itself through the other's eyes, and, in doing so, must confront its displacement from the center of its universe. Richard Wright gives an account of working in a hotel where he was asked to bring "liquor and cigarettes" to white prostitutes: "When you went into their rooms, you were supposed to take their nakedness for granted, as though it startled you no more than a blue vase or a red rug. Your presence awoke in them no sense of shame, for you were not regarded as human."[14] As Wright's account shows, exposure is not enough to make a person feel shame, as shame can only be felt if the judging spectator is thought of as someone who holds power or social status. Indeed, Frantz Fanon criticized Sartre's theories of the gaze in relation to race by focusing on the embodied nature of racism: "Jean-Paul Sartre had forgotten that the Negro suffers in his body quite differently from the white man."[15] In a footnote, he expanded on this difference: "Though Sartre's speculations on the existence of The Other may be correct (to the extent, we must remember, to which *Being and Nothingness* describes an alienated consciousness), their application to a black consciousness proves fallacious. That is because the white man is not only The Other but also the master, whether real or imaginary."[16] This power dynamic transforms shame for African Americans.

In Larsen's *Quicksand,* the white Danish artist Axel Olsen says to the biracial protagonist, "I have offered you marriage, Helga Crane, and you answer me with some strange talk of race and shame. What nonsense is this?"[17] For Olsen, race and shame seem irrelevant, but for Helga Crane and African Americans with middle-class sensibilities, such as the readers of the *Defender,* this "strange talk" was acutely pertinent. As critics have noted, the Harlem Renaissance is generally conceived of as a period of exuberant artistic creation, both producing and driven by racial pride.[18] Arnold Rampersad has provided a necessary counter-narrative by suggesting that the Harlem Renaissance depended "in a fundamental way on the presence of strong feelings of inferiority, cultural and otherwise, at the very moment paradoxically—of the repudiation or transcendence of those feelings of inferiority in the name of progress, emancipation, and independence."[19] Like the project of racial uplift, the Harlem Renaissance relies on the language of shame in concert with that of pride.

In Larsen's novel, as in the *Defender,* the ability to feel shame serves to expose both racial and class affiliations. The novel deals with Helga's futile search for belonging in the American South, Chicago, Harlem, and Denmark. Her sense of racial shame is two-sided in that the internalized observer she imagines is both Black and white, a self-concept reflected in Helga's relationship to art—to theater and portraiture in particular. The Danish vaudeville show with the "cavorting Negroes on the stage" and Olsen's portrait of Helga are the two most striking examples of the novel's representation of the parallels between looking at art and feeling shame.[20] In both cases, Helga is placed in the role of the spectator who watches other African Americans—the vaudeville performers and the representation of herself in the painting, a representation she denies is true to life because it looks like "some disgusting sensual creature with her features."[21] She simultaneously rejects a connection to those she gazes upon and identifies with them through feelings of shame, placing her in dual roles in the shame dynamic: the internalized spectator and the gazed-upon object. This oscillation between roles reveals the extent to which Helga is caught between ideas about Blackness and whiteness, between being watched and watching.[22]

In contrast to the Danish audience of "enchanted spectators," Helga acts as "an ironical and silently speculative spectator" of the vaudeville performance, while also feeling linked to it.[23] Her distance from the audience and the performers is reinforced by her status as a "spectator" who is also "speculative." The two terms refer to looking, and the adjective's relation to thoughtfulness emphasizes Helga's difference from the bodily African American performers, who "danced, pounding their thighs, slapping their hands together, twisting their legs, waving their abnormally long arms, throwing their bodies about with a loose ease!"[24] The "twisting" and "abnormally long" limbs of the performers are depicted as unnatural, and Helga finds herself "filled with a fierce hatred for the cavorting Negroes on the stage. She felt shamed, betrayed, as if these pale pink and white people among whom she lived had suddenly been invited to look upon something in her which she had hidden away and wanted to forget."[25] This revelation of the hidden self through her feeling of shame recalls an earlier scene when Helga finds herself "drugged, lifted, sustained, by the extraordinary music, blown out, ripped out, beaten out, by the joyous, wild, murky orchestra" of the Harlem jazz club. When the music ends, she finds herself filled with "a shameful certainty that not only had she been in the jungle, but that she had enjoyed it."[26] Her "jungle" dancing aligns her with the vaudeville dancers. Despite her sensual enjoyment of the jazz and her disgust over the vaudeville act, she feels equally ashamed in both situations. Her feelings reveal the closeness of Helga's identification with the African American performers and her related refusal of this identification.

In the same chapter, Larsen's protagonist refuses marriage to Olsen; he replies, "I think that my picture of you is, after all, the true Helga Crane. Therefore—a tragedy."[27] In this moment, Olsen aestheticizes Helga in visual and literary (or dramatic) ways by using the word "tragedy." The link he makes between her true self and the portrait compels Helga to come face-to-face with her "disgusting" and "sensual" corporeality; this recognition forces her to confront her racial and sexual anxieties, just as her actions in the jazz club do. Racial shame is linked to shame over sexual desires, desires that confirm, for her, the worst "jungle" stereotypes of African Americans. Visually based art, such as portraiture and stage performances, makes manifest the visual logic of shame, but even an auditory aesthetic experience in the jazz club divides and destabilizes Helga, as afterward she recognizes herself as having been in the "jungle," a term that shows how she has internalized the stereotypes of those whites or upper-class Blacks who watch and judge her for her sensual enjoyment of the music. Although able to recognize the hypocrisy of racial uplift, Helga is implicated in its affective web, which locates racial shame in sexual desire.

Tormented by an inability to feel as though she belongs anywhere, Helga continually insists on her distinctiveness from the masses through what she calls her "aesthetic sense,"[28] overtly manifested in her love of beautiful objects, such as "a blue Chinese carpet" and a "shining brass bowl crowded with many-colored nasturtiums."[29] This aesthetic sense immediately marks her as different from the other people at Naxos, the oppressive Southern school where, early in the novel, she teaches. In Harlem, she meets "people with tastes and ideas similar to her own."[30] For Helga, aesthetics is supposed to oppose suffocating social and bodily discipline, yet this supposedly liberating aesthetic sense is part of the discipline that grounds Harlem society, as represented by her friend, Anne Grey. Anne's aesthetic sense, which is "in complete accord" with Helga's, is linked with the discipline of Naxos.[31] Anne herself seems to fit the "white man's pattern" that Naxos is bent on inculcating; she professes to hate white people even as she has "aped their clothes, their manners, and their gracious ways of living."[32] The use of "aped" here alludes to the racist language of beastliness, which reveals Anne's complicity with the very people she professes to hate. In showing the extent to which Anne is caught up in this discourse, Larsen demonstrates that it spans classes and regions and extends from Naxos to Anne in Harlem, and finally to Helga.

"WHAT THE PEOPLE SAY" ABOUT SHAME

Larsen's novel was not simply part of Harlem Renaissance networks, but it was also part of the same affective network of the *Defender*'s letters, although it was not in direct dialogue with those letters. In this way, the novel's affiliation with this affective network reveals one of the links between the Harlem Renaissance elites and the *Defender* readers with their middle-class aspirations. Larsen, like most writers of the era, was entangled in periodical culture, including a brief stint contributing to the *Brownies' Book* (1920–21), a children's magazine edited by Du Bois and Jessie Fauset. In fact, Larsen's career as a writer was specifically affected by letters to the editor: The widely known accusations of plagiarism leveled at her toward the end of her career as a writer sprang from these periodical networks.

Larsen published her short story "Sanctuary" in the January 1930 issue of the *Forum,* edited by Henry Goddard Leach. The *Forum,* founded in 1886, was an intellectual monthly magazine that would merge with the *Century Magazine* to become *Forum and Century*, along with other metamorphoses on the way to its death in 1950. An issue cost 25 cents in 1930, and the magazine's contributors included Du Bois, Willa Cather, John Dewey, Theodore Dreiser, Bertrand Russell, and Upton Sinclair. According to Frank Luther Mott, it was due to Leach's work that the *Forum* had reached a peak circulation of 92,000 by the end of the 1920s, although this figure would decline with the beginnings of the Great Depression.[33] The periodical called itself "The Magazine of Controversy" and, for example, stated on its January 1930 table of contents that "its method is to give a fair and friendly hearing to both sides, all sides, of important questions of the day."[34] Mott describes the magazine as being guided, in part, by an editorial policy that figured the magazine as "that of the symposium": "Throughout most of its hundred and twelve volumes, the *Forum* was distinguished by joint debates on all kinds of political, economic, social, religious, scientific, and educational subjects."[35] In other words, the *Forum* explicitly presented itself as a site of debate by juxtaposing writers with different viewpoints. Contributors were placed in dialogue with one another, and the readers' letters were also placed side by side to create an appearance of debate between readers, along with the editor and contributors.

The correspondence section, titled "Our Rostrum," contained many letters from readers—the January 1930 issue contained eighteen letters and the May 1930 issue contained thirty-three—with the occasional "Editor's Note" responding to a particular letter. In the April 1930 issue, the editor solicited letters from readers by asking, "Are Outlines Good or Bad?," in a reference to Will Durant's *The Story of Philosophy*, which Durant and Howard Mumford Jones debated in the January 1930 issue.[36] The following issue extended the debate by setting up different readers' letters under the subheadings "Outline Books Are Bad" and "Outline Books Are Good" in the "Our Rostrum" section.[37] In order to highlight its status as a symposium, the magazine also made a point of regularly publishing letters that were complimentary or critical of its openness to debate. In the March 1930 issue, the editor made a point of publishing two letters asking for the cancellation of their subscription alongside two letters that praise the magazine. John D. Leslie of New Castle, Indiana, writes, "Please cancel my subscription. I do not care for magazines such as yours. Great questions cannot be settled by controversy, and doubt leads to cynicism."[38] The accompanying editor's note responds, "We have never heard of any great question that was settled without controversy. And doubt *may* lead to knowledge. To reason what we don't know is the beginning of wisdom."[39] In contrast, J. H. O'Neill, MD, of Morgan City, Louisiana, expresses support for the magazine's emphasis on controversy and writes, "I would not give five cents for a milk-and-water magazine."[40]

Within this context, Larsen's short story "Sanctuary" was published alongside geometric color illustrations by Winold Reiss, whose art had been featured in the Harlem issue of *Survey Graphic* magazine that announced the New Negro Renaissance to the world.[41] The potential plagiarism was called to the attention of the editors and readers of the *Forum* in a letter by a reader named Marion Boyd published in the April 1930 "Our Rostrum" column.[42] In that same issue, William Faulkner's short story "A Rose for Emily" was published alongside an essay by Carl Jung titled "Your Negroid and Indian Behavior," with sketches titled "The Aframerican Cakewalk" by Miguel Covarrubias, multiple book reviews, a feature on Mata Hari, and a debate about the publishing industry. In her letter, Boyd states that the Larsen story has a "striking resemblance" to "Mrs. Adis," a short story by white British author Sheila Kaye-Smith, published in the *Century*'s January 1922 issue with illustrations by George Bellows.[43] The *Century* was one of the most influential magazines of the period with its mix of arts and culture. In that issue, Kaye-Smith's short story was given the place of honor following the table of contents, with one of Bellows's illustrations set as the frontispiece. The editor's note to Boyd's letter in the *Forum* explains that "we, too, were impressed by the 'striking resemblance' between them, and felt it our duty to call the matter to our author's attention, asking her, in fairness to FORUM readers, to explain how she came by her plot and the circumstances under which her story was written."[44] In response, Larsen sent in four rough drafts and also wrote a letter of explanation, which states, "I haven't as yet seen the *Century* story, but it seems to me that anyone who intended to lift a story would have avoided doing it as obviously as this appears to have been done—judging from the excerpts which you have sent me."[45]

This example reveals the workings of a periodical network that is interracial in nature. Larsen published her short story in a white-edited periodical that readers like Boyd read. Because the readers existed in a periodical network in which they read multiple periodicals, they recognized the resemblance between Larsen's story and Kaye-Smith's story published in the *Century*. As a result, Boyd and others wrote in to the correspondence column, causing the editor to write to Larsen, who responded with her own letter; the editor then published Boyd's letter, the editor's note, and Larsen's letter, one after another, in the letters page. These juxtapositions enhanced the magazine's reputation for openness and spelled out the magazine network that connected editor, author, and readers together. Even the plots of Kaye-Smith's and Larsen's stories speak to the power of networks. Set in Sussex with white characters, "Mrs. Adis" centers on Peter Crouch, who seeks shelter with Mrs. Adis, the mother of his friend Tom, after killing an unknown man. As Peter is hiding, Mrs. Adis receives the news that the murder victim is, in fact, her son. Instead of giving up Peter, she tells the searchers that she does not know where Peter is. "Sanctuary," which is set in the American South, tells the story of Jim Hammer, a Black man who seeks shelter with Annie Poole after shooting a man. Jim pleads with Annie to conceal him because her son, his friend Obadiah, would, as he says, "lemme stop ef he was to home."[46] Annie acquiesces and allows him to hide in her bed, which is where he cowers while the sheriff relays the identity of Jim's victim.

While Peter in Kaye-Smith's story leaves Mrs. Adis's home "silently," Jim is confronted by a furious Annie, who says to him, "Git outen mah feather baid, Jim Hammer, an' outen mah house, an' don' nevah stop thankin' yo' Jesus he done gib you dat black face."[47] While Kaye-Smith's story highlights the role of networks by showing that it is Tom's friendship with Peter that causes Mrs. Adis to conceal him, Larsen's story highlights not only friendship and familial networks but also, ultimately, distinctively racial networks. The racial network in which Jim Hammer's "black face" exists obligates Annie Poole to conceal him from the white sheriff's search for the murderer, overriding her maternal desire for justice for her son.

The existence of this racial network was interrogated and shaped in the counterpublic pages of the Black press; however, this racial network was itself grounded in affective networks that complicated the implications of racial affiliation. During the 1920s, at the height of the Great Migration, the pages of the *Chicago Defender* newspaper (1905–2019, and then online only) were filled with discussions of respectability and, consequently, shame. The *Defender*, the preeminent Black newspaper of the period, discloses the political valences of shame in debates about race taking place during the 1920s. Certainly, other Black periodicals, such as the *New York Amsterdam News*, the *Pittsburgh Courier*, the *New York Age*, and the *Half-Century Magazine*, contained discussions of shame—and, indeed, the New York newspapers would have been components of Larsen's Harlem network—but, due to its role as a national force in the movement of Southern Blacks to the North during the Great Migration, the *Defender* was a key site in which the visual dynamics of shame were enacted. In fact, it is important to acknowledge that Jim Crow periodical networks are not bounded by geography, and that Larsen's novel is part of a network predicated on affect, reaching beyond New York City.

Through its printing of cartoons, news articles, features, editorials, and the Bud Billiken children's column, the *Defender* worked to assist readers in racial uplift. While photography and editorial cartoons, especially those by Leslie Rogers, assisted the *Defender* in promoting its mission, it is the visual dynamics of the language in the letters page that reveals the way that readers constituted themselves as being both seeing subjects and seen objects. Significantly, this discourse of shame was produced by the newspaper's readers themselves, rather than by sources such as the National Urban League or elite Black leaders.

The *Defender* was a particularly powerful site in which to discuss shame due to the paper's national reach and influence. Founded and published by Robert Abbott in Chicago, the *Defender* exhorted and encouraged African Americans in the rural South to move to the urban North as part of its Great Northern Drive. This was both a marketing move and part of its activism. The *Defender* also fought for Black rights in general, even as it reported on African Americans in the sports and entertainment fields. As Patrick Washburn notes, Abbott "decided to model the *Chicago Defender* after the sensational Yellow Journalism that William Randolph Hearst and Joseph Pulitzer had popularized in New York City beginning in the 1890s but which now was on the wane."[48] In the early twentieth century, the newspaper championed Jack Johnson, worked to block the screening of *The Birth of a Nation,* and fought lynchings in the South. A large part of the newspaper's success was, as Michaeli writes, that it "could simultaneously offer news for the Pullman porter as well as the social climber, the 'Race Man,' and the businessman."[49] According to Juliet E. K. Walker, "by 1920 the Chicago *Defender* was the first black newspaper to gain extensive national circulation. The black press in America had arrived with power to speak in concert for a people who previously had no advocate that spoke in a collective voice with force and authority."[50] While the *Defender* existed in a network of other Black weekly newspapers—including its hometown competitor the radical *Chicago Whip* and its national competitors, the powerful *Pittsburgh Courier, Amsterdam News,* and *Baltimore Afro-American*—it was a trailblazer and was the most influential and widely read in the first decades of the twentieth century before the Great Depression.

It is difficult to know the newspaper's precise circulation figures, as one subscription might be read by several people. While acknowledging that these numbers are not fully verifiable, Walker states, "By 1918 its circulation had increased to 100,000; two years later the circulation showed an almost threefold increase to 283,571, according to a circulation pamphlet distributed by the paper."[51] Black newspapers were often passed from hand to hand and also read aloud, so, even accounting for the newspaper's potentially inflated self-reported numbers, it is clear that the *Defender* was widely circulated and read: "It has been estimated that each copy was read by five to seven people, and the number might have been even higher if copies had not become worn out."[52]

In the previous chapter, I discussed the *Half-Century*'s positioning of the *Defender* as specifically lowbrow and associated with working-class Southern migrants. However, in this chapter, by examining how the *Defender* readers presented themselves and also how the newspaper presented its readers, I demonstrate how the newspaper and the readers insisted on their affiliation with middle-class respectability. That the *Defender* can be perceived in different contexts as lowbrow and linked with the working class while also as associated with middle-class sensibilities demonstrates the meaning-making power of relationality in networks.

The newspaper's pages during the 1920s, the peak of its national popularity, were filled with discussions of the inferior manners of the same people that the newspaper had encouraged to come to the city. Thus, the newspaper and its readers produced and shaped a shared community grounded in shame. In the pages of the newspaper, the community forcefully combated the national logic of racism through discussions of racial unity and equality alongside blistering criticisms of injustice and racial violence. Yet in its emphasis on uplift ideology, the newspaper affirmed class differences. Michele Mitchell has identified this intraracial class-based focus as a turn "inward" that shaped the race in the decades following Reconstruction; this turn inward, with its focus on sexuality and morality, was central to the "efforts [of African Americans] to preserve themselves" during this period of segregation.[53] The periodical forum is one inward site that allowed African Americans who shared urban middle-class sensibilities to talk about shame and to demonstrate their difference from those who did not share these sensibilities.

Works by Kevin K. Gaines, James R. Grossman, Evelyn Brooks Higginbotham, Anne Meis Knupfer, Jacqueline Najuma Stewart, and others have been pivotal to understanding the workings of class and respectability.[54] This chapter tracks the way affective affiliations are used to form and affirm class hierarchies as a tactic for refuting national racial hierarchies. These affective responses make up networks based in connections facilitated by shared feelings of shame. Ultimately, the letters to the editor are part of an affective network that includes Larsen's novel. This emphasis on shame exposes the simultaneous relational and oppositional dynamics in the construction of collective identity, class affiliations, and perceptions of race during this period.

The Great Migration intensified discussions of shame as urban African Americans in the North came face-to-face with their new neighbors, Black Southern migrants. Feeling appropriately ashamed became a key marker of class affiliation for Black Northerners, and claiming the affect became a notable political move to demonstrate the refinement of African Americans already living in the urban North.[55] In tracking the dynamics of respectability as reflected in the leisure activities—moviegoing, in particular—of urban Black migrants, Stewart has demonstrated how public spaces act as sites where class distinctions within the race were contested and delineated during the early twentieth century. One public site is the Black newspaper, which, as a forum for the debate of intraracial concerns, facilitated the inward turn. The correspondence page of the *Defender*, labeled "What the People Say," was an especially rich site for these inward discussions, as it allowed the readers to delineate what it meant to be Black in the twentieth century through the writing of letters and reading the letters of others.

The correspondence section or letters to the editor page of periodicals has been understudied. The majority of the scholarship on these letters comes from outside of literary studies and focuses on magazines published since 2000.[56] Notable exceptions include works by Teresa

Zackodnik, Barbara Green, and Janet Galligani Casey.[57] While there has been a recent flurry of attention on African American readers, the readers who write letters to the editor have been mostly overlooked; however, the space of the letters page, I argue, provides a significant glimpse into the readership.[58] The question of readership as opposed to circulation numbers is a fraught one in periodical studies, as it is in literary studies in general. As Green rightly points out, "Correspondence columns certainly count as some of the more ephemeral aspects of weekly papers—their authors largely unknown, their reference points sometimes too distant to resonate today. And they are among the least likely materials to circulate in any manner after the periodical ceases publication: letters are unlikely to find their way into an anthology."[59] Determining who the readers of a periodical were often requires material that was not deemed worthy of archiving, such as letters and subscription information.

In discussing readership, Robert Scholes and Clifford Wulfman observe that "every magazine must give the public what it wants, but different magazines have very different publics in mind."[60] Scholes and Wulfman avoid the problems inherent to discussions of readership by focusing not just on circulation numbers but also on the "implied reader," rather than the actual readers, a notoriously elusive group.[61] Notably, their focus is on the publics that the magazine itself has "in mind" as data about contemporary periodical readers is lost in a vast majority of cases—or often never recorded. Thus, as Scholes and Wulfman assert, our access to the implied reader is limited to "clues in and around the magazine itself," particularly in terms of subject matter and advertisements.[62] While the recovery of data on the readers of a given periodical—if it even existed—is not the task of this book, I propose, in this chapter and the next, strategies for reading the letters to the editor as a method of gaining limited access to the readers and their concerns.

Instead of treating letters to the editor as, to use Gérard Genette's term, paratextual elements in a periodical, I read them as text. Zackodnik maps the critical conversation around these letters: "Media history tends to take up letters to the editor as a press form through which editors construct and shape perceptions of their publications. Journalism scholars tend to understand letters to the editor as a vital public sphere institution where reader debate provides a forum for democracy in action. These rather different understandings of letters to the editor together emphasize the individual—whether as controlling editor or empowered reader—and the capital each asserts, both economic and cultural."[63] Reading letters to the editor in terms of a network between readers and as belonging to a network of which the periodical is a part allows us to see this genre as encompassing both the individual and the collective. The constitutive difference between these letters and personal letters exchanged between individuals is, of course, that letters to the editor are meant to be read by more people than the presumptive direct addressee (the editor). The letters are public and written with this fact in mind. In letters to the editor, the individual voice is privileged; Casey usefully describes letters to the editor as "a particular form of self-narrative."[64] At the same time, this individual voice is categorized as representative of other voices and a participant in a community of debate.

In her work on the letters to the editor of Black periodicals, Zackodnik has linked these letters to Michael Warner's discussion of the "cross-citational field."[65] Focusing on texts like periodicals and pamphlets, Warner writes that they each, in effect, assert: "I don't just speak to you; I speak to the public in a way that enters a cross-citational field of many other people speaking to the public."[66] This cross-citational quality is an affordance of the letters page that highlights their individual and collective dynamic. Writing about farm women's letters to the editor in the early twentieth century specifically, Casey has argued that these letters allowed women to "[share] their personal experiences within a discursive context that not only permitted, but actively encouraged, public revelations concerning what previously had been viewed as the private domain of home and family" and, in doing so, created "the cultivated notion that editors and readers constituted a community wherein, among other things, personal problems could be aired."[67] Green also highlights this twinned public and private stance within the letters in looking at feminist periodicals of the early twentieth century: "Through fragmented autobiographies and confessional gestures, the authors of letters engaged one another in dialogue, critiqued the positions held by editors and authors, and tried on the new subjectivities being offered by those papers."[68] Casey's and Green's claims are useful to understanding the "inward" work of the *Defender*'s letters page in facilitating intraracial discussions that were figured as private within the safe space of the Black newspaper but at the same time public in its formation of a community around the shared attention to shame and shaming within Jim Crow networks.

These letters provide an important, although limited, glimpse into the readership or, at the very least, the periodical's self-presentation of its readership. The problem with reading these letters is, of course, that what they can tell us is limited due to the fact that the letters may be fabricated and that they are most likely not representative of all the readers or even all the letters since the letters page is a curated space wherein editors make decisions on what letters are published. Casey, Green, and Zackodnik implicitly accept the letters, their objects of analysis, as real enough, and, despite recognizing the limitations of reading these letters in this way, I too read letters to the editor in the *Defender* as being real enough. Reading these letters as real enough is an imperfect way of developing a sense of the readers but this does not mean that it is not worth doing so. Discussing these letter writers and their letters as being "real enough" acknowledges that the readerly positions in the letters tell us something real about the periodical's self-positioning as well as the different subject-positions that the periodical's readers hold or repudiate—or can imagine themselves as holding or repudiating. I contend that the letters have value, first, in providing a flawed and limited understanding of the readers through the presentation of readerly subjectivities and, second, in developing insight into the editors' construction of the periodical—in other words, how the editors curate a picture of the readership and the appearance of readerly interaction in order to exert a measure of control over public perceptions of the periodical.

The letters offer a picture of the often-understudied readerly networks that encompass the readers' relationships with one another and also their connections to the magazine. Editors use the letters with their attendant political positions to allow their readers to imagine themselves in one position or another—what Green describes as "[trying] on the new subjectivities being offered by those papers." The letters page is, in part, a space where the magazine can construct itself, but it does not allow magazine editors to simply fabricate whatever perspectives they may like; they must offer up perspectives that readers recognize as possible. The letters also tell us something of how the periodical sees itself due to the editorial choices made in publishing the letters (or fabricating them, if that may be the case). In essence, the correspondence page of the *Defender* reveals the newspaper's embrace of the appearance of readerly debate and commentary within its pages. By labeling the column "What the People Say," the newspaper highlights the supposed voices of its readers, identifying them as part of a periodical network of newspaper and reader that extends to readers speaking to one another. It also emphasizes the newspaper's status as a forum for the ordinary folk to voice their opinions and debate with one another. This network of "what the people say" produces a discourse of shame based in visuality in relation to uplift.

This can be seen in a letter to the editor that complains of "'down-home' people moving to Chicago," in which a Mrs. James writes, "I am from 'down home' myself, but you would never know it unless I told you. I know the white folks are watching our Race and trying to get what they can on us, and it hurts me to see some of our people acting as they do."[69] By saying that it "hurts" her to see the bad manners of "our people," Mrs. James alludes to feeling ashamed for the actions of those with whom she would normally be grouped; her language is explicitly linked to visuality in the form of surveillance. Her sense of shame is not for herself but stems from the idea that "white folks" are watching the bad behavior of migrants. At its core, shame is based on a sense of exposure in relation to a real spectator or to "the imagined gaze of an imagined other" and, as Bernard Williams notes, involves a sense of a "loss of power."[70] Yet Mrs. James derives power from her feelings; being ashamed permits her to see the race through the judging eyes of whites, while also allowing her to see herself in contrast to the "down home" community despite her affiliation with that group. Due to the economic and social constraints of the Jim Crow era, social class for African Americans depended not only on economic status and family background but also on affective responsiveness. These readers like Mrs. James may or may not have been of the middle class but they highlighted middle-class sensibilities and aspirations in order to signal their distance from working-class migrants.

In response to perceived uncouth behavior, such as "women wearing house slippers and boudoir caps while during shopping [*sic*]," one *Defender* editorial states, "There is no excuse for such conduct in [a] city like Chicago. People who have been residents here for years and are acquainted with newcomers who violate former customs should call their attention to this unbecoming conduct even if they have to do it by anonymous letters."[71] In effect, this editorial works to instill a system of surveillance within the race to discipline those new to the city; the possibility that disembodied anonymous gazes will be watching ill-mannered and fully bodied newcomers suggests an inescapable panopticism. The 1927 editorial affirms the newspaper's central role in this surveillance by stating that the newspaper "has engaged the services of two photographers who will make pictures the coming week of such scenes and later publish them to let these people see themselves as others do."[72] Through the modern technology of photography, the newspaper can shame the misbehaving newcomers by embodying the perspectival shifts of shame, which causes people to "see themselves as others do."

Although the *Defender* did not, it seems, actually publish any of these photographs in subsequent issues, the threat of photographic policing reveals the extent to which double consciousness is institutionalized as a kind of panopticism within the newspaper. Mrs. James's statement—"I know the white folks are watching our Race"—becomes, in effect, the claim that "we" (the newspaper and its readers) are watching the newcomers. Through its letters page and the threatened photographs, the newspaper provides a way to watch those from "down home," just as it offers a venue to "see" the leaders of the race as a means of instilling race pride. For the readers of the *Defender,* shame is not only a dynamic between self and the other, but a triangulation among those with middle-class sensibilities, working-class migrants, and the white gaze. The newspaper is repeatedly the site by which conduct advice from one Black person to another is refracted through the lens of an imaginary white observer, as in the case of Mrs. James. That this refracted gaze is articulated in a nationally circulating newspaper reinforces the status of shame as a source of panoptic power.

This emphasis on surveillance is part of the "inward turn" that Mitchell has noted; the "intimate public" of the newspaper's letters page is a key site for this inward turn. As Lauren Berlant has stated in explaining her conception of intimate publics: "Publics presume intimacy."[73] This sense of intimacy allows Mrs. James to affirm the bonds of the community through her shared feelings of shame. Berlant emphasizes that "what makes a public sphere intimate is an expectation that the consumers of its particular stuff *already* share a worldview and emotional knowledge that they have derived from a broadly common historical experience." She continues: "Whether linked to women or other nondominant people, [an intimate public] flourishes as a porous, affective scene of identification among strangers that promises a certain experience of belonging and provides a complex of consolation, confirmation, discipline, and discussion about how to live as an *x*."[74] An intimate public, in other words, is a network that is grounded in affective bonds. The intimacy of Mrs. James's letter is grounded in the understanding that her worldview will be shared by those of her fellow readers, and her letter, alongside the other letters, provides for herself and others a way of navigating what it means to "live as an *x*," where *x* in this case is an African American person who desires to attain the appearance of middle-class status. The intimate public, shaped by an investment in shame, allows strangers, the readers, to come together and feel as part of a community, which provides "an ongoing potential for relief from the hard, cold world."[75] "Indeed," as Berlant notes, "the offer of the simplicity of the feeling of rich continuity with a vaguely defined set of like others is often the central affective magnet of an intimate public."[76] The newspaper's emphasis on respectability provides belonging for those who coalesce around *x* and separation from those who do not.

The *Defender* column "What the People Say" consists exclusively of text, with readers' letters placed one after another without editorial comment, aside from section headings; this placement conceals the editorial hand and conveys the idea that this page is indeed for the people. The juxtaposition of the letters creates the sense of a conversation among the readers, with multiple opinions being represented within the network of readers. While the column does not contain any photographs or images, it reflects not only what the people say but also what they see; the readers formulate a mode of surveillance founded on an intraracial gaze that is highly conscious of being watched by those outside the race. It is worth noting the distinction between surveillance as shame versus Foucault's model of surveillance. Foucault's model relies on a disembodied and impersonal observer, one who "sees everything without ever being seen";[77] in contrast, the pages of the newspaper are filled with observers who are anything but impersonal, as seen in their insistence on talking about themselves. While double consciousness and shame intersect with Foucauldian panoptic surveillance and discipline, for the readers, they also appear to offer a way out of discipline by institutions and structures through an emphasis on the individual. Shame can discipline, but, by multiplying people's perspectives, it can also help them understand how they are perceived; then they can use this knowledge to control how they are seen. According to the *Defender*'s letters column, seeing the structures by which one is governed is a step toward transforming them.

In the *Defender,* Du Boisian double consciousness in the form of shame becomes not just a condition of all African Americans but a tool to control perceptions of the individual and the race in the pursuit of social transformation. In one letter, a reader named Starnes S. Peak Jr. praises the newspaper's efforts: "Not as a means of inducing you to publish this article, but for your honest effor[t]s with cartoons and articles to teach shame—as some may say—our people proper conduct [*sic*] in public, permit me to heartily congratulate you on your policy."[78] Shame is seen as a valuable affect that induces people to behave properly; crucially, it can be taught through practices of reading that develop the awareness of how one is perceived. It allows people to imagine alternative possible lives and see how they can live in the world with others in different ways. According to Peak, the newspaper reveals the malleability of the seemingly fixed Jim Crow United States, which could be transformed through an awareness that one's behavior is continually being watched by whites and by other African Americans.

A reader who signs himself "O. B." urges, "Please talk a little more about Race pride and self-respect in the columns of your paper. . . . I am a member of the dark Race, but I am heartily ashamed of the way the majority conduct themselves."[79] O. B.'s feeling of shame over the bad conduct of other people is portrayed as a good quality; as it does for Mrs. James, shame allows O. B. to distinguish himself from the ill-mannered (and shameless) "majority." Nevertheless, racial pride in this letter is linked to feeling shame, implying that a collective sense of pride is attainable through shame. Tomkins has pointed out that the affect provides "powerful negative sanctions against the transgression of shared social norms"; a "sense of community" is constructed when an individual feels shame for another because it indicates that he identifies with the other.[80] In the case of O. B., feeling shame allows him to affirm this sense of identification and disavow it. As both spectator and gazed-upon object, he feels responsible for the race as a whole and, simultaneously, affirms that he is different from its badly behaved members.

The importance of the press in teaching good behavior is not exclusive to the African American community of the early twentieth century. Rather, in engaging in these conversations about behavior, the *Defender* and its readers took part in more than two centuries of conduct advice in the public sphere. The most influential periodicals in this history are, of course, Joseph Addison and Richard Steele's *Tatler* (1709–11) and *Spectator* (1711–12, 1714), which sought to reform British society through their focus on decorum, taste, and social life. Directed mainly at the rising middle class, the twentieth-century *Defender* and Addison and Steele's popular eighteenth-century periodicals defined norms and educated readers about proper taste. In discussing the public sphere, Jürgen Habermas famously argues that these British periodicals' focus on "manners and morals" acted as a "mirror" for the public: "The public that read and debated this sort of thing read and debated about itself."[81] The discussions within the *Defender*, by contrast, constitute what Warner has called a counterpublic, a public that is "defined by [its] tension with a larger public" and that "maintains at some level, conscious or not, an awareness of its subordinate status."[82] Although defined by its difference from the larger public, this counterpublic is in many ways invested in the norms that define the larger public of the dominant social group. The letters page, in conjunction with other articles in the *Defender,* formed a counterpublic sphere that was concerned with being in public; the readers of the newspaper explicitly saw one of the jobs of the *Defender* as teaching shame to ill-mannered people who dragged down the race with their conduct.

Discussions of shame are also relevant to queer studies scholars, who, influenced by Sedgwick, have analyzed the effect of shame on those who identify with sexualities outside of the dominant heterosexual paradigm. The shame of the closet, however, is markedly different from the shame that preoccupies the readers of the *Defender.* While shame can be linked to feelings of debasement, as Kathryn Bond Stockton has shown in analyzing the intersection of Black and queer identities, *Defender* readers do not perceive their feelings as related to debasement; rather, those who do not feel shame are the debased ones. Like the readers' characterization of the affect as being positive for the race, Stockton emphasizes the "social nature of self-debasing acts," which can create "a kind of social solitude of people who are set, in some deep measure, apart from each other—but in an apartness they create together and in which they are held (sometimes sexually by a lover, sometimes mentally in someone else's mind)."[83] This social quality resembles the way readers of the *Defender* use shame, although the affective language in this case is grounded in pride and racial uplift.

While Du Bois affirmed that the Black upper classes must act to instill a feeling of racial pride and thus diminish the power of racial shame, the letter writers of the *Defender* saw shame as an instrument that can provoke pride in two contradictory ways. On the one hand, teaching shame to working-class migrants teaches respectability, which facilitates a sense of pride in the race as a whole; on the other hand, feeling shame instills class pride, which creates divisions within the race. In the pages of the *Defender,* shame was mainly available to African Americans with middle-class sensibilities; the working-class Black body, from the point of view of those with these sensibilities, was in fact a source of shame in its shamelessness.

"WITHOUT FEAR OR SHAME"

The contrast in the attitudes of Du Bois and Hurston regarding shame, as outlined in this chapter's opening, illustrate that there were multiple discourses of shame during the period, and they lie at the heart of the aesthetic debates among the Harlem Renaissance networks of artists and intellectuals. While he did not go so far as to characterize the shame associated with Blackness as "nonsense," Langston Hughes advocated for an African American aesthetics "without fear or shame," a sentiment shared by other Harlem Renaissance artists.[84] In contrast, for Larsen, shame was an unhealthy affect but one that was a key component of the Black experience, and thus must be represented in African American art. In *Quicksand,* as in the *Defender,* the experience of shame is not simply imposed by a racist society that forces African Americans to see themselves as inferior; it also emerges from an uplift ideology of a disciplined Black body that must only feel socially appropriate desires. Although Helga's "aesthetic sense" is represented as an escape from this ideology, in fact it covers up reality and thereby reveals the inefficacy of art that does not engage with the "strange talk" of shame.

The debate over the political power of art is central to the Harlem Renaissance, as Du Bois's equation of art with propaganda encapsulates. Standing in explicit opposition to Du Bois's formulation were those artists associated with the only published issue of *Fire!!* magazine, founded by Wallace Thurman. In the issue, Thurman includes his short story about a prostitute, titled "Cordelia the Crude," while Richard Bruce Nugent, writing as Richard Bruce, presents a story about a man who desires another man in "Smoke, Lilies and Jade." These stories do not provide conventional moralistic frameworks for interpreting their characters; the lack of shame in these stories thus sets the magazine in opposition to Du Bois's *Crisis* with its commitment to Black middle-class morality as a path to political and social change for African Americans.

Yet it is too simple to place Du Bois and his *Crisis* in opposition to Thurman's *Fire!!,* as Du Bois himself highlighted the negative consequences of racial shame. In condemning the ways African Americans have been ostracized, Du Bois calls for spurning racial shame through a new "organized group action" that would "involve deliberate propaganda for race pride. That is, it is going to start out by convincing American Negroes that there is no reason for them being ashamed of themselves."[85] Unlike Thurman's *Fire!!*, the *Crisis* under Du Bois's editorship (1910–34) engaged in uplift propaganda with, for example, articles about the great men of the race and photographs of children. However, Du Bois also puts the blame for racial shame directly on the class divisions displayed in such sites as the *Defender* letters page, arguing that the upper class's "secret shame of being identified with [the lower classes]" lies in the sense of double consciousness that makes them aware of the white gaze: "Because the upper colored group is desperately afraid of being represented before American whites by this lower group, or being mistaken for them, or being treated as though they were part of it, they are pushed to the extreme of effort to avoid contact with the poorest classes of Negroes."[86] Du Boisian social philosophy pinpoints these class conflicts within the race as a factor in creating feelings of shame over racial identity. His aesthetic philosophy, with its emphasis on propaganda that focuses on the achievements of the race over that which depicts African Americans in a negative light, is in tension with his insistence that the shame causing the upper class to shrink from "contact with the poorest classes of Negroes" is harmful to racial unity. In other words, while his comments about shame reveal the harm that class divisions inflict, his views on art often led him to conceal the perceived negative qualities of the lower classes.

This dynamic is apparent in Du Bois's notorious review of Claude McKay's *Home to Harlem* (1928), in which he compares the novel to *Quicksand*, positioning Larsen's novel as an antidote to the "drunkenness, fighting, lascivious sexual promiscuity and utter absence of restraint" that, according to him, characterize McKay's novel.[87] This comparison aligns Larsen with the Black bourgeois values that Du Bois and readers of the *Crisis* espoused. Du Bois overlooks the depiction of female sexual desire in Larsen's novel, while condemning McKay's novel for setting out "to cater for that prurient demand on the part of white folk for a portrayal in Negroes of that utter licentiousness which conventional civilization holds white folk back from enjoying—if enjoyment it can be called."[88] His praise for Larsen and vehement condemnation of McKay are grounded in class distinctions. Larsen's discussion of sexuality is perceived as more refined—Du Bois uses the words "subtle" and "delicately" to describe the plot—in comparison to McKay's novel with its concentration on the lower class, which, famously, "nauseate[d]" Du Bois and caused him to "feel distinctly like taking a bath."[89]

Du Bois's condemnation of *Home to Harlem* employs visual language that echoes the letters of the *Defender* readers. His real criticism lies in McKay's supposed "cater[ing]" to "that prurient demand on the part of white folk," while his praise for Larsen includes the assertion that "white folk will not like this book."[90] Like *Defender* reader Mrs. James, who knows that "the white folks are watching our Race," Du Bois's primary concern in this review is the white gaze; at least part of this concern revolves around the emphasis on lower-class characters in *Home to Harlem,* in contrast to the upper-class characters of *Quicksand.* In this review, then, Du Bois's equation of art with propaganda leads to the very type of triangulated thinking that he previously identified as race suicide. Despite his rejection of racial shame, Du Bois, like the *Chicago Defender* readers, argues for class-based shame through a concern with the gaze.

In a scathing June 18, 1928, letter to Du Bois, McKay responded to the review, contending that Du Bois's emphasis on racial propaganda "has precluded [him] from contact with real life, for propaganda is fundamentally but a one-sided idea of life. Therefore I should not be surprised when you mistake the art of life for nonsense and try to pass off propaganda as life in art!"[91] McKay's emphasis on the "art of life" dismisses any attempt to shame him through the rhetoric of dirtiness, and he defends the aesthetic validity of his representation of the prostitutes, gamblers, and jazz clubs that make up *Home to Harlem.* Similarly, Hughes—who along with Thurman and Hurston was involved with *Fire!!*—insists in his important essay "The Negro Artist and the Racial Mountain" that shame over the lower class is a key hindrance to the development of an authentically Black art.[92] While the *Defender* readers posit that the ignorance of the migrants, which leads to their supposed shamelessness, is something to be reformed, Hughes maintains that this seeming lack of knowledge produces a fearless, and thus great, "art of life."

Throughout his essay, which must be read as a proclamation against shame as much as an aesthetic manifesto, Hughes relies on visual language to make his point. While Hughes does refer to literature and jazz, he also mentions portraiture, just as Larsen does. He uses the example of a "Philadelphia clubwoman" who "doesn't care for the Winold Reiss portraits of Negroes because they are 'too Negro.' She does not want a true picture of herself from anybody."[93] In this acidic example, Hughes points to the visual logic of shame by literalizing the gaze of the imagined other in portraiture, specifically the iconic images of Reiss, whose pictures of African Americans were included in the Harlem number of *Survey Graphic* magazine. Hughes's visual language affirms that the "true picture" of African Americans is not something to be ashamed of, whether in portraiture, literature, or in everyday life outside art.

Hughes and Larsen, much like readers of the *Defender*, use the language of visual art to highlight the visual character of shame as well as Ellison's un-visibility of the highly visible. In the critical conversations about the aesthetic debates of the Harlem Renaissance, Larsen is not given a key role, but it is a mistake to ignore her aesthetic philosophy as presented in *Quicksand,* with its protagonist who values art so highly. However, her approach to aesthetics cannot be designated as Du Boisian, despite his positive review of her novel, nor can it be aligned with Hughes, McKay, and the contributors to *Fire!!,* for whom art was its own end, not a vehicle for propaganda. Unlike the latter group of artists, Larsen completely refutes the characterization of the folk as beautiful in any way through her bleak portrayal of female lives in the rural South; indeed, she seems to mock this view by depicting Helga's initially naïve love for the rural South and her eventual recognition of its horrifying oppression. Similarly, Larsen suggests that Hughes's view of being unashamedly Black is unrealistic in the Jim Crow era, particularly for Black or biracial women.

Larsen's criticism of the Black elite, including race leaders as embodied in the figures of Mrs. Hayes-Rore and Anne Grey in *Quicksand* (and by Irene Redfield in her second novel, *Passing* [1929]), hints at a rejection of Du Bois and his Talented Tenth. However, her art is not explicitly propagandistic, since *Quicksand* refuses a clear moral ending and represents Black female sexuality without judgment. The novel reserves its condemnation for a repressive society, whether at Naxos or in Harlem. But despite the inefficacy of Helga's aesthetic sense and the novel's undeniably tragic conclusion, it would be a mistake to conclude that Larsen refuses the transformative potential of art. Like the *Defender,* Larsen's novel acts as a tool for shaming even as it condemns the concealment of shame. By holding up a mirror to uplift ideology and to elite Harlem coteries, Larsen asks the reader to see the resemblance between the two. This shift in perspective asks the reader to engage in a potentially socially transformative way of looking that acknowledges the hypocrisy of racial uplift, elite coteries, and an aesthetics that conceals the ugliness of shame.

A NEW "AESTHETIC SENSE"

Although Hughes proclaims, "We younger Negro artists who create now intend to express our individual dark-skinned selves without fear or shame," Larsen advances the idea that shame and fear of shame are essential aspects of Black (and biracial) female experiences, and that shame must play a role in art that represents those experiences.[94] Hazel V. Carby and Ann duCille have examined Larsen's radical alternative depictions of Black women in American fiction in relation to more traditional depictions by Black and white authors, male and female. Carby calls Helga "the first truly sexual black female protagonist in Afro-American fiction."[95] Similarly, duCille asserts that Larsen and her peers, including Fauset and Hurston, revise the traditional marriage plot by depicting Black women as "actively sexual beings, implicitly questioning their positioning as objects of male desire and contemplating, if not fully exploring, their sexual selves."[96] It is not an accident, of course, that the discussions of shame are centered on Black women's bodies; the stereotypes around Black female sexuality and bourgeois norms around female sexuality in general made Black women's bodies sites to be regulated. However, I wish to emphasize that it is through *Quicksand*'s modernist experimentation that Larsen creates a different kind of aesthetic; this new aesthetic aims for authenticity, links social transformation with aesthetic transformation, and shows how old repetitive structures, social or aesthetic, can be made new.

Larsen criticizes social convention through her use of a novelistic form that permits different points of view—a form that parallels shame's form with its perspectival shifts and reveals the ethical possibilities of shame. Thaggert correctly notes that, as in *Quicksand*, "visuality and appearance are central issues in *Passing*. An exchange of glances between and among women occurs repeatedly in the text—glances that the main character, Irene, can never fully comprehend."[97] Thaggert concludes that *Passing* "denies ready access to both the external and intimate aspects of a black woman, rendering ineffective any reading of black femininity based solely on a woman's body or appearance."[98] In echoing *Quicksand*'s themes of respectability and female sexuality, *Passing* thus denies the gazes of the reader and Irene the power to interpret Clare Kendry. By contrast, *Quicksand* provides access to oscillating perspectives, facilitating the reader's knowledge of Helga, even though her own desires remain mysterious to herself.

Most critics take it for granted that *Quicksand* is told from Helga's perspective. One exception is Claudia Tate, who notes one instance of a shift from Helga's thoughts to the third-person narrator's perspective at the novel's end, but even she does not remark upon other shifts in viewpoint.[99] Another exception to this consensus is Sianne Ngai's compelling analysis of the minor affect of irritation in Larsen's novel; Ngai fixes attention on the novel's "oscillation between insides and outsides," reflected in the formal move to "merg[e] aspects of Helga's 'silent but implied speech' with the narrator's 'factual reporting.'"[100] This continual exchange of perspectival positions—what Ngai calls "narrative lesions or ruptures"—prevents the reader from fully identifying or disidentifying with Helga or the narrator, thus "foreground[ing] *Quicksand*'s larger effort to distance itself from the sentimental tradition of mulatta fiction and its politics of compulsory sympathy, while also enabling the text to resist the imperative that productions by African-American artists *fill in their blanks,* facilitating *either* identification *or* disidentification with existing constructions of black identity."[101] In contrast, a consideration of the major affect of shame reveals the process by which Helga and the reader both experience identification *and* disidentification, paralleling the structure of shame that places the ashamed person simultaneously in the positions of self and observer.

The novel's opening reveals that Helga's point of view is not the only one available. In describing Helga's physical appearance in her darkened room, Larsen writes, "An observer would have thought her well fitted to that framing of light and shade."[102] With this statement, Larsen places the reader at a distance from Helga by aligning the reader with the observer; she also explicitly stages Helga's narrative as an aesthetic object by calling attention to the "framing" of the scene. This "observer" both resembles and differs from the status Helga has as a spectator to the vaudeville show. Throughout the novel, the reader oscillates between seeing through Helga's eyes and being placed at a distance from Helga; this oscillation resembles Helga's own experiences, and her feelings about Olsen's portrait literalize this oscillation between spectator and object. Helga acts as a spectator in looking upon the painted representation of herself; she distances herself from the portrait by describing it as "some disgusting sensual creature with her features," but she also identifies with it through her feelings of shame. Helga is both an observer with an aesthetic sense and an aesthetic object.

Indeed, Helga is continually described as someone who has an acute sense of double consciousness, a quality she shares with the *Defender* readers who continually characterize themselves as seeing and being seen. After she is rejected by her uncle's white wife, Mrs. Nilssen, she thinks: "Worst of all was the fact that under the stinging hurt she understood and sympathized with Mrs. Nilssen's point of view, as always she had been able to understand her mother's, her stepfather's, and his children's points of view. She saw herself for an obscene sore in all their lives, at all costs to be hidden. She understood, even while she resented it. It would have been easier if she had not."[103] Sympathizing with others' points of view is suffocating for Helga because she can see herself as others see her—or, to put it in Sartrean terms, she sees herself as an object through the eyes of the other. At the same time, Larsen is careful to show that Helga's sympathetic viewpoint is not all-encompassing or omniscient. There are six major occasions when the omniscient narrator gives the reader access to the thoughts of other characters, thoughts that are about Helga but not accessible to her: the perceptions of the strangers in Chicago, Mrs. Hayes-Rore's point of view, Herr Dahl's reaction to Helga's tears, Anne's thoughts about Helga's relationship with Robert Anderson, the rural women's disapproval of Helga's plans for uplift, and Miss Hartley's knowledge of Helga's thoughts.[104] These moments of rupture from Helga's perspective force the reader to see her from the outside and confront other points of view that come from both within and outside the race.

Larsen's interest in calling attention to the aesthetic nature of the reading experience prevents the reader from reading passively, forcing the continual interrogation of the subject positions of the reader and the characters within the novel. This interrogation compels the reader to recognize that "naturalization" or conformity to the social order is not inevitable. I take the term "naturalization" from the word "naturalized," which Helga and James Vayle use to describe those who fit into the "unmistakable Naxos mold."[105] This word is echoed later in the novel when a pregnant Helga asks the rural Southern women of her husband's congregation how they manage with so many children; Sary Jones, "who, as Helga knew, had had six children in about as many years," answers by saying, "Tain't nothin', nothin' at all, chile. . . . Yuh all takes it too ha'd. Jes' remembah et's natu'al fo' a 'oman to hab chilluns an' don' fret so."[106] Sary Jones's words assume that there is only one "natu'al" path for a woman, but her claim is called into question by the novel's different perspectives that disrupt the naturalness of social and aesthetic scripts and conventions. At the same time, the rural women's earlier rejection of Helga's uplift project provides a class critique of her Talented Tenth condescension. In public, the women go along with Helga's plans to "subdue the cleanly scrubbed ugliness of her own surroundings to soft inoffensive beauty," but "she was unaware that afterwards they would shake their heads sullenly over their wash-tubs and ironing-boards."[107] This perspectival shift generates a class-based critique: Helga's point of view is challenged by that of the lower-class rural women.[108] In other words, the novel has the capacity to hold "strange talk" and different perspectives, including those from different classes and races. By embracing multiple points of view, Larsen's novel relies on the imaginative and potentially ethical power of shame to refute a script that will end in the birth of "more dark bodies for mobs to lynch."[109] While the novel emphasizes the harmful effects of shame, it also depicts shame's constitutive power of seeing through the eyes of others as a tool for refuting racist ideology that refuses the humanity of others.

For Helga, irony often attaches itself to shame, and irony as an aesthetic tool—specifically, a visual one—offers a solution to deadening art. In the beginning of the novel, when she thinks about her resistance to conformity, she realizes that "she hadn't really wanted to be made over. This thought bred a sense of shame, a feeling of ironical disillusion. Evidently there were parts of her she could not be proud of. The revealing picture of her past striving was too humiliating."[110] Irony's double vision gives her distance from the situation at hand and an ability to see herself from a position of remove, but it is tied to shame, which forces the self to identify with a past that is "too humiliating." Shame as a way of looking asks the self to oscillate between a perspective of intimacy with the self and a perspective of distance in which one sees the self through the eyes of a judging spectator. The aesthetic metaphor of the "the revealing picture of her past" crystallizes this point: Helga, the spectator, distances herself from the past by seeing it as a "picture," while also being able to see it more clearly because it is imagined as a painting or photograph. Shame, coupled with irony, prevents Helga from simply experiencing the aesthetic in a wholly immersive and passive way, as Helga's experiences watching the vaudeville show in Copenhagen also illustrate. Her distance as a "speculative spectator" is reinforced by her "ironical" attitude, which emphasizes her doubling and removes her from passive enjoyment of the scene; she is forced to realize that her life is governed by "a suspensive conflict in which were fused doubts, rebellion, expediency, and urgent longings."[111] Her shamed and ironical gaze stops Helga from falling into a passive reception of the aesthetic experience, but she cannot maintain this perspective indefinitely.

The alternative reality that Larsen creates is evident in her formal experimentation, which represents both bleak societal facts and the possibilities for changing dominant discourses. Larsen's novel, in other words, criticizes the passive and deadening effects of not only social but also aesthetic conventions. An art that does not shy away from representing shame allows for the revelation of different ways of being. Bernard Williams points to the power of shame: "By giving through the emotions a sense of who one is and of what one hopes to be, [shame] mediates between act, character, and consequence, and also between ethical demands and the rest of life."[112] Larsen's plot offers no alternatives for Helga, but the fact of Larsen's multiplication of perspective reveals to her readers that there are different ways of seeing, and thus living, than those privileged during the Jim Crow period. Although Helga Crane is finally unable to move outside of her own point of view, Larsen's experiments with conventions and perspectives expose the fact that they are neither fixed nor natural.

Recognizing the malleability of these conventions opens up new ways of seeing oneself, others, and one's relations to others. We must reexamine Sartre's claim that the other causes the individual to be "put in the position of passing judgment on [one's] self as on an object, for it is as an object that [one] appear[s] to the Other."[113] As Williams suggests, shame as the multiplication of perspectives leads to reimagining the self and others, and provides the foundation for an ethics that allows the recognition of the self and others as subjects, rather than simply as Sartre's objects. The discourse of shame insists on a different perspective on the self in relation to societal norms. Such an experience, according to the *Defender* readers and Larsen's novel, has the potential to lead to an ethics that allows for new ways of living during the Jim Crow period.

Essentially, shame can be socially transformative through its perspectival shifts between self and imagined other. The modernist formal experimentation of *Quicksand* follows this dynamic of perspectival shifts. These shifts reveal the potential to change seemingly fixed aesthetic and social conventions by demonstrating an alternative way of looking at the world. Larsen suggests that the disciplinary powers of social and aesthetic conventions are related and can be resisted by disrupting the illusion of their fixity. The *Defender*'s letters page (comprised of readers' multiple viewpoints) and Larsen's formal experimentation allow their readers to experience shifts in viewpoint that parallel the dynamics of shame. Reading shame through multiple discourses reveals that such shifts in perspective do not necessarily replicate the ontological condition of racial shame equating Blackness with inferiority; instead, these shifts offer alternative perceptions of the race that can dispel the seeming fixity of racial stereotypes and roles.

These shifts also have the capacity to expose shame as a tool of the power order that is used both to suppress the self and then to do the work of suppressing others. In other words, one might say that perspectival shifts call attention to the cruel optimism of shame and shaming. Berlant states, "A relation of cruel optimism exists when something you desire is actually an obstacle to your flourishing."[114] In this case, the desire for respectability is the object of desire and the obstacle. An essential part of race shame is the internalization of white hegemonic norms; the identification of these norms as being worth striving for is grounded in the assumption that they are achievable if one only plays the game correctly—that, ultimately, the system is a just one. However, this optimism is cruel because the rules of the game do not allow for African Americans to achieve these norms no matter how much one works for them, as the system is, by design, not just. The perspectival shifts expose the cruelty of this optimism by revealing the path to rejecting the norms altogether; seeing *otherwise*—seeing beyond these hegemonic norms—can expose the rigged nature of the game.

A clear understanding of the network that exists between Larsen's novel and the *Defender* readers reveals the way that a novel and newspaper are involved in producing a shared discourse of shame even though they themselves are not directly linked. Affective networks map onto periodical networks as the networked connections between novel and newspaper produce and are influenced by a common concern with shame. Networks, due to the dialogic relationships between their nodes, bring up the question of what we owe others. In other words, networks are imbued with ethical concerns since the position of one node affects the positions of other nodes. Perspectival shifts that provide alternate views allow for an ethics that refuses the inevitability of Jim Crow conditions and definitions; ultimately, connections within the networks have the potential to be destabilized and re-formed into new configurations.

CHAPTER THREE
Readerly Networks
William Faulkner's Magazine Publics

In a 1956 letter to his friend Ralph Ellison, the writer Albert Murray wrote, "Saw that Faulkner piece in *Life*. Sad, pitiful and stupid thing for a writer like that to do. That underdog shit makes me puke. How can a son of a bitch sit up and fuckup morality like that?"[1] The "Faulkner piece" that provoked such nausea is "A Letter to the North," published in a 1956 issue of *Life* magazine. In this essay, William Faulkner argues for racial gradualism by advising African Americans to "go slow now'" in the wake of the *Brown v. Board of Education* decision.[2] In a letter to Murray, written less than two weeks after the publication of Faulkner's essay, Ellison wrote that Faulkner forgets that the Negro "isn't in the market for his advice, because he's been knowing how to 'wait-a-while'—Faulkner advice—for over three hundred years, only he's never been simply waiting, he's been probing for a soft spot, looking for a hole, and now he's got the hole."[3] Ellison and Murray see Faulkner's advice as ignoring the realities of what it means to be Black in the Jim Crow United States. Faulkner's failure of the imagination is seen as a product of a flawed moral system, and, as Ellison notes, despite his ostensible intentions, Faulkner remains markedly ambivalent about the possibility of sociopolitical change for African Americans.

While Faulkner's influence on and intersections with African American writers like Toni Morrison and Ellison have been discussed by other critics, his relationships with his Black magazine-reading publics have been understudied. While his readership certainly included elite writers like Ellison and Murray, it was also composed of ordinary readers of middlebrow periodicals like *Ebony* magazine. In this chapter, then, I call attention to the ways that magazine letters pages offer insight into the interactions between the author and his publics—Faulkner and the readers of *Life* and *Ebony*—during the critical period following the

Brown v. Board of Education decision (see figure 3 for a timeline of relevant events). In the previous chapter, I argued that the visual logic of shame has the potential to open up space for perspectival shifts. In this chapter, I build on my discussion of the *Defender*'s letters to the editor to demonstrate the way that such letters in *Life* and *Ebony* magazines work to affirm and refute the perspectival imagination that lies at the heart of Faulkner's racial politics. The letters to the editor provide a glimpse into both the readers' negotiation of the authority of a celebrity author and into the magazine's self-presentation through those letters; in other words, this magazine section allows access into the networks of reader, author, and periodical.

The 1956 *Ebony* issue in which Faulkner was published featured a Black woman in a bathing suit—Ramona Carlene Bruce, a model—to match the feature on "How to Handle Beautiful Women." In reference to the cover image, the table of contents page states, "Typical of young Negro beauties, Ramona says marriage is the height of her ambition."[4] The cover also advertised Faulkner's essay and a story on "Billie Holiday's Tragic Life." Faulkner chose to publish his essay in *Ebony* in order to reach a different audience from that of *Life*. According to the magazine, while Allan Morrison, the New York editor of *Ebony*, was walking with Billie Holiday, the pair bumped into Faulkner on the street. The "Backstage" column of the issue states, "In the course of the brief river side conversation, Mr. Morrison told Mr. Faulkner what a figure of controversy Faulkner had become among Negroes since so much had been printed about his stand on desegregation. The Mississippi author insisted that he had been greatly misquoted and said that he would like to clarify his position."[5] While he was paid $250 to write the essay, Faulkner claimed that the money was unimportant. In a June 23, 1956, letter to Harold Ober, he wrote, "I assume that EBONY may wish to pay for it, simply as a token that they consider worthwhile. But the money will not matter. I would rather have it in the Negro journal, even at no price, if they will print it intact, unedited. If they dont want it, hold it and write me; it may take some elaboration for a white publication."[6] Faulkner was clearly aware that the readerly networks of *Ebony* were different from those of a white-focused periodical, and he leapt at the

November 1950	Faulkner awarded 1949 Nobel Prize for Literature
September 28, 1953	Coughlan's "The Private World of William Faulkner" published in *Life*
October 5, 1953	Coughlan's "The Man Behind the Faulkner Myth" published in *Life*
October 5, 19, and 26, 1953	Letters to the editor about Coughlan's piece published in *Life*
May 17, 1954	*Brown v. Board of Education* decided
1955	*A Fable* awarded both the Pulitzer Prize and the National Book Award (*A Fable* published in August 1954)
July 1955	"On Privacy (The American Dream: What Happened to It?)" published in *Harper's* magazine
February 1956	Autherine Lucy became the first African American student at the University of Alabama; Faulkner refers to her as the impetus for his essays on gradualism.
March 4, 1956	Russell Warren Howe interview published in the London *Sunday Times*
March 5, 1956	"A Letter to the North" published in *Life*
March 16, 1956	Ellison's letter to Murray about Faulkner's "wait-a-while" comment
March 22, 1956	Howe interview published in a different version in the *Reporter*
April 19, 1956	Albert Murray's letter to Ellison about that "underdog shit"
Fall 1956	Baldwin's "Faulkner and Desegregation" published in the *Partisan Review*
September 1956	"If I Were a Negro" published in *Ebony*
November 1956	*Ebony* letters to the editor about Faulkner
December 1956	*Ebony* letter to the editor—only one letter about Faulkner

FIGURE 3. Timeline of events related to Faulkner's magazine publications. Created by the author.

opportunity to use the Black publication as a platform for explaining his racial philosophy. In fact, Faulkner's choice of multiple publication venues in the 1950s in responding to the debates surrounding integration reflected his understanding that he would be most effective by targeting his message to different audiences, in terms of periodical networks of diverse regional, racial, national, and cultural affiliations.

Recent critical works on Faulkner, such as *William Faulkner in the Media Ecology* and *William Faulkner in Context,* do not consider his work in the periodicals other than in glancing ways.[7] A notable exception to this trend is the *Faulkner and Print Culture* collection, which contains several essays on Faulkner's relationship with middlebrow magazines (along with other kinds of periodicals).[8] It is fair to say that Faulkner's imbrication in periodical culture, particularly Jim Crow periodical culture, is understudied despite its importance to his writing and life. As Jaime Harker and Jay Watson write, "*Book* history can tell only part of the story of the author's imaginative investments in print culture. He published in, and wrote about, a wide variety of other print media: newspapers, slicks, little magazines, pulp periodicals, academic journals. Throughout his career, he was remarkably opportunistic and savvy about the trends and conventions that governed print publication in the United States."[9] In discussing Faulkner's savviness about the workings of print culture—in particular, print media networks—this chapter extends the argument of the previous chapter in making a claim for the importance of the letters to the editor. However, rather than focusing on the way that readers speak back to one another and to larger debates about uplift, this chapter analyzes the author-reader interactions, facilitated and encouraged by periodical editors, that the letters allow.

In the previous chapter, I argued that the letters page deserves serious attention because it contains valuable information about a periodical's strategies in presenting itself and equally valuable though limited information about its readership. In the cases of *Ebony* and *Life,* as discussed in this chapter, this magazine section offers insight into the way readers negotiate the authority of a celebrity author at the beginning of the end of the Jim Crow period. These readerly negotiations reveal the shifting network connections between author, readers, and magazine, and highlight the authority that the network offers readers in speaking back to a celebrity writer; networks allow for authority to be contested and for often-unrecognized forms of authority to be asserted. This kind of work, like the discourse of shame produced by the juxtapositions of the *Defender*'s letters to the editor, is one of the affordances of the periodical form that distinguish it from the work that a novel engages in. In his novels, Faulkner produces a dominant world-making artistic voice that does not contain the capacity to include other authorial voices; one of the affordances of the novel as a genre is that its linguistic code generally does not include other authors, even though it may contain a multiplicity of voices in terms of characters and in the sense of Bakhtinian heteroglossia. Rather, reviews by critics and readerly responses are external to the novel's code, although they may be present in the bibliographic code—for example, on the back cover. In contrast, one of the affordances of a periodical is the capacity to contain external voices to produce a network between author, reader, and editor (among others, like advertisers and photographers) to allow for the destabilization of the authorial voice.

In September 1956, a few months after the publication of Faulkner's *Life* magazine essay, *Ebony* published "If I Were a Negro," Faulkner's attempt to clarify his notoriously controversial views on race.[10] The essay's title refers to *Negro Digest*'s popular regular feature, "If I Were a Negro," in which well-known white figures like Eleanor Roosevelt were given the opportunity to discuss how they would respond to racial problems if they were Black.[11] This essay includes a quotation from his *Life* essay in which he tells "the NAACP and the other organizations working actively for the abolishment of segregation" to "go slow now."[12] It is also a clarification of his earlier quoted and widely circulated controversial statement—a statement that he would ascribe to his inebriation during the interview and that would lead W. E. B. Du Bois to challenge him to a debate on race issues—that he would choose Mississippi over the United States "even (at the price or if it meant) shooting down Negroes in the street."[13] The essay calls for gradualism as a solution to the race problem, and, notably, it also contains a strong claim for the efficacy of the imaginative enterprise of seeing through the eyes of others. Presented as a four-page photo spread, the essay is marked by the repetition of the striking phrase "If I were a Negro" followed by various explanations of what Faulkner would do if he were Black. Faulkner's assumption of authority through the act of imagining himself Black is not left unchallenged, however, and the consecutive issue of the magazine is filled with responses. In their letters, the readers of the magazine provide counterpoints to the essay by arguing for the authority that comes through lived experience, in opposition to the aesthetic imagination. The letters page ultimately works as a site where the celebrity author's authority risks destabilization while the ties between the readers and the magazine are affirmed.

In his *Ebony* essay, Faulkner's notorious assertion that he would choose Mississippi even if it meant "shooting down Negroes in the street" is a quotation of himself; the quotation's origin comes from an interview with Russell Warren Howe that was published in the London *Sunday Times* on March 4, 1956, and an edited version was published in the *Reporter* on March 22. James B. Meriwether and Michael Millgate in their introductory notes to the interview state, "Excerpts from the *Reporter* version received wide circulation in the American press within the next few weeks, and one sentence, quoted out of context, soon became notorious."[14] In the published *Reporter* interview, Faulkner declares, "But I don't like enforced integration any more than I like enforced segregation. If I have to choose between the United States government and Mississippi, then I'll choose Mississippi. What I'm trying to do now is not have to make that decision. As long as there's a middle road, all right I'll be on it. But if it came to fighting I'd fight for Mississippi against the United States even if it meant going out into the street and shooting Negroes. After all, I'm not going out to shoot Mississippians."[15] With regard to Faulkner's comments, Catherine Gunther Kodat notes that "however much he intellectually understood the issues at stake, desegregation and civil rights were fundamentally personal issues for Faulkner."[16] Although Howe stood by his reporting, Faulkner immediately repudiated these widely circulated comments in letters to the editor, including to the *Reporter* and *Time* magazine. In his April 19 letter to the *Reporter*, he wrote that his comments "are statements which no sober man would make, nor, it seems to me, any sane man believe"; he continued, "The statement that I or anyone else would choose any one state against the whole remaining Union of States, down to the ultimate price of shooting other human beings in the streets, is not only foolish but dangerous."[17] This interview and the less inflammatory *Life* essay, published around the same time, had wide repercussions, reverberating through Jim Crow networks grounded in periodicals. In dealing with the fallout, Faulkner sought out *Ebony* as a venue to explain his position to African Americans, even as readers like Murray and Ellison discussed his views on integration in both private letters and public letters to periodical editors.

Critics have long grappled with Faulkner's often-complicated public statements on race and his complex depictions of African Americans in fiction. In engaging with Faulkner's comments during 1956, particularly those he made sober or not over the course of the Howe interview, critics historically have often mitigated their force and acted as apologists for them, suggesting that they are not in fact representative of Faulkner's racial views. Meriwether and Millgate, for example, suggest that Faulkner's statement in the Howe interview about choosing Mississippi over the United States "was inconsistent with the rest of the interview and with the stand Faulkner had elsewhere taken upon the racial problem, and he went to some pains to repudiate it."[18] Similarly, in calling this period of Faulkner's career "the racial crisis," Louis Daniel Brodsky has stated that "Faulkner's position on civil rights . . . was ethical and universally humanitarian in its Ghandian [*sic*] non-violent posture" and argues against "focusing on individual lapses," like the statements made in the Howe interview.[19] Brodsky dismisses two critical letters published in the March 26 issue of *Life* as being "written by Negroes with grievances."[20] Charles D. Peavy has noted that "some of Faulkner's statements are ambivalent or contradictory, and many are controversial, particularly when they are viewed outside their original context."[21] About the Howe interview, Peavy has commented, "It is unfortunate that so much attention was focused on this somewhat notorious interview, and so little attention paid to Faulkner's many public letters on integration."[22] In analyzing this tumultuous period in Faulkner's career, I demonstrate the circulations of Faulkner's racial politics in the networks; the affordances of networks allowed letter writers to be more than mere "Negroes with grievances" and to be authorities themselves who counter Faulkner's authority. Faulkner's statements, once released into these networks through publication and circulation, were examined and debated by readers, who countered and complicated the perception of Faulkner's humanitarianism by refuting his power to speak for African Americans.

James Baldwin once famously declared that "Faulkner means everything he says, means them all at once, and with very nearly the same intensity."[23] It is important to keep the contradictions of Faulkner's racial philosophy, which is inextricable from his aesthetic approaches, in mind. These contradictions were ones that Ellison, for example, acknowledged in his criticism and praise for Faulkner. Despite his evisceration of Faulkner's racial gradualism, Ellison famously named Faulkner as one of his literary "ancestors."[24] Critics have argued that Faulkner's representations of Black characters changed with the publication of *Go Down, Moses* in 1942. George Hutchinson, for example, makes claims for the "increasing centrality and complexity of Faulkner's black characters in the 1940s—that is, their increasing humanity."[25] Hutchinson points to three factors: Faulkner's reading of Richard Wright's *Native Son* (1940) in 1945; his realization that Caroline Barr, his family's long-time Black servant, had a "life [that] was outside his ken"; and "World War II, which struck him as a fundamental challenge to racial tyranny in the United States."[26] This narrative posits a shift in Faulkner's fictional engagements with African Americans—from Dilsey Gibson in *The Sound and the Fury* to Mollie Beauchamp in *Go Down, Moses*.

Yet, as this chapter demonstrates, despite his literary work, Faulkner's public pronouncements in response to desegregation do not dramatically reflect a deepening understanding of Black lives and, particularly, of the limits of his imagination in piercing what Du Bois would call "the Veil" or "the strange meaning of being black."[27] Regardless of this, as Kodat maintains, "we should not conclude that Faulkner's writing lost all salience to Baldwin or later authors (or, to put it another way, that Faulkner's late-1950s civil rights implosion gives the lie to the work of the 1930s). To the contrary, Cold War readers and writers maintained an active creative engagement with Faulkner, picking and choosing their way through his oeuvre, keeping what was useful, setting aside what was not, and frequently taking issue with both his claims and his techniques—habits of critical reading practiced especially skillfully by African American authors who came of age during the civil rights movement."[28] In examining ordinary (and some not-so-ordinary) readers' use of periodical networks to push back against a celebrity author, this chapter highlights these habits of Black critical reading. The periodical network facilitates these habits through a shift in power dynamics that affords readers the ability to speak back to an author, an affordance that the novel does not provide.

In so doing, the readers push back against Faulkner's claims about privacy, claims that argue for his status as a private individual who, despite his celebrity status, should not have his life pried into. Instead, the readers refuse Faulkner's insistence on his privacy and make the case for Faulkner's place in a network that affords the authority of other voices. While critics have not generally linked Faulkner's insistence on privacy to his racial politics, these views are relevant to an understanding of his social philosophy; the limits he placed on what others deserved to know about his life stand in contrast with his belief in his imagination's power to understand Black life. His commitment to upholding his personal privacy intersects with his argument for a sense of Southern privacy, what can also be described as a Southern exceptionalism that focuses on the white South's primacy in understanding how to confront the race problem. His *Life* essay and the reader responses to it reveal the way an influential mainstream magazine presented Faulkner's views on the race question. This is contrasted with the way his essay is handled in *Ebony,* in which the editorial strategies work instead to bring Black life to forefront. Like the previous chapter, this chapter emphasizes perspectival shifts but those shifts are Faulkner's work in imagining what it means to be Black—with all the limitations that implies—and also the readers' use of their opposing perspectives to criticize Faulkner's imaginative work. Faulkner's words and the "speaking back" that the readers engage in are both possible through a periodical network that allows for the destabilization of authorial authority. Thinking about this relationship as a network highlights the affordances of the magazine form with its facilitation of dialogues between author, readers, and editors.

FAULKNER AND PRIVACY

Although Faulkner had mostly fallen into obscurity in the United States—only his novel *Sanctuary* (1931) was still in print—by the time Malcolm Cowley published *The Portable Faulkner* in 1946, "a book that many literary historians and critics see as the turning point in Faulkner's literary reputation," by the 1950s he had become a feted author and public figure due to the turn in critical and public interest in his work.[29] His book *A Fable* was awarded both the Pulitzer Prize and the National Book Award in 1955. Before that, he had received the 1949 Nobel Prize in Literature in November 1950, and his Nobel speech had received great acclaim from the public due to its discussion of the artist's role in maintaining universal human values. Faulkner used his celebrity status to speak to the nation and the world, and, in doing so, he became a public voice of authority on the American South and on the United States—and received all the fame and publicity that came with this role. As a result, he became, as Kodat phrases it, "one of America's first Cold War cultural celebrities."[30] Murray, in fact, criticized Faulkner's role as a kind of cultural ambassador for the U.S. State Department during the Cold War and as a spokesperson during the desegregation crisis, linking these two roles together and suggesting that, in these two roles, Faulkner does not engage in true sociopolitical change. In a letter to Ellison, Murray states, "Imagine a fatass travelling all around the world selling humanity for the State Dept and then going back home pulling that kind of crap at the first sign of real progress . . . Sounds like all of the other 'safe liberals.'"[31] Yet, despite his public role "travelling all around the world selling humanity," Faulkner insisted on the sanctity of his private life.

Three years before the publication of "A Letter to the North," *Life* magazine published a two-issue spread on Faulkner titled "Private World of William Faulkner" and "The Man Behind the Faulkner Myth" on September 28 and October 5 in 1953.[32] This two-part essay, written by Robert Coughlan, highlights Faulkner's biography. Coughlan would go on to publish a biography titled *The Private World of William Faulkner* (1954). As the titles in *Life* suggest, the feature, which is complimentary overall and in line with Faulkner's self-narrative, delves into the private life of a public figure. In a letter about Coughlan's essays, Faulkner wrote, "Sweden gave me the Nobel Prize. France gave me the Legion d'Honneur. All my native land did for me was to invade my privacy over my protest and my plea."[33] Faulkner himself did embrace his status as a public figure in the context of his work as a cultural ambassador for the State Department and an essayist responding to the desegregation debate; at the same time, he was famously ambivalent about the effects his public life had on his privacy (and his feelings about the Coughlan essay seem related more to the very fact of the publicity thrust on him after its publication than to the details of its content). The letters to the editors in response to Coughlan's essay reflect this ambivalence on the part of the readers, too.

As a whole, the letters, which ran in the October 19 and 26 issues, mostly contain praise for Coughlan's essay, including a commendation from novelist John Dos Passos. They also contained insults directed at Faulkner himself, such as the letter from Donald Wetzel of Santa Fe, New Mexico, who writes, "Faulkner is obviously an idiot who stands two feet high and writes drivel."[34] However, other letters suggest that the private life of a public figure has no place in the public sphere and that this type of exposure is unseemly. John H. Snow writes, "What purpose is served by the revelation of Faulkner's personal life, except perhaps the enormous pleasure Mr. Coughlan must take in rubbing a great man's face in the mud."[35] Betty Ann Calvert of Indiana condemns the two-part essay as a "vicious spate of derogatory propaganda," and states, "No wonder Mr. Faulkner so diligently seeks privacy if Robert Coughlan is representative of available biographers!"[36]

This readerly criticism is in line with Faulkner's thoughts about privacy, although he certainly benefited from the publicity generated by Coughlan's articles. In Faulkner's essay "On Privacy (The American Dream: What Happened to It?)," originally published in *Harper's* magazine in July 1955, he links privacy's role in maintaining personal individuality in the nation to a personal account of having his privacy violated by interviewers: "The American sky which was once the topless empyrean of freedom, the American air which was once the living breath of liberty, are now become one vast down-crowding pressure to abolish them both, by destroying man's individuality as a man by (in that turn) destroying the last vestige of privacy without which man cannot be an individual."[37] In his logic, privacy is necessary for individuality, and individuality is necessary for American freedom and democracy; thus, without privacy, America would not exist. For Faulkner, a democracy is made up not of the undifferentiated masses but of autonomous individuals bound together in a collective. Faulkner's democracy, as Richard Gray claims, is based on a paradox: "The paradox is that we exist apart, as autonomous subjects and authors of our own discourse, and as part of what Bakhtin called 'a speaking collective' from whom our words are derived and to whom, however implicitly, they are addressed."[38]

Faulkner ultimately sees democracy as consisting of individuals making up nodes that are bound together into a collective network. He argues that the American Dream began with "individual men and women who said as with one simultaneous voice: 'We will establish a new land where man can assume that every individual man—not the mass of men but individual men—has inalienable right to individual dignity and freedom within a fabric of individual courage and honorable work and mutual responsibility."[39] Notably, this vision of America is not based simply on self-interested individuals, but rather on individuals who share a "mutual responsibility" to one another and whose behaviors and decisions influence one another's. While Faulkner was deeply interested in the private consciousness of individuals in his fiction, he was also deeply committed to the public role of the artist in promoting universal values. Faulkner's relationship with public life was a conflicted one because, even as he took on an increasingly public role, he raged against the breaches of his private life.

Kodat notes that Faulkner's essay is "informed by the agonistic logic of going public in the name of privacy."[40] As Robert Jackson observes, Faulkner assisted in Coughlan's reporting in various ways despite his claim that he had not: Faulkner "had become, in the end, famously private, and the Faulkner brand was a performance of a well-publicized privacy."[41] In one of the few studies that notes the tie between Faulkner's views on privacy and his racial politics, Jackson perceptively comments that "Faulkner's formulation of privacy arises from the fact that it is implicitly racialized . . . because his model of individualism was grounded in the culture of whiteness in which he had lived all his life and beyond which he never quite traveled—except, perhaps, fictionally."[42]

Understanding Faulkner's privacy is necessary to understanding his racial politics during the 1950s for two key reasons. First, Faulkner insists on Southern exceptionalism and the concomitant claim that the American South is best equipped to understand and handle Black and white relations; thus, Southerners should be given the privacy to deal with this problem on their own without interference from others, including the U.S. government. Faulkner's focus here springs, in part, from a very real (and ultimately realized) fear that top-down integration from the federal government would lead to violence against African Americans. Second, Faulkner argues that private interactions between individuals are the central sites where real racial change can take place, not in top-down public legislative actions. However, as some of his readers implicitly point out, Faulkner's emphasis on privacy does not encompass African Americans and the integrity of their experiences. In his essays, as I will demonstrate, Faulkner presents African Americans as members of a race, not as individuals in their own rights; in other words, individuality is raced as white. In claiming that he understands what African Americans must do in order to create sociopolitical change, he intrudes on their authority, individualism, and, ultimately, privacy.

FAULKNER IN *LIFE*

Faulkner's publication of his essay in *Ebony* (1945–present, largely online with an uncertain future), a glossy monthly periodical aimed at middle-class and aspirational African Americans, highlights an audience different from that of *Life* (1936–72, 1978–2000), which billed itself as a weekly news magazine, although both shared similarities as coffee table periodicals with an emphasis on photographs, news, culture, and American life. As Maren Stange notes, "A heavily illustrated 'consumer' magazine with feature stories in photo-essay format as well as other modes of photojournalistic display, *Ebony,* though monthly, was consciously modeled on the weekly *Life,* by 1945 the primary vehicle for conveying the news visually to a mass American (and, increasingly, international) audience."[43] Brenna Wynn Greer observes that *Ebony*'s tactics "reveal that the representation and marketing strategies of the most powerful black media- and imagemaking institution of the postwar United States did not emerge purely out of black culture or a set of black sensibilities or politics, or even from methods and models defining black publishing or the black press at the time."[44] These two magazines are mass-market magazines, rather than little magazines with the attendant narrow readership and avant-garde focus; instead, their abundant advertisements mark them as popular, even though they were not generally labeled as lowbrow. These choices of venues for transmitting his views on desegregation were not out of line with Faulkner's overall periodical affiliations despite his highbrow authorial reputation for experimentation and difficulty as a modernist writer. As Harker and Watson note, Faulkner worked to publish in the *Saturday Evening Post* specifically so that he could reach a wide audience and, importantly, be paid well for his short stories. Though it was a middlebrow magazine, considered to be one of the big "slicks" with its glossy paper and numerous advertisements, the *Post* was one of Faulkner's frequent publication venues.[45]

In publishing with *Ebony*, Faulkner's motivation was to reach a particular audience. *Ebony* was founded by John H. Johnson; *Life* was founded by the influential periodicals magnate Henry Robinson Luce. In 1956, an issue of the weekly *Life* cost 20 cents, while an issue of *Ebony*, as a monthly, went for 30 cents. While they were not quite as focused on the domestic life as the *Half-Century*, they were middlebrow in their aspirationality, and they were not particularly focused on literature. *Life*'s audience was broader and larger than *Ebony*'s, and it was interracial while *Ebony*'s was predominantly Black. *Life* attempted to speak to Americans, which for the most part meant white Americans despite its interracial readership, while *Ebony* constructed and took part in a counterpublic space where African Americans could speak to other African Americans and read about themselves.

"A Letter to the North," Faulkner's essay that angered Ellison and Murray, was published in *Life* on March 5, 1956, just a few months before the publication of "If I Were a Negro" in *Ebony*. During this period, *Life* was a powerful force in the United States, and the March 1956 issue reflects this with its many glossy and colorful advertisements, such as for

Carnation evaporated milk and Pillsbury cake mix. *Life*'s circulation in 1956 reached 5.8 million, while *Ebony*'s circulation in 1950 was 500,000.[46] Within the pages of the 1956 *Life* issue, which had actress Kim Novak on the cover, Faulkner's photographed portrait is presented on the first page of his essay.[47] This portrait, in which he is presented as a distinguished author, complements the other photograph that accompanies this essay, that of the monument to Faulkner's great-grandfather, William Clark Falkner. The caption reads: "Great-grandfather, William Cuthbert [*sic*] Falkner (as he spelled family name), lies beneath this monument. He had slaves, fought in Confederate army."[48] (It seems that the magazine meant "William Clark Falkner" but used Faulkner's middle name in place of his great-grandfather's. It was Faulkner who added a "u" to his family name.) This presentation reveals the way *Life* shores up the regional exceptionalism that Faulkner argues for in his essay: "So the Northerner, the liberal, does not know the South. He can't know it from his distance."[49] The magazine, in effect, affirms Faulkner's personal mythology, which was initially emphasized in the 1953 Coughlan two-issue biographical pictorial spread in the magazine.

Just as the two 1956 photographs emphasize Faulkner's celebrity status, the form of the essay, which is written as a letter complete with a reproduction of Faulkner's signature at the end, highlights Faulkner's celebrity status. The signature clearly positions Faulkner as a lauded celebrity, whereas the epistolary form places the author in an intimate relationship with the readers. Faulkner's choice to use the form of a letter positions his essay as a private conversation with the readers, specifically those in the North, his addressee, even as it is deliberately public in nature. This authorial intimacy is reinforced by Faulkner's letter to the editor in response to the letters he received following the publication of "A Letter to the North"; the correspondence page of the March 26 issue is filled with letters from ordinary readers responding to Faulkner's essay, plus a letter from Faulkner himself.

In one letter, Borden Deal, a reader who identifies as being from Scottsboro, Alabama, writes that Faulkner "is the voice of wisdom and moderation that is being drowned out by rising extremism on both sides."[50] Directly after Deal's letter, a letter from M. A. Harris of New

York criticizes Faulkner, much as Ellison and Murray did: "In putting his hand to pen, Faulkner resembled the boy who put his hand in a dike to stop a flood. His rhetoric was good but his reasoning was poor."[51] Alongside the letter, *Life* reproduces a photograph sent in by Harris of his or her great-grandfather, George Washington Harris, who was a slave. This photograph adds authenticity and weight to Harris's statement and counters the authority of the Falkner monument photograph; the imaginative eye is rejected in favor of the photographic eye. The visual is used as a claim to identity, as a kind of evidence for authority. In another letter, Lewis Herring of Mobile, Alabama, claims, "Mr. Faulkner has stated the views of myself and many friends," while, directly after, Leslie H. Engram of Cleveland, Ohio, writes, "Mr. Faulkner's ancestors owned slaves. My ancestors were slaves."[52] With this statement and with Harris's photograph, Engram and Harris argue for the fundamental differences between Faulkner and themselves, differences grounded not simply in race but in genealogical history. They argue that Faulkner's gradualist philosophy is grounded in his racial privilege, whereas their perspectives are informed by their ancestral experiences of slavery. (Of course, Faulkner's perspective is itself also informed by ancestral experiences of slavery but from the standpoint of the slave owner, rather than the slave.) With this argument, these letter-writers reject Faulkner's claim to authenticity as derived from his Southern context, and suggest that the true voice of authenticity comes from people who have a family history of enslavement.

Though these letters argue against Faulkner's stance and his assertion of a privileged knowledge of African Americans and the desegregation debate, the magazine shaped the manner in which the debate was perceived through its silent arrangement of the letters. The magazine positioned a letter from the South, which, predictably, is complimentary of Faulkner's essay, against a letter from a self-identified African American person in the North, which criticizes Faulkner's gradualism. Alternating these positions allowed the magazine to create a space that appeared to be diverse. It also reinforced Faulkner's claim for Southern exceptionalism even as it juxtaposed that claim with contradictory claims for the authority that lived experience provides these African American readers. The selection of letters allows for the appearance of debate and conversation within the pages of the magazine while the editorial hand that chose these letters over others is concealed. At the same time, outside the magazine, Ellison and Murray rejected this notion of Southern exceptionalism in their private letters. Murray condemned what he perceived as Faulkner's irrational loyalty to the South: "Son of a bitch prefers a handful of anachronistic crackers to everything that really gives him a reason not only for being but for writing. I'm watching his ass but close forevermore."[53] Ellison and Murray's opinions were, however, not made public in the pages of the magazine since they, like most magazine readers, did not choose to write letters to the editors.

Faulkner's own letter to the editor closes out the commentary on the essay. In this letter, Faulkner writes, "The United States outside the South does not understand the South." He continues, "The reason behind the letter was the attempt of an individual to save the South and the whole United States too from the blot of Miss Autherine Lucy's death."[54] In this response, Faulkner positions himself as a savior for the region and nation even as he insists upon Southern exceptionalism. Faulkner's individual sense of privacy can be applied to his sense of regional privacy that is manifested as a kind of white Southern exceptionalism. In this view, the nation as a whole cannot have any real knowledge of race relations in the South so they ought to afford the South the privacy to deal with its own business. Despite the appearance of debate in the letters page, the magazine ultimately shored up Faulkner's status as an authority on the subject in the March 12, 1956, issue, which is the issue following the one in which his "A Letter to the North" appears and preceding the issue that contained readers' letters responding to Faulkner's essay. This later issue includes an article titled "No Sign of Peace for Autherine"[55] and letters to the editor that discuss Autherine Lucy, who became the first Black student to attend the University of Alabama in February 1956. It also contains an essay by the editors supporting Faulkner's call to "go slow now":

> For when all is said and done, unless the Southern whites accept a Negro as a person—rather than as a cipher bearing a writ of mandamus—he will gain access to nothing more than resentment and hostility. Desegregationists,

> therefore, have a double duty to talk softly, and, as Faulkner urges, 'Go slow, now. Stop now for a time, a moment.' In the great battle of principle, the victory is already theirs; they can afford patience in its execution. There can be no simple, uniform or swift solution to a condition so complex; rather it is a continuing and unfolding drama (which LIFE, incidentally, will explore, in future issues, in many ways) requiring the best efforts of all Americans.[56]

In citing Faulkner in its editorial, the magazine makes explicit an editorial platform that condones Faulkner's essay. Unsurprisingly, *Ebony,* using the affordances of the periodical form, chose to engage with Faulkner's views and celebrity status in a different way than did *Life.*

FAULKNER IN *EBONY*

Faulkner was deeply skeptical of the potential for laws to initiate top-down changes in citizens' everyday behaviors and interactions, mainly because he believed that laws could not change minds. By refuting the government's ability to legislate private selves and advocating for gradualism, Faulkner argues for the autonomy of the individual; at the same time, he emphasizes the way interactions between private individuals in public spaces can eventually lead to social change on a macro level. In his work, both aesthetic and sociopolitical, Faulkner stresses the imaginative work of seeing through others' eyes as allowing one to understand how one must treat others. Faulkner's social philosophy is based on the importance of private individuals interacting with one another in more ways than through simple conversation.

Essentially, his racial politics were grounded in the claim that change in the U.S. South and in the nation as a whole could only come through networks of everyday intimacy. The periodical was a key tool in this social philosophy, as his magazine essays and interactions with the readers built a network between author and reader that allowed him to engage in a kind of intimacy. However, the network also allows the reader to speak back to the author. As the letters pages of *Ebony* and *Life* reveal, one of those public spaces where private individuals can interact is the public (and counterpublic) spheres of the magazines, sites where the networks between readers, authors, and periodical are affirmed and challenged.

In one remarkable paragraph of imaginative—and, arguably, imaginary—sight, Faulkner speaks in the voice of a Negro giving advice to "his people" in *Ebony*: "So if I were a Negro, I would say to my people: 'Let us be always unflaggingly and inflexibly flexible. But always decently, quietly, courteously, with dignity and without violence. And above all, with patience . . . Let us use this patience not as a passive quality, but as an active weapon. But always, let us practice cleanliness and decency and courtesy and dignity in our contacts with [the white man].'"[57] In his discussion of Faulkner's nonfiction statements about race, Peavy has claimed that Faulkner "never really professes to understand [the Negro]."[58] In speaking with students in 1958 at the University of Virginia, where he held the position of writer-in-residence, Faulkner recognized that "it is possible that the white race and the Negro race can never really like and trust the other; this for the reason that the white man can never really know the Negro, because the white man has forced the Negro to be always a Negro rather than another human being in their dealings, and therefore the Negro cannot afford, does not dare, to be open with the white man and let the white man know what he, the Negro, thinks."[59] However, this "white man [who] can never really know the Negro" does not seem to be Faulkner in his *Ebony* essay. At one point in that essay, Faulkner does acknowledge that "it is easy enough to say glibly, 'If I were a Negro, I would do this or that.' But a white man can only imagine himself for the moment a Negro; he cannot be that man of another race and griefs and problems. So there are some questions he can put to himself but cannot answer."[60] The "only" in front of "imagine" is disingenuous, since the rest of the essay speaks to the potency of the imaginative faculty by providing advice on acting in the social and political spheres.

Although Faulkner argues for the integrity of individual privacy, he, at the same time, emphasizes the ability of people to inhabit perspectives that are unlike their own. In other words, Faulkner conceives of the imagination as a powerful tool in responding to the racial tensions of his day. He is deeply skeptical of the potential for laws to initiate top-down changes in citizens' everyday behaviors and interactions because he believes that laws cannot change minds. Imagination, for Faulkner, then functions not simply on the aesthetic level but also in the sociopolitical arena. His own conception of his political responsibilities is crystallized in his 1950 Nobel Prize speech. Delivering this speech under the shadow of the Cold War, Faulkner argues for the artist's responsibility in creating and supporting social change: "The poet's voice need not merely be the record of man, it can be one of the props, the pillars to help him endure and prevail."[61] However, Faulkner's belief in the possibilities of his imagination was not—unsurprisingly—shared by many members of his magazine publics, which included elite figures like Ellison and also the ordinary readers of *Ebony*. The debates that erupted from the publication of Faulkner's essays in the magazines reveal the ways his publics, under the shadow of the 1954 *Brown v. Board of Education* decision, argued for the insufficiency of his sociopolitical imagination at the center of his gradualist philosophy.

Indeed, Faulkner does pose some questions to himself but, contrary to what he says, he manages to answer them with his perceived ability to imagine himself in the place of another human being of a different race. Directly after he states that "there are some questions he can put to himself but cannot answer," he provides a literal question-and-answer session with five questions and answers.[62] In fact, it is not clear what questions Faulkner cannot answer about what it means to be a Negro. It seems that here Faulkner tries to give a nod to the limits of imagining another private self but, instead, he refuses to believe that there are limits to his own imagination, both artistic and social.

Like his character Quentin Compson, Faulkner seems to believe in the imagination's power to lead to insight. In *Absalom, Absalom!* (1936), Quentin famously imagines Thomas Sutpen's experiences during the Civil War: "He could see it; he might even have been there. Then he thought *No. If I had been there I could not have seen it this plain.*"[63] In fact, Faulkner's faith in the sight that his imagination provides is so strong that he spends the rest of the *Ebony* essay ventriloquizing the voice of a Negro speaking to "the leaders of our race." Michael North has discussed the popularity of racial ventriloquism among modernist writers; for North, racial ventriloquism allows writers like Ezra Pound and T. S. Eliot to use dialect to demonstrate their modernity while protecting themselves from the changes of modernity: "Thus white masquerade behind black dialect became a well-established strategy that allowed for both rebellion and a reinforced conformity."[64] Although he does not use dialect in "If I Were a Negro," Faulkner's racial ventriloquism works to signal support for African Americans while also maintaining the boundaries of a past when white voices drowned out Black ones.

The *Ebony* essay was not just a development of Faulkner's thinking later in life, as Donald Kartiganer has shown. This confident belief in the imaginative faculty is a constant through much of Faulkner's life, as reflected in Faulkner's boasts about his mostly fictional accomplishments during the war. For example, Kartiganer suggests that "Faulkner believed that in some strange way he had successfully appropriated the war—not only as a civilian by eventually learning to fly but more by the sheer power of his imaginative empathy."[65] In the *Ebony* essay, Faulkner would use this misguided empathy to position himself as a Negro to lend authority to his call for gradualism. As Thadious M. Davis suggests, "In an artistic sense, he is obsessed not with the Negro as a rounded character or as part of the world of humankind, but with the Negro as an idea which impinges upon the white man's internal world of thought and feeling, and upon the artist's own imaginative world."[66] The letters page of *Ebony* functions in rebuttal to this, as it is a site that works to impinge on one particular white man's imaginative world. While they are an admittedly imperfect way of understanding what ordinary readers thought, the letters to the editor demonstrate that some of his magazine publics did not agree that Faulkner's approach was a "pillar" to help African Americans "endure and prevail." By using Faulkner's own rhetoric of perspective and imagination, the readers, through the magazine letters pages, called into question the artist's authority.

As both the public magazine letters pages and the private letters between Ellison and Murray reveal, Faulkner's *Life* essay (and the Howe interview) generated controversy during the fraught years after *Brown v. Board of Education;* his *Ebony* essay was an attempt to respond to and quell that controversy. To his credit, Faulkner himself seemed aware that the September 1956 *Ebony* essay also had the potential to ignite controversy: In a June 23, 1956, letter to Allan Morrison, the New York editor of *Ebony,* Faulkner wrote, "It may not please your publisher and other editors. But I assume that we both assume that our dilemma and problem can be solved only by men of good will regardless of race, stating their honest ideas to one another that the erroneous ones can be corrected."[67] In this letter, Faulkner, in effect, acknowledged that the periodical network affords debate, and the readers eagerly accepted his invitation to engage. In responding to Faulkner's "If I Were a Negro" essay, many readers of *Ebony* rejected the authority of his perspectival imagination. In the November 1956 issue, the letters to the editor page was filled with six responses to Faulkner's essay.[68] Out of the published letters, only one praises it, while the December 1956 issue contains one neutral response that simply commends *Ebony* for "procuring such a controversial literary giant."[69] Like Ellison and Murray, the other five letter-writers condemned Faulkner's racial politics. One reader named Donald C. Wilson suggests that Faulkner's essay would have been better titled as "If I Were An Uncle Tom," and he pointedly closes his letter with the phrase "From a Negro who is a *Negro.*"[70] While it is important to acknowledge that the racial backgrounds of the letter-writers can only be accessed through these self-identifications, this letter with its carefully italicized word emphasizes the authority of experience by suggesting that racial barriers are not simply legal and social but also imaginative; in doing so, the letter undercuts Faulkner's implicit claim for the power of the authorial imagination by suggesting that simply saying "if I were" is not equivalent to being able to say "I am."

Another reader, Mrs. Wanda Pittman, points out the limitations of Faulkner's imagination: "If Mr. Faulkner were a Negro, it is more likely he would comprehend that it is not the Negroes and their leaders that need advice on how to conduct themselves during this 'dilemma' of equal rights. On the contrary, he would pray to God that the elders and leaders of the white race might first themselves learn and practice decency, dignity, moral and social responsibility that that they might then be more capable of advising a more moral code of conduct to members of their own race."[71] Throughout her letter Pittman playfully but seriously signifies on Faulkner to refute his authority in the matter of race relations even as she calls attention to her own understanding of both Faulkner and the racial situation. Henry Louis Gates Jr. has famously identified "signifyin(g)" as a Black rhetorical strategy that relies on wordplay, specifically "repetition with a signal difference."[72] Using this tactic, which stems from Black vernacular culture and folklore, Pittman repeats and revises Faulkner's own writing and words. In the first line of her letter, for example, she states that he is "apt at writing 'fables,'" an allusion to his *A Fable*.[73] She repeats "If Mr. Faulkner were a Negro" four times in the letter to reflect Faulkner's own repetition of "If I Were a Negro" in his essay and to highlight the conditional "if" to demonstrate the distance between Faulkner's self and Black lives.[74] Her tactic of signifying then uses Black strategies of resistance to wittily condemn Faulkner's advice and call attention to her own readerly and writerly mastery.

An even more explicit letter to the editor from Mrs. Corinne Poole Tane, who identifies herself as a white woman, asks, "How, tell me, can anyone who hasn't been faced with misery tell those who have what to do or how to do it?"[75] She goes on to discuss her views against racism, and then ends with an alternative to Faulkner's politics of the imagination by declaring, "I can't think, 'If I Were a Negro'; I can tell you, 'I believe these things being white.'"[76] In saying this, she implicitly argues for the limitations of the imagination in racial politics and suggests that racism can be combated through her experience as a white woman, not by imagining herself Black. She also discusses her own work toward social change, particularly her financial and verbal support of the NAACP and her education of her son, work that does not rely on the assumption of a Black voice, thereby arguing that Faulkner's attempts to dictate behavioral changes in African Americans to create social change are inadequate and presumptuous. Her model of social transformation thus refutes Faulkner's argument that his prescription for African Americans is the most judicious and effective way to create change.

The autobiographical details that appear in the *Ebony* readers' letters, as well as in the *Defender* and *Life* letters, are employed by their authors as markers of authority, allowing them to counter Faulkner's own authority as an elite figure. Janet Galligani Casey has discussed letters to the editor as a form of "autobiographical expression"; these letter-writers argue for the importance of autobiographical authority in speaking about race relations.[77] These letters provide a picture of the multiple strategies of readerly engagement. Jerome McGann outlines one type of this engagement in his analysis of the ways that books can be conceived of as "a code of signals designed to put specific sets of such interchanges in operation."[78] Readers do things with this code: "Readers, for their part, decode the signals, but that is not all they do. They also retransmit, functioning as secondary authorities who interact with other readers, but who also re-act on the initial code of signals, complicating and altering the original messages."[79] In using autobiographical elements, the writers of letters to the editor act as authorities within the periodical network and, in doing so, they refute Faulkner's signals. Like these letter-writers, Ellison also emphasized the importance of experiential knowledge: "Negro writers and those of the other minorities have their own task of contributing to the total image of the American by depicting the experience of their own groups. Certainly, theirs is the task of defining Negro humanity, as this can no more be accomplished by others than freedom, which must be won again and again each day, can be conferred upon another. A people must define itself, and minorities have the responsibility of having their ideals and images recognized as part of the composite image which is that of the still forming American people."[80] As in Ellison's essay, these letters to the editor, taken as a whole, argue for the limitations of empathy by rejecting the artist's ability to see through the eyes of others. These letters then work to push back against Faulkner's assumption of authority as a celebrity author and to affirm the value of other kinds of authority, specifically empirical.

As I have discussed in the previous chapter, the letter-writers can be described as, if not "real," then "real enough." In speaking about the correspondence column of a nineteenth-century British women's magazine, Lynne Warren has observed,

> Because of the difficulties in obtaining information the concept of the implied reader is often substituted for the elusive figure of the real reader—the reader who actually

> paid her penny and read the magazine. The implied reader is a useful critical tool, but it offers only one way into a particularly complex problem. Implied readers are not, and can never be, anything more than approximations of real people. At the same time it is true that the notion of the "real" reader is also problematical in the sense that all readers "construct" themselves in the process of reading. While I would admit that the task of presenting a "real" reading would be both illusory and misleading, I would argue that the "real" reader should not be ignored.[81]

In moving away from distinctions between the "real" reader and the "implied" reader, I suggest that the letter-writers can be described as "real enough" because the significance of their letters does not come from any notion of the particular reality of the readers or the accuracy of their claims. Instead, the letters can be conceived of as placeholders for readerly subject-positions that are part of the network in which the magazine exists; these subjectivities may be actual ones held by actual readers or they may simply be those imagined by the magazine in its address to its public. Warren suggests that "readers engaging with other readers' contributions will be prompted either to identify with, or challenge, the 'voices' of these readers (or those of the editorial respondents)."[82] This process of engagement, as expressed publicly in the letters pages or privately in individual reading experiences, is part of the magazine's facilitation of the creation of readerly networks, what Michael Warner, as discussed in the previous chapter, has identified as the cross-citational field. James Wald, in his history of periodicals as form and object, has claimed that "when periodicals were scarce, the experience of reading them was often collective and oral, but became more individualized and silent after they became a mass medium, reflecting the shift from vehicle of public discussion to object of private consumption."[83] However, Wald's assertion overlooks the genre of the letters to the editor in periodicals, a genre that allows private consumption to become public discussion through this characteristic of cross-citationality. In the letters to the editor section, readers' private reading experiences and private opinions are made public through engaging with others. Like the letters of the *Chicago Defender*, the letters are both individual and collective—individual in their use of autobiographical elements and in the names signed by the writers, and collective in their presentation of perspectives that other readers may imagine themselves sharing or rejecting and in their address to the periodical community.

In a more general sense, the letters are indicative of the magazine's self-positioning—of its editorial curation of its image to its readers, its potential readers, and the general public. The letters page is part of a genre that Bridget Griffen-Foley calls "participatory media."[84] She observes that the strategies used in participatory media "have sought to foster a sense of audience engagement and agency and, by extension, create a loyal community of readers/listeners/viewers."[85] The letters page highlights the role of the reader, certainly, but also that of the editor. With regard to the correspondence column, Warren has argued that "the construction of the textual community, the 'world' in which identities are constructed and challenged, is a two-sided process, albeit an unequal one, in which magazine and readers are involved in a struggle to assert their own meanings, and in which it is not a simple matter of the magazine imposing a way of reading on a passive readership."[86] The inequality of this relationship must be foregrounded since the editor always has the last word in terms of selecting, editing, and presenting the letters. As with the letters in the *Chicago Defender*, the *Ebony* letters provide limited but valuable information about the readers and their interactions with the magazine. The imperfect nature of this knowledge derives not only from the fact that the letters come from a tiny percentage of the readers of the magazine—and that those letter-writers might be particularly motivated. It also comes from the very nature of letters pages themselves. After all, assuming that the letters are not fabricated, the editor (or whomever is responsible for the page) selects (and edits) the letters to be published from a larger pool of letters. The editor's role as decision-maker in overseeing the correspondence page means that the letters provide insight into the editor's attempts to shape perceptions of the magazine.

The letters page affords readers the seeming ability to interact with the magazine, which creates the magazine's appearance as a site of community, openness, and polyvocality. As Warren observes, "The success of a magazine was in large part due to its formulation of a textual or 'corporate' identity—inextricably linked to its successful appeal to its targeted audience, conveyed through the clues provided by title, cover design, editorial content and so on."[87] In the case of *Ebony* and many other periodicals, including the *Defender,* part of the formulation of this textual and corporate identity lies in the letters page. In other words, the appearance of the magazine as participatory media was essential to its self-presentation. As discussed in the previous chapter, the white-edited *Forum* was explicitly invested in this community of debate in presenting itself as a kind of symposium where controversial ideas were discussed from all sides; although *Ebony* itself was not quite as explicitly invested in this specific periodical identity, it fostered an appearance of polyvocality through the curation of readers' letters, along with Faulkner's essay.

However, *Ebony*'s letters page did not simply present itself as a place of debate and controversy as it—at the same time—acted as a site where a particular side of the debate was instituted as the correct one. The letters page offered a space where a Nobel Prize–winning author can be criticized by the readers and, implicitly, by the editors. The editors refrained from arguing against gradualism as a solution to segregation in an explicit way (and, thus, retained the benefits of Faulkner's celebrity and the controversy to follow) but they allowed the space for letters to rebuke Faulkner and, in so doing, revealed the outlines of an editorial platform in the wake of the *Brown v. Board of Education* decision. Rooks has argued that the *Ebony* of the 1950s makes "no mention of tension between the races, or of the civil rights movement at all,"[88] as the magazine was more invested in presenting positive depictions of Black lives, as seen in its celebrity features and articles like "How to Handle Beautiful Women."[89] Rooks claims that "race, and by extension racism, was an issue in the magazine only so we can be told of the narrowing difference between the races, or shown how African Americans had absorbed U.S. consumer culture sufficiently as non-threatening 'good consumers' and ideal U.S. citizens."[90] However, this is not exactly true: a somewhat unified editorial platform against gradualism emerged from the publication of the readers' responses, even as the magazine maintained an appearance of polyvocality. The seeming openness of the periodical facilitates the rejection of Faulkner's authority and its concomitant prescription of gradualism.

Interestingly, Faulkner had engaged in this strategy of openness and judgment as early as 1929 in his modernist novel *The Sound and the Fury*.[91] Faulkner's much-discussed use of modernist techniques of stream of consciousness and the deployment of different perspectives valorizes the individual perspective but acknowledges it as one out of many and lays a mandate to imagine other viewpoints. At the same time, this project resists a relativism that simply gives equal weight to all perspectives, and Faulkner himself once railed against an idea of truth that depends "solely on where you are standing when you look at it."[92] Throughout the novel, it is clear that there are certain points of view that are privileged over others, not in terms of any notion of objective truth, but in ethical and moral terms. For example, Jason Compson's status as a morally reprehensible figure in *The Sound and the Fury* is clear, but why is it clear? Certainly, his actions, such as cheating his niece out of money, tormenting his sister, and refusing to provide Luster with money to attend the carnival, do not mark him as a paragon of virtue, but the form of the novel also assists in the reader coming to this judgment. The reader only encounters Jason's perspective after having seen him through the eyes of his brothers, Benjy and Quentin, and there is little in those sections to suggest that Jason's conduct is one that the reader ought to approve of. By placing Jason's section after those of his brothers, Faulkner directs the reader's response to his character's actions and thoughts by having already weighed the reader with preconceptions.

In some ways, *Ebony*'s editors seem to have taken a similar approach in guiding readers' responses to Faulkner's essay. This guidance is seen in the fact that one of the letters is not like the others; the publication of one letter that praises Faulkner's essay is significant for what it tells us about *Ebony*'s editorial practices and their construction of the magazine's image. In the lone letter of support, Mrs. Clementine B. Spencer writes that Faulkner "indicates that he has a thorough understanding of what appears to be an enormous problem. Even so, he did not spare the colored reader the important information that self-improvement is the order of the day."[93] The publication of this letter solidifies *Ebony*'s pages as sites of openness and dialogue, but the letter's juxtaposition with the other letters reveals its naïveté. The magazine even implicitly comments on Faulkner's own naïveté via the photographs that accompany his essay. While the beginning of the essay is illustrated with photographs of Faulkner and Autherine Lucy, the concluding page includes a photograph of Booker T. Washington at the top and, below, an elderly Black woman in a rocking chair who fits the familiar image of the "mammy." The photograph of the "mammy" figure is accompanied by the caption, "And above all, with patience," a quotation from Faulkner's essay.[94] The inclusion of this weighted and intensely evocative image harkens back to the mythology of the Old South, which Faulkner trafficked in and radically interrogated throughout his fiction, and, in doing so, it subtly comments on Faulkner's views as being relics of the past.

Faulkner, the modernist giant, is then associated with outmoded representations of African Americans, and these representations look out of place in a magazine that, just an issue later, published an article titled "The Fighting Jacksons," which discusses a Baltimore family working to end segregation, and an article titled "The Till Case People One Year Later," which revisits the 1955 Emmett Till case.[95] While John H. Johnson's periodical was, for the most part, not particularly radical, it attempted to portray a new sense of Black identity, and Mrs. Clementine B. Spencer's and Faulkner's claims for Black identity were implicitly rejected as being outmoded and inconsistent with the realities of life in the 1950s during the waning years of Jim Crow. This rejection manifests itself through the magazine's strategy of openness and judgment, a strategy that is made possible specifically through the periodical form and its characteristic network juxtapositions.

Due to the affordances of Jim Crow networks, Faulkner's comments circulated far and wide. Aside from the writers of the letters to the editor (which included Dos Passos) for *Life* and *Ebony*, notable figures like Ellison and Murray were also discussing them. Elite readers and ordinary readers alike were simply readers engaging with the work of a celebrity author; in their negotiation of Faulkner's racial politics, these readers often made links between his public pronouncements and the personal.

While the letter-writers of *Ebony* provided snippets of autobiographical details, Ellison and Murray discussed Faulkner's comments in private letters in which they addressed only one another with the colloquial language of friendship. Baldwin, however, used a different strategy in his engagement with Faulkner when he turned to a public setting—but one with an elite audience. In publishing his essay "Faulkner and Desegregation" in the *Partisan Review* (1934–2003), Baldwin made the choice to speak not to the readers of large glossy magazines like *Life* and *Ebony*, but to elite intellectual readers. The *Partisan Review* is one of the most important little magazines of the twentieth century, best known for its status as an anti-communist leftist quarterly that focused on cultural and political issues and the arts. As Frances Stonor Saunders puts it, the journal is notable for "creating a counter-language to articulate anti-Stalinism and redefine radicalism in a non-Communist context."[96] Its influence, like that of many little magazines, was greater than its subscription figures in that it was responsible for solidifying a Cold War modernism through its publication of the writings of significant figures, including Faulkner. That fall 1956 issue of the *Partisan Review* includes pieces by Saul Bellow, John Berryman, Irving Howe, Robert Lowell, and Marianne Moore, and reviews of John Ashbery's *Some Trees* (1956) and Vladimir Nabokov's *Lolita* (1955).[97] The magazine, edited by William Phillips and Philip Rahv, was published in New York City and sold for one dollar an issue; the relatively high issue cost—in contrast, a contemporary issue of *Life* cost 20 cents—highlighted its status as a highbrow publication that did not have the luxury (or inclination) of relying on advertisements to stay afloat.

In this essay, Baldwin summarizes Faulkner's use of the South in the desegregation debate: "[Faulkner] concedes the madness and moral wrongness of the South but at the same time he raises it to the level of a mystique which makes it somehow unjust to discuss Southern society in the same terms in which one would discuss any other society."[98] Like the letter-writers, Baldwin begins his criticism with autobiography by referring to his racial identification. He opens by discussing in general terms how "one clings to what one knew, or thought one knew" in the face of change that causes "the breakup of the world as one has always known it"; he states, "It is one of the irreducible facts of life. And remembering this, especially since I am a Negro, affords me almost my only means of understanding what is happening in the minds and hearts of the white Southerners today."[99] Unlike Faulkner, Baldwin highlights the limits of his perspectival imagination; he claims that being Black means he has a limited range of pathways into white Southern viewpoints on desegregation. Instead, he turns to the universal experience of coming to terms with "the breakup of the world" as a way for him to understand Faulkner and others who share his views.

In doing so, he, as Tyler Williams has noted, describes Faulkner's views as significantly not distinctive to the author as they align with a hegemonic ideology that has historically afforded power to white Americans: "The image of Faulkner one gets from Baldwin is neither the ur-modernist sage nor the exceptionally untimely liberal Southerner adorned with world-renowned literary accolades. Baldwin's Faulkner, when denied the protection of individuating laurels and celebrity mystique, is instead rendered basely prototypical, a product and personification of the white tide of hereditary prejudices against which black 'salvation' ineluctably struggles."[100] At the same time, Baldwin's reference to his Blackness—"especially since I am a Negro," his only explicitly personal note in the essay—also serves to emphasize his credentials in the debate and undermine Faulkner's authority to speak for African Americans.

In using the genre of the essay, rather than that of the letter to the editor with its fiction of a reader addressing an editor, Baldwin meets Faulkner on the same level—author to author—in the pages of a highbrow intellectual periodical. This act demonstrates his understanding of the periodical field. The *Partisan Review*, from the 1930s to the 1970s, contained multiple discussions of Faulkner, discussions that ranged from casual references to the author as a representative, like James Joyce, of the literary avant-garde, to more substantive analyses of the author and his work. For example, the summer 1957 issue contained a Steven Marcus review titled "Snopes Revisited" of Faulkner's *The Town*, even as it opened with Baldwin's short story "Sonny's Blues," while the summer 1955 issue included a substantial essay by Ursula Brumm titled "Wilderness and Civilization: A Note on William Faulkner."[101] As a way of drawing attention to the upcoming release of his novel, an excerpt from Faulkner's *Requiem for a Nun*, titled "The Jail (Nor Even Quite Relinquish—)," was published in the September–October 1951 issue of the journal.[102] In that issue of the journal, Faulkner was inscribed as an important author deserving of attention from intellectuals. Baldwin's focus on Faulkner in the pages of this influential journal then also had the effect of highlighting Baldwin's status as a significant author and thinker. In fact, Baldwin had recently published his second novel, *Giovanni's Room*, a point noted by the journal's brief contributor biography that states, "JAMES BALDWIN'S new novel, Giovanni's Room, has just been published by Dial."[103] Baldwin is presented in the pages of the magazine as an equal to Faulkner, while the publication of his essay on Faulkner in the *Partisan Review* drew attention to the novel, particularly from the intellectual and cultural elite, who would have been most receptive to it. In these ways, Baldwin negotiated the workings of authority within periodical networks.

The spring 1968 issue of the *Partisan Review*, which featured a symposium on "Black Power," included a reflection by Calvin Israel titled "The Last Gentleman."[104] This essay, published six years after Faulkner's death, discusses Israel's brief happenstance encounter with Faulkner in New York City in 1956 when he was a college senior. This encounter, which may have occurred during the same trip when Faulkner bumped into the *Ebony* editor walking with Billie Holiday, adds to the Faulkner myth with descriptions of his pipe smoking and his extreme reticence. Israel recounts how he told Faulkner that he disagreed with his advice to "go slow." In this essay, Faulkner is described as being agitated by the reference to the controversy and by Israel's claim that violence "is worth all the chance" in the case of ending segregation.[105] Israel writes, "'You don't understand, son,' he said again. 'You can't understand that kind of violence.' He offered me his hand and I shook it."[106] Israel's account of Faulkner's response certainly matches the assertion of Southern exceptionalism that Faulkner provided in his essays. While the title of the essay—"The Last Gentleman"—shores up the Faulkner myth, the essay's placement in an issue on Black Power emphasizes Faulkner's distance from the contemporary moment of the 1960s. The *Partisan Review*'s publication of this essay puts Faulkner's racial philosophy squarely in the past, acting as a nail in the coffin that Baldwin's essay began to build.

Examining Faulkner's *Life* and *Ebony* essays highlights the expansiveness of the periodical network, especially when it comes to the case of a celebrity author. The network in which these essays are embedded is sprawling and is made up of pathways between periodicals, including the *Partisan Review,* and between author, readers (both elite and ordinary), and editors. While this chapter has had as its focus the networks between author, editor, and readers, it has also revealed the wider network in which author, editor, and readers exist by examining the dialogues between multiple periodicals (beyond *Ebony* and *Life*) and between readers, such as Ellison and Murray, outside of the letters page.

The concept of the "network" can provoke unease with its impreciseness and with its voraciousness of connection and inclusion, and can propel critics to define it and make it more containable (and thus, perhaps, more meaningful). Part of this critical unease comes from the concept's present-day associations with the language of computation. This borrowing of computational language seems to be part of a push to make the humanities more precise and more quantifiable—more "useful"—but, at the same time, the concept's portability and flexibility—its capacity to be used in different situations and contexts, from studies of friendship to terrorism to the natural world to the internet—seem to make it devoid of rigor and meaning. Throughout this chapter (and this book overall), I insist on the usefulness of conceptual impreciseness when it comes to networks that engage with Jim Crow segregation. Ellison opens his essay "Twentieth-Century Fiction and the Black Mask of Humanity" with the declaration that "perhaps the most insidious and least understood form of segregation is that of the word."[107] Examining the sprawling networks in which Faulkner's racial politics existed reveals Faulkner's attempts to counter this segregation by speaking to diverse audiences and, at the same time, exposes criticisms of these attempts as manifestations of this segregation of the word, which was itself essential to de jure and de facto Jim Crow practices of segregation. Focusing on Faulkner's essays means—to mix metaphors—going down rabbit hole after rabbit hole of connections, expanding our picture of their places in networks that were being used both to sustain and to interrogate Jim Crow systems of inequality in the wake of *Brown v. Board of Education*.

CHAPTER FOUR
Global Networks
Cane *in the Magazines*

In the long-awaited second edition of the Norton critical edition of *Cane,* an edition that received a flurry of media attention when it was published, a key opening page from the original 1923 edition of Jean Toomer's masterpiece is missing, as it usually is in subsequent editions.[1] This page, written by Toomer, simply states: "Certain of these pieces have appeared in *Broom, Crisis, Double Dealer, Liberator, Little Review, Modern Review, Prairie,* and *S 4 N*. To these magazines: thanks."[2] While this acknowledgement of magazines is not particularly extraordinary, it does demonstrate Toomer's debts to the periodicals. At the same time, it represents Toomer's explicit attempt to shape his reputation by directing the reader's experience of the book by revealing the periodical family tree that produced *Cane.* Contemporary readers most likely came to Toomer's book through advertisements placed in magazines, his writings published in those periodicals, and magazine reviews of *Cane.* While critics generally give a nod to the fact that sections of *Cane* had pre-book lives in the periodicals, they often do not substantively examine the meanings of *Cane*'s (and Toomer's) entanglements with the press.[3] *Cane*'s existence as a book owes much to the magazines, and my goal is to trace some of those debts and read *Cane* through the magazines, rather than simply reading those periodicals or reading the text as separate from its pre-book existence in the magazines. Reading through the magazines provides a deeper picture of the periodical networks in which the book was enmeshed and reveals the way examining these networks brings to light the aesthetic and political negotiations involved in publication and the regional, national, and, ultimately, global scope of Toomer's ambitions and concerns in writing and publishing *Cane.*

Thus far, *Jim Crow Networks* has examined networks in the geographical context of the United States; however, periodical networks create and often demand global connections due to authorial interests, the broader readerships that modern technologies allow, publishing exigencies, and the office locations of publishers. In the previous chapters, this focus on the national, rather than the global, obscures the hidden world within the works—for example, Ida B. Wells's British lecture tours, James Weldon Johnson's turns as consul in Venezuela and Nicaragua, Helga Crane's Denmark in *Quicksand*, the *Chicago Defender*'s global coverage, the *Crisis* as an international "record of the darker races," and Faulkner's travels to Japan. In this chapter, I see *Cane* through the magazines in order to re-imagine it as a text embedded in expansive temporal and geographical networks. This chapter makes the case that the study of periodical networks reveals the global.[4] It calls us to see U.S. literature as world literature and, at the same time, the world in U.S. literature.

Over the course of the book's argument, I have demonstrated the different strategies harnessed in resisting the hierarchies of the Jim Crow era. Central to these strategies is the network's resistance to hierarchy. Jerome McGann's notion of radial reading speaks to the periodical affordance of a less rigid adherence to the dictatorship of linearity in reading magazines and newspapers. The book's titular cane, along with the line drawings of arcs that introduce each section and the cyclical structure of the book, emphasizes Toomer's rejection of hierarchies and demand for radiality; at the same time, his pre-book publication history expands the radius of our reading. In the epigraph for the book, which was omitted from the second Norton critical edition, Toomer opens with, "Oracular. / Redolent of fermenting syrup. / Purple of the dusk, / Deep-rooted cane."[5] The notion of cane's rootedness plays a role throughout the text, but this rootedness is radial in its reach; in "Box Seat," for example, Dan sees "a portly Negress whose huge rolls of flesh meet about the bones of seat-arms. A soil-soaked fragrance comes from her. Through the cement floor her strong roots sink down. They spread under the asphalt streets. Dreaming, the streets roll over on their bellies, and suck their glossy health from them. Her strong roots sink down and spread under the river and disappear in blood-lines that waver south."[6] *Cane* and cane stretch throughout the urban North with its "asphalt streets" and then extend into "blood-lines" that course through the rural South. This spatial language is key to *Cane,* but, at the same time, the epigraph also reveals the temporality of *Cane* and cane. While "deep-rooted" evokes rootedness in space, it also emphasizes the fact that growing things become deeply rooted over time. "Oracular" and "fermenting" (as a method of preservation) also evoke temporality that extends forward and backwards. Taken together, these words underscore the cyclical nature of the natural world and thus the text. The text's figuring of cane as characterized by a spatiotemporal quality elaborates on the nonhierarchical nature of the workings of the network.

This chapter exposes the global networks at work, networks that connect nation, region, and world by focusing on Jean Toomer and the publication history of *Cane.* At the same time, these global networks are themselves temporal ones—chronotopic networks, to use Bakhtin's terminology—as Toomer's use of cane demonstrates. Thinking globally exposes the temporal scales of networks. Levine has argued that "humanists interested in networks have almost always privileged space over time."[7] I take seriously Levine's call to pay attention to time in relation to networks; in fact, the affordance of juxtapositions within the periodical allows us to read more fully the global and temporal contexts in which the book is embedded. Understanding the periodical history of *Cane* highlights not just the global networks of which the book is a part but the very temporality of those networks. Periodicity, the feature that gives periodicals their name, is grounded in temporality. In examining the features that other scholars have seen as constitutive to magazines, Robert Scholes and Clifford Wulfman pinpoint "periodicity—the interval between issues" as key: "Every publication issued periodically is a periodical."[8] Similarly, James Wald states, "The essence of the periodical is periodicity."[9] As Scholes and Wulfman note, these intervals can range from daily (as in the case of many newspapers) to irregular (as is the case for some little magazines). While Bakhtin applies the concept of the chronotope—"the intrinsic connectedness of temporal and spatial relationships that are artistically expressed in literature"—to the genre of the novel, the chronotope is a particularly rich concept for periodicals.[10]

A magazine as a periodical is defined, in part, by its temporality, as seen in the way readers identify issues by their dates of publication. At the same time, periodicals circulate, moving spatially in their distribution networks. Ultimately, periodicals traverse chronotopic networks.

In his pre-book publications, Toomer worked to highlight these global and temporal networks, which are indeed present as themes in the book itself through the choices he made in publication venues (see figure 4 for the timeline of *Cane*'s appearances in the magazines). The publication history, then, can reveal something of the ambitions of the author for his book by providing a sense of how he perceived his intended and ideal readership, along with the cultural categories into which he thought the book would fit. Situating *Cane* in its periodical networks reveals it to be a heterogeneous literary work that lies at the intersection of different aesthetic, political, and social projects and, consequently, the intersections of different reading audiences and networks.

This reading of *Cane* through the magazines springs from two challenges that I see in Toomer criticism. The first has already been mentioned: the importance of magazines to Toomer's writings has been understudied, even though the Jean Toomer Papers at the Beinecke Rare Book and Manuscript Library are rife with letters to and from magazine editors, letters about magazines, and even several issues of magazines that published Toomer's writings and some that did not. The second challenge is more evident—and one with which all Toomer scholars must engage—and that is the question of *Cane*'s formal and generic experimentation. Critics have certainly puzzled over the book's hybrid form due to its highly experimental mélange of line drawings, songs, poetry, prose, and dramatic elements, many of which depict African American experiences in the South and the North. These two challenges are not generally thought of in relation to one another, but I want to suggest that in thinking about *Cane*'s form, we must also consider its pre-book publication history in its magazine networks.

Cary Nelson has gestured toward *Cane*'s resemblance to a periodical (or, rather, to the way periodicals can resemble *Cane*), but it seems clear that to read *Cane* as a magazine is to ignore salient details about the nature of magazines and of *Cane* itself, such as the fact that it was written

April 1922	"Song of the Son"	*Crisis*
Autumn 1922	"Fern"	*Little Review*
September 1922	"Carma" and "Georgia Dusk"	*Liberator*
	"Storm Ending" and "Nora" (titled "Calling Jesus" in *Cane*)	*Double Dealer*
October 1922	"Becky"	*Liberator*
December 1922	"Seventh Street"	*Broom*
December 1922	"Harvest Song"	*Double Dealer*
January 1923	"Esther" and "Georgia Portraits" ("Face," "Portrait in Georgia," and "Conversion")	*Modern Review*
January 1923	"Karintha"	*Broom*
March-April 1923	"Blood-Burning Moon"	*Prairie*
May-August 1923	"Her Lips Are Copper Wire"	*S4N* (which was, in an earlier incarnation, the *Modern Review*)
Summer 1923	"November Cotton Flower"	*Nomad*
August 1923 and September 1923	"Kabnis" (in two parts)	*Broom*

FIGURE 4. Timeline of *Cane* in the magazines. Created by the author.

September 1923 *Cane* published by Boni & Liveright

The magazine versions of the poetry and fiction differ in some minor and some substantive ways from the versions published in *Cane*. Some of these differences seem interesting, others less so. However, for the most part, these differences are not within the scope of this chapter.

"Reapers," "Cotton Song," "Nullo," "Evening Song," "Rhobert," "Avey," "Beehive," "Theater," "Box Seat," "Prayer," and "Bona and Paul" were not published in the magazines.

by a single author and not by a team of contributors.[11] At the same time, *Cane* is embedded in and shaped by magazine culture by virtue of its pre-book history and its fragmented and collage-like form, what Rachel Farebrother has called its "collage aesthetics."[12] Ultimately, reading *Cane* through the lens of periodical studies reanimates our understanding of the text and its readerly networks—and of the periodicals themselves. This chapter then takes seriously Sean Latham and Robert Scholes's observation that periodicals "create and occupy typically complex and often unstable positions in sometimes collaborative and sometimes competitive cultural networks. Uncovering these sorts of connections . . . adds new layers of density both to the magazines themselves and to the work of individual contributors."[13]

While not always focusing on periodical networks, critics such as Wesley Beal, Jennifer J. Sorensen, and John K. Young have recently begun to trace out *Cane*'s status within networks and as a network itself. Beal, for example, has discussed the book as "a network of forms"; for him, the cane is the "most important networking device in the content of the text."[14] Sorensen has examined the book's network of linguistic and bibliographic codes in relation to Toomer's publishing and marketing networks.[15] In focusing on Toomer's pieces in the *Double Dealer,* Young has sketched a picture of "those stories and magazine issues as objects in their own right, moving through particular networks in the early 1920s and becoming visible again retrospectively through this book's longer history."[16] Young's focus is narrower than that of this chapter as he focuses mainly on the *Double Dealer,* but his work, along with that of Beal and Sorensen, extends critical conversations about the complexities of form, content, and context in and around *Cane.* In looking at the pathways between *Cane* in the magazines and *Cane* as a book, I add to the critical conversations about the work's form and its audiences, but my overall goal is to highlight the possibilities of periodical studies in illuminating the temporal and global networks that magazines and individual works of literature construct and engage with.

According to Charles Scruggs and Lee VanDemarr, "Jean Toomer wrote *Cane* over a period of two years, from its beginnings in Georgia in the fall of 1921 until it was published by Boni & Liveright in the fall of 1923. The task of making a book out of Toomer's various poems, sketches, and stories was largely accomplished between March and December 1922."[17] They note that Toomer "first brought up his idea for a book" in a July 19 letter to his friend and fellow writer Waldo Frank in 1922. While *Cane*'s various parts were published in many magazines (and, according to Toomer's letters, rejected from many others) before its publication as a book in September 1923 by Boni & Liveright, I will focus briefly on *Cane*'s positions in the periodical networks of the *Double Dealer* (1921–26), with its emphasis on the American South; the *Little Review* (1914–29) and *Broom* (1921–24), with their international affiliations; and the *Crisis* (1910–present, largely online), which was, of course, the official organ of the NAACP. Despite the differences in their audiences and concerns, these magazines were united by their oppositionality to the mainstream, however it may be defined, and Toomer's decision to publish in these magazines provides insight into his places in cosmopolitan modernism, American regional modernism, and the Harlem Renaissance. Critics have tended to read *Cane* as a farewell to a rural Southern way of life, and, in doing so, they cast *Cane*'s concerns as regional and national.[18] However, such a reading of the text bypasses the complex world network of which Toomer's text is a part and which it, in fact, comments on.

"NEW PEOPLES, CUSTOMS PREVAIL"

The two magazines Toomer published in the most frequently in the months leading up to the publication of his book were the little magazines the *Double Dealer* and *Broom*. *Broom*, along with the more influential and better-known *Little Review*, explicitly saw itself as part of a loose network of little magazines that placed themselves in opposition to popular tastes and mass market magazines, while the *Double Dealer* positioned itself in opposition to the national emphasis on Northern writers, artists, subjects, and magazines. What does it mean that parts of Toomer's *Cane* were published in both international magazines and a magazine focused on regional issues?

Toomer's pre-book publications were imbricated in a network of little magazines. While James Weldon Johnson, as discussed in chapter one, serialized *The Autobiography of an Ex-Colored Man* in a middlebrow magazine aimed at African Americans as part of his activist outreach to a wide audience, Toomer pinpointed little magazines as venues for his work. His work was explicitly meant for highbrow intellectual publications, but, as I demonstrate, his audience was meant to be broad not in terms of brows but in terms of race and geographical reach. Despite recent scholarship on middlebrow and popular periodicals, elite little magazines have been an object of comparatively greater critical interest among scholars of modernism. Though modernist writers like Faulkner published in middlebrow and pulp magazines, they are most often tied to the networks of little magazines. As Eric Bulson has stated bluntly, "No little magazines, no modernism: it's as simple as that."[19] Frederick J. Hoffman, Charles Allen, and Carolyn F. Ulrich note that these magazines were parts of counterpublics: "Little magazines usually come into being for the purpose of attacking conventional modes of expression and of bringing into the open new and unorthodox literary theories and practices."[20] Little magazines are defined in opposition to the mainstream, however the category of the "mainstream" may be regarded. In their foundational study, Hoffman, Allen, and Ulrich define the little magazine as "a magazine designed to print artistic work which for reasons of commercial expediency is not acceptable to the money-minded periodicals or presses."[21] Practically speaking, what this meant was that these little magazines had small circulation figures. The *Double Dealer* at its peak had a circulation of 1,500, while the *Little Review* had approximately 700–1,500, and *Broom* had 4,000 in 1923.[22] The *Crisis* had the largest peak circulation figure out of these magazines, with 100,000 in 1919.[23] Its relatively substantial circulation figures and affiliation with the NAACP suggest that it cannot be categorized as a little magazine, but its oppositionality to the mainstream Jim Crow system gives it a kinship with the oppositionality that defines little magazines.

Published in New Orleans, the *Double Dealer* was a little magazine that had a Southern—although not exclusively so—focus, and it would eventually publish William Faulkner's fiction and essays plus works by writers who would later be connected to the Fugitive poetry and Agrarian movements. The founding of the monthly magazine by Julius

Weis Friend, Albert Goldstein, John McClure, and Basil Thompson was a clear response to H. L. Mencken's famously biting condemnation of Southern culture and art in his 1917 essay "The Sahara of the Bozart." The April 1921 opening editorial stated that the *Double Dealer* is "a movement, a protest, a rising up against the intellectual tyranny of New York, New England, and the Middle West."[24] Although the magazine clearly positioned itself against the more cosmopolitan art centers of the nation, it also took an oppositional stance to a certain Southern aesthetic tradition associated with the past: "The old traditions are no more. New peoples, customs prevail. The Confederacy has long since been dissolved. A storied realm of dreams, lassitude, pleasure, chivalry and the Nigger no longer exists. We have our Main Streets here, as elsewhere."[25] In referring to Sinclair Lewis's *Main Street* (1920), the magazine links the South to the nation and the new art, although it does not completely push aside claims of Southern exceptionalism. This unsigned editorial also explicitly rejects the tradition of the "nigger story" à la Joel Chandler Harris's "Uncle Remus" tales, and suggests that the arts must change in order to more truly represent the contemporary South, "the physical, mental and spiritual outlook of an emerging people—the soul-awakening of a hardy, torpid race, just becoming reaware of itself."[26]

Toomer published the short prose piece "Nora" (which would be titled "Calling Jesus" in *Cane*) and the even shorter poem "Storm Ending" in the September 1922 issue of the *Double Dealer* and "Harvest Song" in the December 1922 issue. Initially, Toomer had submitted his manuscript with the title "Calling Jesus" to the *Double Dealer* but an editor, John McClure, asked him to change the title before publication. In an August 14, 1922, letter, McClure wrote, "Will you give us an alternative title on 'Calling Jesus'? There is an objection to it on the staff here—though why, I can't quite see—and we should like very much to print the sketch."[27] This rather unsatisfying account of the story behind the switch in the title hints at the influence of the editor and at Toomer's pragmatic willingness to bow to external demands in order to publish his work. (It seems that Toomer preferred his first title, as he reverted to it in *Cane*.)

Toomer emphasized the Southern inflection of his art and concerns, something that would become even clearer with the first and third sections of *Cane*, which sprang out of Toomer's trip to Sparta, Georgia. He also aligned himself with the magazine's call for a Southern art that represents the "spiritual outlook of an emerging people," even as he famously called *Cane* a "swan-song."[28] McClure's *Double Dealer* review highlights *Cane*'s Southern emphasis by stating, "This volume reflects the Negro's South. Jean Toomer derives from the South and the South is in his work. The feel of southern air and southern twilight and southern pine is in this book more than in the work of any all-Caucasian writer that I know of. But 'Cane' reflects the black man's life and not the white man's life in the South."[29] Notably, this review also stresses Toomer's racial background and places the text in the overlapping but not equivalent categories of Black literature and of Southern literature. The initial publication of "Nora," "Storm Ending," and "Harvest Song" in a little magazine with a regional emphasis highlights the importance of region to Toomer's art.

This highlighting of region is not a provincial or narrow response, and it does not preclude cosmopolitanism, which, as Tom Lutz has argued, is grounded in local commitments. According to Lutz, regionalist writers in the late nineteenth and early twentieth centuries were driven by a concern with "the relation of different groups to ongoing technological, economic, and social change, or, in other words, the relation of the region to the rest of the world."[30] In fact, the magazine itself refuted an equation of regionalism to provincialism in the July 1921 issue; announcing its new self with its opening editorial "A National Magazine from the South," stating that it would "provide a national medium for Southern writers and readers" but it would still include what it called the "imported stuff."[31] The magazine then is both national and Southern, making the argument that these two categories do not have to be exclusionary. After all, while "Nora" describes "the bare feet of Christ moving across bales of Southern cotton," the Imagist-influenced "Storm Ending" does not explicitly refer to a Southern setting.[32]

The *Double Dealer* issue in which Toomer published those two pieces opens with a short prose piece by Thornton Wilder on Rome, Pierre

Loving's essay titled "Towards Walt Whitman," and an Arthur Symons piece on the modern poster movement. The books reviewed by the magazine have a similarly non-regional focus, covering books on German hedonism, Anatole France, the correspondence of Nietzsche and Wagner, poetry inspired by the American West, Edith Wharton's *The Glimpses of the Moon,* and others that cannot be labeled Southern. Significantly, as Craig Monk notes, "the magazine was known throughout North America and amongst English speakers in Europe, though it never did make a name by commenting on the political and social goings-on in New Orleans."[33] Through its juxtapositions, the magazine argues that regionalism must be included within global networks, that the region is part of the cosmopolitan modern age, and that Toomer's "Nora" can coexist with Anatole France.

The essay on Whitman discusses the influence of the poet on the "experimental moderns" like Eliot, Lawrence, and Pound, and, considering Whitman's importance to Toomer, it is not a reach to categorize Toomer with these "experimental moderns."[34] As John N. Duvall has acknowledged, "Any attempt to link regionalism to American modernism may seem, at first blush, a perverse enterprise. After all, definitions of modernism tend to cast it as nearly the antithesis of regionalism."[35] Toomer's regionalism, in other words, does not negate his embeddedness in modern national and global networks; the periodical context unearths Toomer's place in these networks. *Cane*'s formal experimentation is one of the reasons that today's critics see it as a modernist work, but the fact that Toomer situates and is situated within these networks also demonstrates that he was considered a part of the loose modernist networks of the time. Toomer was befriended and supported by important figures like Sherwood Anderson, Waldo Frank, Georgia O'Keeffe, and Alfred Stieglitz, among others. His involvement with the mystic Gurdjieff and his circle also testifies to his inclusion in modernist networks, as Gurdjieff's other famous disciples included Katherine Mansfield and A. R. Orage. *Cane,* however, was never as successful as Toomer's supporters thought it would be, and, eventually, Toomer faded away from these modernist circles. But at the time of the publication of *Cane,* he was a Harlem Renaissance figure who was recognized and institutionalized as a modernist writer by elite editors and other modernist artists.

Links to global networks notwithstanding, there were certain constraints to be considered when it came to the magazine's Southern audience. In a July 5, 1922, letter to Toomer about his stories "Fern" and "Karintha," McClure wrote, "We should have been glad to print them, but we were frankly afraid. The bigotry and the prejudice of the South do not permeate our subscription list to a great extent, but undoubtedly do to a certain extent. Also there are the guarantors on whom we depend for support. There would have been hostility which, in all probability, would have sent The Double Dealer on the rocks. We felt that the existence of the magazine was more important than any single manuscript."[36] What made "Karintha" (and "Fern") particularly unsuitable for a magazine that billed itself as a "National Magazine from the South" is not entirely clear, but one could speculate that the depiction of Black female sexuality was a source of potential controversy. This letter exposes the editor's role in making publication decisions and that those decisions were not necessarily grounded in aesthetic values alone but also in market pressures. Not only does this letter reveal the distinctive practical constraints that the *Double Dealer* had to face, but it also showcases Toomer's need for multiple venues for his work. His work's variety in content and form demanded a corresponding variety of sites for publication.

ZOOMING THROUGH DEEP TIME

International little magazines offered Toomer publication sites free from the constraints of an American Southern-based magazine. *Broom* and the *Little Review* were responsible for publishing the writers (and visual artists) who are now thought of as high modernists and, essentially, for helping to construct the movement we know now as modernism. When Scholes and Wulfman claim that "modernism began in the magazines," they are referring to *Broom* and the *Little Review*, among others.[37] The *Little Review* is, of course, the better known and more influential of the two, and it was famous (or infamous) for its serialization of Joyce's *Ulysses*. As Alan Golding puts it, "*The Little Review* has always been particularly associated with the promotion of experimental modernism, with its epigraph 'Making No Compromise with the Public Taste' often taken as a synecdoche for the magazine's relationship to a wider audience."[38] It was published in the United States (Chicago, San Francisco, and New York) and later in Paris, and its contributors (as well as its readers) were international in origin and focus. Under the editorship of Margaret Anderson and, later, Jane Heap (often known as jh), the avant-garde magazine also published work by Djuna Barnes, T. S. Eliot, Wyndham Lewis, Ezra Pound (who was the magazine's foreign editor from 1917 to 1919), William Carlos Williams, and other well-known names in modernism. In the *Little Review,* Toomer's "Fern," the short narrative piece that the *Double Dealer* had shied away from publishing, appeared in the autumn 1922 issue, alongside works by Guillaume Apollinaire, Kenneth Burke, Man Ray, and Gertrude Stein; this issue was called the "Stella Number" as it contained fifteen reproductions of Joseph Stella's Futurist paintings, including *New York*, *Brooklyn Bridge*, and *Mardi Gras* (see figure 5).[39]

Initially, these images seem a strange fit for "Fern," which details the narrator's feelings for the eponymous woman who, it is suggested, is Jewish and biracial. This Georgia story does not seem to fit with Stella's focus on an industrialized urban future. Yet this dynamic between the spiritual past of the rural South and the future-oriented temporality of the urban North is one that Toomer himself shows interest in throughout *Cane,* as seen in the implicit links between the quick tempo of Washington, DC, with its "zooming Cadillacs, / Whizzing, whizzing down the street-car tracks" and the "soft listless cadence of Georgia's South."[40] Golding has described the *Little Review* "as internally dialogic, enacting an ongoing and often heated conversation about modernism within its own pages."[41] In this case, the inclusion of the Futurist paintings in the magazine contextualize Toomer's "Fern" within other places and times; it asks us to look at *Cane* in terms of not only an expanded geography but also in terms of "deep time," Wai Chee Dimock's term for an approach to the "continuum of historical life" that takes a long temporal view by rejecting the isolation of historical moments from one another.[42]

This dynamic of deep time between modernity and the past is extended in *Broom.* While "Karintha" was rejected by McClure's *Double*

FIGURE 5. Cover of *Little Review* 9, no. 3 (Autumn 1922). Courtesy of the *Modernist Journals Project* (searchable database), Brown and Tulsa Universities, http://modjourn.org.

Dealer due to its unsuitability for the Southern audience, this prose piece, which would go on to open *Cane* (and it also had another life in Toomer's posthumously published play, *Natalie Mann*), was ultimately published in *Broom*.[43] That "Karintha" found a home in *Broom*, even as it was rejected by the *Double Dealer*, suggests the capaciousness of Toomer's project, a capaciousness that does not simply include region and nation but also the globe. In December 1922, Toomer's brief sketch "Seventh Street" marked his introduction to *Broom*'s readers. He then published "Karintha" in the January 1923 issue; "Kabnis" in two parts during August and September 1923 just before the publication of *Cane*; and a review of D. H. Lawrence's *The Captain's Doll* in the same issue that contained the first part of "Kabnis."

"Karintha" made its *Broom* appearance in an issue devoted to Mayan art and history, and the story itself is punctuated at the very close with a line drawing of a Mayan figure. While an acknowledgment of contingency is important here, as it is to periodical studies in general, this issue embeds Toomer's story of a Southern Black woman in a deep time that is associated with the so-called primitive and the spiritual. The Mayan imagery compels the reader to see Toomer's text in light of the ancient civilization. Unlike the book version, the magazine version of "Karintha" includes this parenthetical direction before the text: "(To be read, accompanied by the humming of a Negro folk-song.)"[44] Reading this statement in relation to the Mayan imagery found throughout the magazine issue suggests parallels between the Negro folk song and Mayan art. *Cane* highlights geographic and temporal networks that reach out beyond regional and national boundaries and beyond the contemporary moment to the past and the future. In effect, these expansive networks point to Toomer's overall project of pushing beyond limited definitions of racial categories. For Toomer, the folk song as an ancestral form is worthy of being studied, much like the Mayan images; seeing *Cane* in these chronotopic networks allows for the reintegration of the African American past into the world history to which the Mayans also belong. This alternative world history—or, one could say, this more capacious world history—shares resemblances to the world histories recounted by African American writers in an attempt to reclaim Black history. From

Pauline E. Hopkins's revelation of Ethiopia's wonders in *Of One Blood* (1902–3) to Langston Hughes's tracing of the connections between different rivers across space and time in "The Negro Speaks of Rivers" (1921), African American writers worked to present a history of the world that recognized the rich and deep history of African Americans beyond slavery in the United States. These historical reclamation projects demanded the acknowledgment of Black humanity and the beauty of Black people and culture.

Broom was published monthly by American Harold Loeb (and then eventually Matthew Josephson) first in Rome, then Berlin, and, finally, New York City during its short life. In discussing *Broom*'s status as an "exiled" magazine, Bulson writes about the difficulty of categorizing it in terms of nationality: "*Broom* may have ended up in the hands of American readers, but it was made in Europe; and the people who flipped through its pages consistently remarked on the quality of the paper (Fabriano when made in Italy, an unnamed 'exclusive paper' when printed by Labisch and Co. in Berlin), the oversized format, and the page layout (with three-inch margins). It was this materiality and design as much as the physical journey through the international postal system that made *Broom* American and something else: a foreign import that looked like a little magazine from Europe."[45] Toomer's project then is not simply about global connections; in fact, through his choice of periodical networks he becomes part of these global connections. Much of his periodical history was marked by the search for the right home for his experimental texts, which is a polite way of saying that Toomer, like many writers, was rejected by various magazines. Yet, the submission of his work was guided in some measure by the periodical networks of which he was already a part. For example, McClure specifically suggested to Toomer that he submit "Karintha" (and "Fern") to *Broom;* in a July 5, 1922, letter, McClure wrote, "If The Dial does not use them, it seems to me almost certain that Broom would use them, as well as much more of your work."[46] In essence, Toomer relied on one node of his periodical network to suggest another site for publication. The avant-garde nature of *Broom* with its international affiliations proved to be a good fit for

Toomer's writing. *Broom* published images by artists like Picasso and Man Ray; critical essays and reviews; and poetry, drama, and fiction by authors like Hart Crane, William Carlos Williams, and Virginia Woolf. Toomer was published, advertised, and reviewed in its pages, which suggests a strong tie between his work and the aims of the magazine before and directly after the publication of *Cane*.

Like the *Little Review*, *Broom* was aimed at an international and cosmopolitan audience interested in experimental art. The magazine itself as a physical object was designed to be beautiful and eye-catching. Not only did his affiliation with this magazine help construct Toomer's status within the arts, but, in choosing to publish in *Broom*, Toomer worked to portray himself specifically as an American artist with international import. Josephson's October 1923 book review of Toomer's text is titled "Great American Novels," which riffs on the other book Josephson reviewed at the same time as *Cane:* William Carlos Williams's *The Great American Novel*, a highly experimental work that, it must be noted, is not a novel in the conventional sense and, in fact, asks, "What then is a novel?"[47] In placing Toomer alongside Williams and in naming *Cane* a "great American novel" (even though it too is not a novel in any conventional sense of the term), *Broom* positioned Toomer as a modernist American writer, an author who writes about America—an America that includes African Americans.[48] In this same issue, Toomer's mostly negative review of Zona Gale's novel *Faint Perfume* appears under the byline "J. T."[49] Directly before and during the time of the publication of his book, Toomer was deeply entrenched in the periodical culture of the time. Yet it is important to note that Toomer's relationship to this culture was often tied to failure; his papers at the Beinecke Rare Book and Manuscript Library testify to his many rejections from magazines ranging from the *Atlantic Monthly* to the *Dial* to the *Hound and Horn*. After the publication of *Cane* and with his rejection of racial categories, Toomer would retreat from these periodical networks more and more. His post-*Cane* publication history reveals a move away from modernist little magazines and to Quaker newspapers and newsletters toward the end of his life.

CANE IN THE *CRISIS*

Little magazines such as the *Little Review* and *Broom* advertised and referred to one another to varying degrees, and existed within overlapping periodical networks. The *Crisis,* under the editorship of W. E. B. Du Bois from the years of 1910 to 1934, does not fit as easily into these overlapping networks because its aesthetic, political, and social priorities were markedly different from those of the *Double Dealer,* the *Little Review,* and *Broom.* Yet this magazine is where Toomer first began publishing what would eventually become *Cane* (see figure 6).

In the April 1922 issue of the *Crisis,* Toomer published "Song of the Son," a poem that grapples with the legacy of slavery and lynching through son/sun imagery.[50] Interestingly, this issue also discusses the death of P. B. S. Pinchback, who was a former governor of Louisiana, and, more importantly for our purposes, Toomer's grandfather with whom he had a difficult relationship. The five-stanza poem is given its own page and framed by a border of repeated flowers. Generally, poems were not given their own pages in the issues, and they were most often highlighted by empty space or line drawings of open books and swastikas (used, presumably, in its traditional meaning as an auspicious symbol). In a scan of all issues published in 1922, it is clear that not even the poetry of Hughes merited the treatment that "Song of the Son" received that year. The one exception is an anonymous short story titled "The Great Surgeon," which is framed by a border of leaves and takes up the entirety of three pages in the December 1922 issue.[51] The unusual method of presentation in the case of "Song of the Son" highlights the poem as a significant aesthetic object within an issue that deals heavily with lynching.[52] Of course, the *Crisis* and the NAACP were established, in part, to combat the lynching of African Americans during the Jim Crow period, and, at this time, the Dyer Anti-Lynching Bill was a topic of especially heated discussion in the Black press.[53] This particular issue of the *Crisis* is filled with different discussions of the Dyer bill. The opening section of the magazine, titled "Opinion of W. E. B. Du Bois," discusses the bill even as it talks about global affairs, individual African Americans, Missouri schools, Africa, and fundraising; in moving effortlessly from the global to the individual to the national, Du Bois (and the *Crisis* itself)

THE CRISIS

A RECORD OF THE DARKER RACES

PUBLISHED MONTHLY AND COPYRIGHTED BY THE NATIONAL ASSOCIATION FOR THE ADVANCEMENT OF COLORED PEOPLE, AT 70 FIFTH AVENUE, NEW YORK CITY. CONDUCTED BY W. E. BURGHARDT DU BOIS; JESSIE REDMON FAUSET, LITERARY EDITOR; AUGUSTUS GRANVILLE DILL, BUSINESS MANAGER.

Vol. 23—No. 6 APRIL, 1922 Whole No. 138

Page

THE MAY CRISIS

The cover will be Albert Smith's fine painting of René Maran. The special articles will be on the late Bert Williams and on the leaders of Negro fraternities.

FIFTEEN CENTS A COPY; ONE DOLLAR AND A HALF A YEAR

FOREIGN SUBSCRIPTION TWENTY-FIVE CENTS EXTRA

RENEWALS: The date of expiration of each subscription is printed on the wrapper. When the subscription is due, a blue renewal blank is enclosed.

CHANGE OF ADDRESS: The address of a subscriber can be changed as often as desired. In ordering a change of address, both the old and the new address must be given. Two weeks' notice is required.

MANUSCRIPTS and drawings relating to colored people are desired. They must be accompanied by return postage. If found unavailable they will be returned.

Entered as second class matter November 2, 1910, at the post office at New York, New York, under the Act of March 3, 1879.

FIGURE 6. Table of Contents of *Crisis* 23, no. 6 (April 1922). Courtesy of the *Modernist Journals Project* (searchable database), Brown and Tulsa Universities, http://modjourn.org.

demonstrates his understanding of these interrelationships, much as Toomer does in his linkages between the regional, national, and global, and educates his readers in these connections. Lynching is embedded in all of these sites, even though it may be seen as a race-specific and even region-specific problem.

Robert Bagnall's short story "Lex Talionis," published in the same issue, also engages with the horrors of lynching but from a fictional perspective with elements of science fiction.[54] "Lex Talionis," appearing almost a decade before George Schuyler's *Black No More,* is an astonishing tale about a Black man named Flournoy who develops a chemical process to transform whites into Blacks, and he uses this process to attain revenge against his sister's white rapist, Langston. After his transformation into a Black man, Langston attempts to embrace his wife and is lynched for seemingly trying to assault a white woman. This story provides a different perspective on lynching by literalizing the notion that white people must put themselves in the shoes of Black people in order to understand the terrors of racial violence. Fictional clippings transcribed from white newspapers are also embedded within the story; these clippings present Langston's attempted embrace of his wife as an assault by a brutish Black man. In embedding these clippings into the narrative, Bagnall, who was the NAACP's national director of branches, mimics the form of the *Crisis* itself, as several sections of the magazine frequently included newspaper excerpts compiled into what Anne Elizabeth Carroll has called a collage of Black lives in the United States.[55] The story is, in part, about the need to be suspicious of different discourses, particularly those, as represented by the newspaper clippings, that suggest that African Americans deserve to be lynched. The inclusion of the different fictional and nonfictional discourses about lynching throughout the issue then compels the reader to recognize the heterogeneous discourses that surround lynching and, at times, propel lynching.[56]

Toomer's "Song of the Son" with its reference to slaves as "dark-purple ripened plums, / Squeezed, and bursting in the pinewood air," is one of those heterogeneous discourses about lynching, and its placement in the issue gestures to the cultural moment from which *Cane*'s exploration of lynching springs. Not only is the poem placed directly before the NAACP report on the Dyer Bill, but it follows Jessie Fauset's review of Benjamin Brawley's *A Social History of the American Negro;* as part of the historical reclamation project to uncover Black history, the book, Fauset says, "presents American history as it must have appeared to black men."[57] The review of the book, which looks at the history of African Americans from the earliest days to the contemporary present, faces the full-page "Song of the Son." The poem with its repeated reference to the "souls of slavery" offers a retrospective look at Black life; in this way, it extends the work of Brawley's book in a poetic format. The magazine's deep discussions of lynching embed the poem in contemporary discussions, discussions that would later emerge in *Cane*'s overall attempt to grapple with lynching, especially in its citation of Mame Lamkins's baby in "Kabnis."[58]

Mary Turner, the real-life basis for Mame Lamkins, was killed, along with her unborn child, in 1918; Barbara Foley notes that she was the source for "numerous artistic representations," including Anne Spencer's "White Things" published in the *Crisis* in 1923 as a "testament to the horrors of southern violence."[59] Foley observes that Layman's description of Mame Lamkins's death in "Kabnis" parallels Walter White's report in the *Crisis* about Turner's murder.[60] In his report as assistant secretary of the NAACP, White recounts the lynching with vivid language:

> The method by which Mrs. Mary Turner was put to death was so revolting and the details are so horrible that it is with reluctance that the account is given. It might be mentioned that each detail given is not the statement of a single person but each phase is related only after careful investigation and corroboration . . . At the time she was lynched, Mary Turner was in her eighth month of pregnancy. The delicate state of her health, one month or less previous to delivery, may be imagined, but this fact had no effect on the tender feelings of the mob. Her ankles were tied together and she was hung to the tree, head downward. Gasoline and oil from the automobiles were thrown on her clothing and while she writhed in agony and the mob howled in

> glee, a match was applied and her clothes burned from her person. When this had been done and while she was yet alive, a knife, evidently one such as is used in splitting hogs, was taken and the woman's abdomen was cut open, the unborn babe falling from her womb to the ground. The infant, prematurely born, gave two feeble cries and then its head was crushed by a member of the mob with his heel. Hundreds of bullets were then fired into the body of the woman, now mercifully dead, and the work was over.[61]

Toomer likely learned about Turner's death from the Black press, revealing the ways *Cane*'s content itself was influenced by periodical reading. In effect, by turning Turner's death into art, Toomer establishes literature as a tool of self-help, matching Ida B. Wells's suggestion of one function of the Black press. Ultimately, Turner's horrific death became an integral impetus in the activism for the Dyer Anti-Lynching Bill, activism that the *Crisis* itself was committed to. Toomer's depiction of Mame Lamkins's death, in effect, condemns the horrors of lynching, alongside the *Crisis*'s factual and artistic accounts of Mary Turner's murder.

Although Toomer famously disavowed the label of "Negro," the placement of "Song of the Son" in the *Crisis* reveals that Toomer was initially, at least, interested in reaching a Black, politically engaged, and elite readership and in being a part of the network of the Black elite and the Harlem Renaissance.[62] While Toomer's biography and complicated relationship with racial identity are certainly important to understanding his work, they are often too central to analyses of *Cane;* my argument foregrounds his periodical networks to provide a sense of how Toomer positioned himself racially, culturally, politically, and aesthetically. The variety of periodicals with which Toomer associated himself reveals something of the variety of identities with which he affiliated himself.

As early as February 1922, Toomer and Fauset, the literary editor of the *Crisis,* were corresponding with each other about the possibility of publication. In a February 17, 1922, letter, Fauset wrote, "I am particularly impressed with your 'Song of the Son.' The more I read it, the more I like it."[63] Demonstrating his early investment in this network, Toomer chose Du Bois's magazine as the first publication site of a poem that would eventually become a part of *Cane,* and he would also go on to publish the poem "Banking Coal," which did not become part of *Cane,* in the June 1922 issue.[64] The publication of Toomer's "Song of the Son" shows the *Crisis* recognized the confluence of Toomer's poem with the project of the magazine and, vice versa, Toomer's understanding of his poem's affinity with the political and social goals of the *Crisis.*

Cane also resembles the *Crisis,* and magazines in general, in its form and layout. As Scholes and Wulfman have noted, "A magazine was originally a periodical in which a miscellany of texts was collected and presented; the magazine is defined by its capacious and diverse nature."[65] Carroll has noted the *Crisis*'s multimedia activism in its use of multiple genres, including news stories, essays, visual art, and fiction, to approach the "problem of the twentieth century." Further, the diversity of texts found in the magazine reveals "that a true understanding of a subject required information gleaned from multiple sources."[66] This aesthetic and textual density, which does not rely on one source to represent experience, is matched by the multiple genres found within Toomer's *Cane.* It approaches Black experiences from many different perspectives and genres, and, in doing so, it refutes the notion of a monolithic Black experience even as it reaffirms the connections among Black people across the region, nation, and globe. If magazines, as the word's etymology suggests, are storehouses of different kinds of texts, *Cane* is a storehouse of Black experiences and connections in the world.[67]

THE DIXIE PIKE

A review of the magazines in which various parts of *Cane* were published exposes the book's global nature and encourages us to look more carefully for elements of what Dimock has called "scale enlargement," both in terms of the spatial and the temporal.[68] In the end, we have to take seriously Toomer's claim that "the Dixie Pike has grown from a goat path in Africa."[69] This quotation comes from his story "Carma," which depicts "a girl in the yard of a whitewashed shack"; she "is in the forest dancing. Torches flare . . . juju men, greegree, witch-doctors . . . torches go out."[70] In the backwoods of Georgia, Toomer finds connections to

African spirituality (which itself is connected to Eastern spirituality in the character's name).

The title character's story then is particular to the Dixie Pike but is also global in its bridge to that goat path in Africa. The Pike's geographical reach is long, but its textual reach within *Cane* is also extensive. The narrator of "Fern," for example, "walked up the Pike on purpose" to the title character, while a "nigger woman driving a Georgia chariot down an old dust road" traverses the Pike in "Carma."[71] At the same time, the reader is also characterized as a potential traveler on this path. In attempting to capture Fern's appeal, the narrator of "Fern" states: "Anyone, of course, could see her, could see her eyes. If you walked up the Dixie Pike most any time of day, you'd be most like to see her resting listless-like on the railing of her porch, back propped against a post, head tilted a little forward because there was a nail in the porch post just where her head came which for some reason or other she never took the trouble to pull out. Her eyes, if it were sunset, rested idly where the sun, molten and glorious, was pouring down between the fringe of pines."[72] This shift from "anyone" to "you" in the first two sentences acknowledges the reader as a fellow traveler on the Pike. The text expands to map "you" onto that Dixie Pike, that one strand within regional and national networks that are themselves parts of a global network that includes "witch-doctors," Fern, "the nigger woman," the male narrator, "you," and "anyone."

The network for "Carma" began with its publication in the September 1922 issue of the *Liberator* magazine (1918–24), a socialist monthly magazine. Founded by Max Eastman and Crystal Eastman as a successor to the *Masses* (1911–17), the *Liberator* cost 20 cents per issue in 1922 and had a peak circulation figure of 50,000 to 60,000.[73] Claude McKay was closely associated with the periodical. Works from the first section of *Cane, such as* "Carma," "Georgia Dusk," and "Becky," were published in the *Liberator* in the September and October issues of 1922. Toomer's interest in publishing in a magazine with a leftist international focus highlights his imbrication in these global networks and, in particular, these radical ones.[74] Although the magazine's approach changed over time, Max Eastman's opening 1918 editorial emphasized its international concerns via its affiliation with the Russian Revolution of 1917: "Never was the moment more auspicious to issue a great magazine of liberty. With the Russian people in the lead, the world is entering upon the experiment of industrial and real democracy."[75] It continued by listing what the magazine would focus on, from the labor struggle to women's rights to access to birth control. Included within this list was the magazine's aim to "assert the social and political equality of the black and white races, oppose every kind of racial discrimination, and conduct a remorseless publicity campaign against lynch law."[76] The placement of "Georgia Dusk," which explicitly focuses on lynching, in the *Liberator* highlights racial violence as a socialist issue and a global concern; it ties the struggles of African Americans in the U.S. South to the Russian Revolution. The publication of these Southern-focused pieces reveals the place of the South (and Black Southerners, in particular) in these radical international networks.

This insistence that the American South is imbricated in a global network is most obviously amplified by the eight-line poem "Conversion," which was originally published in the *Modern Review* and which is part of the first section of *Cane*.[77] "Conversion" depicts the displacement of the "African Guardian of Souls" for "a white-face sardonic god" associated with the Judeo-Christian tradition. In referring to the West Indies export of rum, the poem reveals the spiritual effects of the triangular trade of human beings and sugar cane between Africa, the West Indies, and the American South.[78] This reflection on the circulation of human beings, goods, and religion across continental borders is itself embedded in a publication history that peripatetically circulates within interlocking global networks of periodicals. Paul Gilroy has discussed "the image of ships in motion across the spaces between Europe, America, Africa, and the Caribbean" as a chronotope: "Ships immediately focus attention on the middle passage, on the various projects for redemptive return to an African homeland, on the circulation of ideas and activists as well as the movement of key cultural and political artefacts: tracts, books, gramophone records, and choirs."[79] Gilroy's chronotope of the ship contains temporal resonances extending from the time of slavery to the twentieth century; it circulates human beings, objects, and ideas across the seas throughout the globe. Toomer's magazine history enacts these circulations even as the content of his work meditates on them.

Although Toomer declined to be classified as a "Negro" writer and refused identification with the Harlem Renaissance—James Weldon Johnson and Nancy Cunard were denied permission to reprint parts of *Cane* in the revised 1931 edition of *The Book of Negro American Poetry* (originally published in 1922) and in the *Negro* anthology (1934), respectively—he is undeniably a central figure in the Harlem Renaissance. Whether or not he saw himself as a Harlem Renaissance author, his contemporaries did. (He claimed that he "viewed the movement as a splendid thing but as something that had no special meaning for [him]."[80]) "Song of the Son" was included in the Harlem number of *Survey Graphic* magazine that launched the New Negro onto the world's stage, and along with it, "Carma," "Fern," and "Georgia Dusk," were later included in Alain Locke's *New Negro* anthology (1925), which sprang from that pivotal issue. Toomer famously stated that he felt he had been "tricked and misused" by Locke and that he had not "want[ed] *Cain* [*sic*] dismembered" by having its parts placed in an anthology.[81]

The chronotope of the Harlem Renaissance is youth-oriented and centered in Harlem, although the rural South haunts many works. Kenneth W. Warren has commented that "despite the attention given to the folk past and the artistic achievements of past greats whose work had gone unacknowledged, African American literature was prospective rather than retrospective."[82] In the dedicatory note to his anthology, Locke wrote, "THIS VOLUME IS DEDICATED TO THE YOUNGER GENERATION."[83] Toomer's stories and poems were placed in the section of the anthology titled "Negro Youth Speaks." Similarly, in his essay "The Negro Artist and the Racial Mountain" Hughes orients the temporality of the New Negro to the future by closing with his famous declaration: "We build our temples for tomorrow, strong as we know how, and we stand on top of the mountain, free within ourselves."[84] However, in his poem "The Negro Speaks of Rivers" (1921), Hughes looks to the past and connects it with the present and future through his speaker's recitation of different rivers that are not simply geographical features but are also temporally located in the history of Black people.[85] The speaker declares, "I've known rivers: / Ancient, dusky rivers." These rivers—the Euphrates that he "bathed in . . . when dawns were young," the Congo, the Nile, and the Mississippi with its "muddy bosom"[86]—are chronotopes with their geographical specificity and temporal situatedness rooted in the past and present. In a similar vein, Locke's dedicatory note to the younger generation is followed in the opening pages of *The New Negro* by a bar of music with the lines "O, rise, shine for Thy Light is a'com-ing," parenthetically identified as a traditional spiritual.[87] This juxtaposition between the spiritual and the dedication to the youth highlights that, despite the rhetoric of newness that is so central to the Harlem Renaissance (and to literary modernism in general), the past haunts. Toomer's tracing of the Dixie Pike to that goat path in Africa makes visible this chronotopic network.

In his poem "Heritage," Cullen figures Africa as a chronotope. Published in 1925, the poem appeared in the pivotal Harlem number of *Survey Graphic,* republished from Cullen's first collection of poetry, *Color,* in a somewhat different form. When it was published in *The New Negro* anthology, it was placed in the section titled "The Negro Digs Up His Past," suggesting a temporal orientation to the past in contrast to the categorization of Toomer's works in relation to youthfulness. The *Survey Graphic* presentation of the poem contextualizes it with black-and-white photographs of African sculptures and masks. Throughout the poem, the speaker asks himself "What is Africa to me?"; his stance toward Africa is ambivalent throughout. The closing lines of the first stanza of the version printed in *Survey Graphic*—which serve as the epigraph to Larsen's *Passing*—ask: "*One three centuries removed / From the scenes his fathers loved, / Spicy grove and banyan tree, / What is Africa to me?*"[88] Cullen's speaker displays an ambivalence in his question that could be read as a refutation that Africa means anything to an African American person in the twentieth century and as an expression of longing for a continent that seems so far ("three centuries removed") and so close ("scenes his fathers loved"). The gorgeousness of description—"spicy grove and banyan tree," along with many other lines in the poem—highlights the appeal of this faraway land even as it makes it seem impossibly foreign to the readers in Harlem and other American urban centers. Africa is positioned not necessarily as an actual place but as a chronotope, with its links to the past and its possible implications for the speaker's present and future ("What is Africa to me?"). The presentation of the poem in *Survey Graphic* with African sculptures and masks evokes the stereotypical primitivism ascribed to Africa along with the modernity associated with it in the modernist visual art of the period, such as that of Picasso, most notably in his 1907 masterpiece *Les demoiselles d'Avignon*.

Cullen's "Heritage" is similar to Toomer's "Conversion" in that it discusses religion with ambivalence: "My conversion came high-priced. / I belong to Jesus Christ, / Preacher of humility: / Heathen gods are naught to me—"[89] After admitting that he sometimes imagines Christ with "dark, despairing features," the speaker ends the poem with the couplet, "Lord, forgive me if my need / Sometimes shapes a human creed."[90] (The original version of the poem that appears in *Color* ends with a different stanza.) Here, the speaker displays ambivalence about this centuries-old conversion to Christianity, suggesting an affinity to those heathen gods (such as Toomer's "African Guardian of Souls" in the first line of "Conversion")—even as he says that they are "naught" to him—due to their racial resemblance and ancestral significance. This look at religion, as in "Conversion," reaches across space and time. Like Gilroy's ship, Cullen's poem circulates temporally and spatially, traversing what Toomer sees as the African goat path that leads to the Dixie Pike.

Toomer's *Cane* has often been characterized in terms of migration due to the trajectory of the text's foci from South to North to South again, and, certainly, the text stands as an artifact of and meditation on the Great Migration, which so transformed the rural and urban landscapes of the United States during the twentieth century. What the link between the book's content and its publication history reveals, however, is that the text's interest in mobility is broader than the movements that take place within national borders, and, in fact, reveals the artificiality of containing the Great Migration to the simple vertical action of the movement from South to North; rather, *Cane* tracks movements from South to North and back to South again, and exposes the global movements that haunt the national ones, forming networks between unlikely or forgotten aesthetic, historic, and geographic sites.

Cane's links reach inward as well, as the African goat path winds its way throughout the text. The sun in "Carma" is described as "hammered to a band of gold" and "pine-needles, like mazda, are brilliantly aglow."[91] These images bind this early story with the final section of *Cane* and its final lines: "Outside, the sun arises from its cradle in the tree-tops of the forest. Shadows of pines are dreams the sun shakes from its eyes. The sun arises. Gold-glowing child, it steps into the sky and sends a birth-song slanting down gray dust streets and sleepy windows of the southern town."[92] The rising sun calls attention to temporality through the reference to the periodicity of the sun's rising; while Toomer called the book a "swan-song . . . a song of an end," the child-sun with its "birth-song" suggests the cyclical nature of time and the potential for swan songs to lead to birth songs.[93] "Karintha," the short story that opens *Cane,* begins with a description of Karintha's skin as being "like dusk on the eastern horizon / . . . When the sun goes down."[94] The final line of the book begins the cycle anew with the sun rising up. The "gold-glowing child" encapsulates and reanimates all the infants found within the pages of Toomer's work, beginning with Karintha's baby who "fell out of her womb onto a bed of pine-needles in the forest" to Esther's dreamed-up "black singed, woolly, tobacco-juice baby—ugly as sin" to the moon figured as a "white child that sleeps upon the top of pines" to Mame Lamkins's baby ripped out of her womb to Kabnis himself, whom Stella wishes to "nurse and mother."[95]

This child-sun, of course, reminds us of the son and sun in the poem "Song of the Son," and it implicitly connects the *Crisis* (where the poem was originally published) to *Broom* (where "Kabnis" was originally published). Scruggs and VanDemarr rightly point out that reading the ending of *Cane* in hopeful terms is problematic, as "everything leading up to the 'gold-glowing child' of the final sentence contradicts such optimism": "Although the ending of *Cane* sees the cellar as a womb, birth as a symbol of the future is heavily qualified by the defamation and death of so many black children" throughout the text.[96] Reading the book through the magazines also reveals the futility of pure optimism, since the original readers of "Song of the Son" would have confronted it in the context of the *Crisis*'s accounts of lynching. However, alongside these accounts, readers would have also encountered the *Crisis*'s and the NAACP's activism against racial violence and the written and visual portraits of successful African Americans, a strategic combination that Carroll has called "the juxtaposition of protest and affirmation."[97] Reading the book in its networks shows how Mame Lamkins's baby becomes part of world concerns with the book's imbrication in a global periodical network that includes *Broom* and the *Little Review*. Lynching and racial violence are not uniquely regional or even national problems but they are global ones.

That the child in the final sentence of *Cane* is "gold-glowing" also suggests a biracial or multiracial child whose race is indeterminate, a product of miscegenation or, perhaps, more appropriately, amalgamation. In an essay titled "The Americans," which was not published during his lifetime, Toomer wrote that America is "the place where mankind, long dismembered into separate usually repellant groupings, long scattered over the face of the earth, is being re-assembled into one whole and undivided human race."[98] Similarly, *Cane,* with its amalgamation of different genres, works to reassemble different groups into a whole network. These connections, which are made possible through Toomer's formal experimentation, reveal the universality of the local and the region's relevancy to nation and world while still insisting on the distinctiveness of the particular in this capacious text. The Dixie Pike winds its way through the text and throughout the periodical networks; it is a textual, temporal, and global network. Paying attention to overlooked periodical networks then reminds us that the goat path in Africa extends far beyond the Dixie Pike, even as Toomer's *Cane* returns again and again to that Southern road.

CONCLUSION

Media Networks and Activism

In 2018, almost a century after the defeat in the U.S. Senate of the Dyer Anti-Lynching Bill—a bill that was championed in the pages of the *Crisis*—the National Memorial for Peace and Justice, an anti-lynching memorial, opened to the public in Montgomery, Alabama.[1] This memorial provides something of a long-awaited counter to the "Mammy Monument" proposed in the Senate in the same year that the Dyer bill was defeated. This proposal, a brainchild of the Richmond, Virginia, chapter of the United Daughters of the Confederacy, worked to build a statue to the memory of faithful Southern "mammies" on the National Mall in Washington, DC.[2] The monument, which, predictably, provoked strong reactions in the Black press, was considered a slap in the face to the supporters of the Dyer bill. Along with the nearby Legacy Museum, the Montgomery National Memorial for Peace and Justice testifies to the brutal history of racial violence in the United States. In response to the opening of the memorial and museum, the *Montgomery Advertiser* published a news article titled "'There Will Be Lynchings': How the *Advertiser* Failed Victims of Racial Terror," and an editorial titled "Our Shame: The Sins of Our Past Laid Bare for All to See," admitting to its own historical complicity in lynchings.[3]

In 2019, the Justice for Victims of Lynching Act, introduced by Senators Kamala Harris, Cory Booker, and Tim Scott, passed the Senate, while its companion bill, the Emmett Till Antilynching Act, sponsored by Representative Bobby Rush of Illinois, was passed by the U.S. House of Representatives in 2020. These bills aim to finish the work of the Dyer bill (and the more than two hundred other anti-lynching bills that were struck down before they could become laws) to make lynching a federal crime. In speaking about his sponsorship of the bill, Rush invoked the famous *Jet* magazine photographs of the battered body of Emmett Till, the fourteen-year-old lynching victim in Mississippi in 1955, as foundational to his support of the bill.[4] *Jet*, a sister publication to *Ebony* magazine, is part of the media networks of activism opposing Jim Crow. Those searing 1955 magazine photographs extend their reach to the twenty-first century and demonstrate the persistence of Jim Crow media networks.

Throughout *Jim Crow Networks*, I have traced the ways lynching and racial violence in general were driving forces in animating and forging networks. Jacqueline Goldsby notes, "During the period 1882–1930 (the years, scholars agree, when the most reliable lynching statistics were kept), 3,220 African American men, women, and children were murdered by lynch mobs."[5] While the Jim Crow networks that I have examined had periodicals and literature as key nodes, they were energized by social, political, cultural, and aesthetic oppositions to racial violence. In speaking about Jim Crow literary production, Kenneth Warren has made the controversial and influential argument that "African American literature itself constitutes a representational and rhetorical strategy within the domain of a literary practice response to conditions that, by and large, no longer obtain."[6] He observes that "throughout the Jim Crow era, African American writers have sought to build support for a racial project by giving their readers a glimpse of the emptiness, or at least the insufficiency, of dominant white American ideals."[7] What I am arguing is that these Jim Crow networks in which periodical culture was enmeshed sprang to life through different kinds of engagement with the de facto and de jure conditions of the Jim Crow system. Networks with their rhizomatic affordances of proliferation, resistance to vertical structures, connectivity, and interactivity provide counters to the hierarchies of the period, even as they at times reified them. Thinking about these periodical and literary networks allows us to see the multiple pathways activism can take through network affordances.

These networks confronted lynching as a threat and object of activist energy—from Ida B. Wells's anti-lynching campaign to James Weldon Johnson's work with the NAACP to Nella Larsen's description of Helga Crane's children facing the lynch mob to William Faulkner's approaches to racial violence in the aftermath of *Brown v. Board of Education* and, finally, to *Cane*'s complex engagement with the reality and legacy of lynching, an engagement that was magnified by its relationship to the *Crisis.* My claim, however, is not that Jim Crow is still alive and well in the media networks but that its legacies endure through twenty-first-century networks, which are shaped in part by the activism of the first half of the twentieth century. It is important to acknowledge that the specific conditions under which the Jim Crow networks came to life "by and large, no longer obtain," as Warren claims, although this is not to say that racism, racial violence, and structural inequality have been vanquished—something that would be laughable to say in the twenty-first-century United States with its police killings of unarmed African Americans, mass incarceration of Black men, overt demonstrations of white supremacy, and crises of refugees and undocumented immigrants.

As Wells understood, the press was an essential weapon in fighting against racial violence precisely because it was deployed in aid of this violence and other injustices. In *Southern Horrors,* Wells indicted the white press by declaring that it "contains unreliable and doctored reports of lynchings, and one of the most necessary things for the race to do is to get these facts before the public. The people must know before they can act, and there is no educator to compare with the press."[8] The *Advertiser*'s editorial begins: "We were wrong." It goes on to say that "the *Montgomery Advertiser* recognizes its own shameful place in the history of these dastardly, murderous deeds."[9] This 2018 editorial uses the language of shame to acknowledge the immorality of the press's role in lynching. The newspaper apologizes: "We take responsibility for our proliferation of a false narrative regarding the treatment of African-Americans in those disgraceful days." In responding to its central role in legitimizing the dehumanization of African Americans in Montgomery, the newspaper acknowledges its historical place in Jim Crow media networks even as it gestures toward the continuity of those networks to the present day.

In thinking about these newspapers as nodes of media networks that reach back to Jim Crow networks, I want to discuss the extensions and transformations of the earlier networks in our current century. The twenty-first-century network affordances, despite significant differences, produce a counterpublic that shares a kinship with those found in the magazines and newspapers of the first half of the twentieth century. What

I have been examining throughout this book have been, in effect, the media networks that connected people with one another, with different types of texts, and with cultural, social, and political concerns. The interactions of these networks produced political and aesthetic meanings, meanings that extended beyond those produced by any individual actor. In other words, these interactions must be taken as a whole, rather than seen in isolation, to garner a deeper and more complex picture of the political and aesthetic work of American citizens within a period that defined hierarchies of citizenship.

These hierarchies certainly, as Michelle Alexander has convincingly demonstrated in *The New Jim Crow* (2010), have continuity with the hierarchies of the present day. Media networks, particularly social networks, remain powerful sites of resistance and solidarity even as they can be used to maintain privilege and dominance. While mainstream print media remains a part of these media networks even when transferred to the digital environment, it is clear that social media has become a significant component of these nodes. Despite our cultural emphasis on the newness of this century's social media, the periodical networks of the previous century were also "social" in their interactions; this sociality is central to the power and appeal of these old and new media networks. These networks relied on "participatory media," to refer back to Bridget Griffen-Foley's phrase.[10] However, like the letters to the editor, these media forms are themselves not completely participatory as the lack of access to and lack of facility with technology act as barriers to engagement for many people, even in the United States. In discussing participatory media, like social media, it is essential to avoid a triumphalist narrative since "participatory" does not mean universal participation is possible. On the flip side, social media also offers participation for those who wish to maintain power and engage in violence and bigotry toward others, as seen in the use of Twitter by white supremacist groups and individuals and the spread of lies by the alt-right.

It is also important to acknowledge that the media networks are truly social in that activism and political resistance did not simply reside in words and images on the page, whether that page be made of newsprint or of pixels on a screen. A movement like Black Lives Matter, begun in

2013, couples its use of Twitter hashtags with protests in the streets—like the 2014 Freedom Ride to Ferguson, Missouri, and the uprisings of 2020 in response to the murder of George Floyd—bringing the counterpublic sphere into public spaces and vice versa. In analyzing the responses to the shooting death of seventeen-year-old Trayvon Martin in 2012, Keeanga-Yamahtta Taylor writes:

> No one knew who would be the next Trayvon, but the increasing use of smartphone recording devices and social media seemed to quicken the pace at which incidents of police brutality became public. These tools being in the hands of ordinary citizens meant that families of victims were no longer dependent on the mainstream media's interest: they could take their case straight to the public. Meanwhile, the formation of organizations dedicated to fighting racism through mass mobilizations, street demonstrations, and other direct actions were evidence of a newly developing Black left that could vie for leadership against more established—and more tactically and politically conservative—forces. The Black political establishment, led by President Barack Obama, had shown over and over again that it was not capable of the most basic task: keeping Black children alive. The young people would have to do it themselves.[11]

This twinned work in the counterpublic media sphere and in the public spaces is an essential part of the media networks that I have identified and, I would argue, for activism in general. Although the Black Lives Matter networks are fluid and still evolving, both by design and by nature, and, thus, challenging to characterize, its networks are clearly part of a longer history of activism.

Black Lives Matter shares resemblances with other movements of the twenty-first century, like Occupy and the Arab Spring, movements that sprang into being in this century but have roots in previous centuries. These movements were facilitated by modern media networks, notably social media, as some formats, particularly Twitter, offer immediacy and decentralization, factors that are key to twenty-first-century activism. The Black Lives Matter movement sprang from a Facebook post by Alicia Garza after the 2013 acquittal of George Zimmerman in the shooting death of seventeen-year-old Trayvon Martin. Her post ended with the phrase "Black Lives Matter," which Patrisse Khan-Cullors (at that time Patrisse Cullors) turned into the hashtag phrase "#BlackLivesMatter." Garza, Khan-Cullors, and Opal Tometi began the movement to protest the systemic racism that leads to the devaluation of Black lives. In her account of the founding of the movement and the reasons for it, Garza describes it as such: "Black Lives Matter is an ideological and political intervention in a world where Black lives are systematically and intentionally targeted for demise. It is an affirmation of Black folks' contributions to this society, our humanity, and our resilience in the face of deadly oppression."[12]

Taylor argues that the work of Black Lives Matter, with its emphasis on organizing at local levels within decentralized national and international networks, is a response to failures in the top-down model of Black political leadership that had become standard. Her critique of the African American political elite, including Black mayors and extending all the way to President Barack Obama, highlights the complicity of politicians with the dominant powers that have produced and protected structural racism through a focus on respectability politics. She says, "Focusing on individual failure and lapsed morality—instead of structural inequities—justifies the budget cuts and the shrinking of the public sphere that Black political elites help facilitate. What African Americans in cities around the country need, according to this narrative, is personal transformation, not expanded social services—and the converse is that the poor behavior and attitude of young Blacks explains why their neighborhoods lack resources."[13] The focus on personal transformation has, as we have seen, a long history in the United States, from the *Half-Century*'s emphasis on etiquette and fashion, the *Defender* readers' calls for respectability, and Faulkner's advocacy for gradualism. However, as Taylor states, this focus often covers over the necessity for structural transformation. For this reason, she argues, we must move away from a reliance on the Black elite and turn to other ways of creating sociopolitical change: "Not only did the Ferguson rebellion expose the racism and brutality of American policing, it also exposed Black elected officials' inability to intervene effectively on behalf of poor and working-class African Americans."[14] The Black Lives Matter movement and affiliated groups provide a counter to the status quo and work specifically to dismantle this status quo.

The language of networks has an ambivalent status in these discussions of power and resistance. I want to make it clear that networks have been and can be used to maintain and assert power by the dominant class. Networks can be used to oppress, and it is specifically the decentralized quality of networks that can facilitate oppressive power, as Caroline Levine has noted. Patrick Jagoda has also discussed the uses of the network as a strategy for the United States military: "As outlined in numerous US military documents, a network-oriented strategy depends on easier intelligence sharing, greater command speed, self-synchronization of low-level units, noncontiguous organization, increased integration of information technologies, and the 'demassification' of forces."[15] Jagoda continues, "Network warfare, then, seeks to respond to enemies that are multimodal, distributed, and unpredictable."[16] He also pinpoints the way the concept of the terrorist network, "fundamentally oxymoronic in its connotation of both a destructive force and a creative matrix of connectivity," remains useful to U.S. military aims.[17] Imagining the enemy as a network "enables a perpetual war against an enemy construct too formless and fluid to defeat" due to the "distributed nature" of networks.[18]

The Black Lives Matter movement, however, relies on this distributed nature to respond to structural inequality. Structural inequality is itself often distributed and, thus, more challenging to identify and battle. Angela Y. Davis warns, "Racism is so dangerous because it does not necessarily depend on individual actors, but rather is deeply embedded in the apparatus."[19] Khan-Cullors characterizes events such as the 2014 killing of Eric Garner by police officers in New York City as "part of a movement that says Black Lives Do Not Matter."[20] In response, those associated with Black Lives Matter often emphasize local networks in a decentralized overall network that allows for nimble mobilization in responding to ever-shifting conditions. In recounting the origins of the Black Lives Matter Global Network, the "Herstory" section of the website declares, "It became clear that we needed to continue organizing and building Black power across the country. People were hungry to galvanize their communities to end state-sanctioned violence against Black people, the way Ferguson organizers and allies were doing. Soon we created the Black Lives Matter Global Network infrastructure. It is adaptive and decentralized, with a set of guiding principles. Our goal is to support the development of new Black leaders, as well as create a network where Black people feel empowered to determine our destinies in our communities."[21] Throughout the pages of her memoir *When They Call You a Terrorist: A Black Lives Matter Memoir* (2017), written with asha bandele, Khan-Cullors explicitly calls Black Lives Matter a "network" multiple times (and, in fact, its website now calls the movement the Black Lives Matter Global Network), emphasizing the need for a decentralized network to combat the distributed and yet hierarchical power of structural inequality.[22] While the website blacklivesmatter.com represents only one part of the Black Lives Matter movement, it highlights the movement as local chapters loosely organized into a collective network. In a speech delivered in St. Louis about the resistance in Ferguson, Davis declared, "When various public figures asked, 'Where are the leaders?' the movement said we are not a leaderless movement, we are a leader-*full* movement."[23] The affordances of these networks, in other words, are being used for resistance (although it is arguably the very decentralized quality that makes the movement, in some ways, fragile).[24]

In setting up a contrast between the activists of the Black Lives Movement and those like the NAACP and Al Sharpton's National Action Network, Taylor states, "Not only do the 'new guard's' politics stand in sharp contrast to those of the 'old guard' but so does their approach to organizing. Beyond being led by women, the new guard is decentralized and is largely organizing the movement through social media."[25] The network's decentralization is important in providing it with an energy different from that of what Taylor calls the old guard. (Of course, Taylor's picture of this "old guard" is itself a simplification since local grassroots activism was essential to the civil rights movement.) Social media has often been discussed as a savior of democracy as it allows the people to be heard, but, in practice, as concerns over the Cambridge Analytica Facebook scandal have played out and as the simple fact of the class economies of technology makes clear, this is not always the case. Social media has often left out people on the "lower frequencies," the words with which Ralph Ellison closes *Invisible Man;* the question of who has access—who has the means to gain access to these technologies—is occluded by social media's ostensible promise of providing voices for all in the public sphere.[26] However, by coupling social media with on-the-ground organizing, the Black Lives Matter movement uses networks in a way that strives to be more inclusive.

"Hashtag activism," which Black Lives Matter often relies on—the movement's origins lie, after all, in a hashtag that was disseminated widely—might seem to be a kind of "slacktivism," the pejorative word coined to describe the performance of online activism without deep engagement, such as signing an online petition or clicking the "Like" button on Facebook. While it can be, it can also generate energy in the online world and in the outside world. Most notably, the death of Trayvon Martin created online outrage that led to Zimmerman being charged. Relatedly, the hashtag #IfTheyGunnedMeDown was used in response to the shooting death of Michael Brown by a police officer in Ferguson, Missouri, in 2014. Twitter users would post this hashtag along with two photographs of themselves, asking which photograph the media would use if the user were killed. One photograph would show the user in a manner that fit negative stereotypes of Black criminality, while the second photograph would depict the user engaged in normal or even high-status behaviors. The most famous example was that of Tyler Atkins, a high school student, who posted one picture of himself in a bandanna gesturing in a way perceived as a stereotypical gang pose and one picture of himself in a tuxedo with his saxophone.[27] The implication was that the former photograph, which was taken from a rap video he made for a school math assignment, would have been used by the mainstream media because it fit cultural assumptions about Black criminality, even if he had been the victim.

This hashtag was used to protest the criminalization of African Americans, like Martin and Brown—which happened even after their deaths—to demonstrate the ways African American lives are devalued in the public sphere and to clearly illustrate the stakes of the politics of representation. As Wells wrote, "No other news goes out to the world save that which stamps us as a race of cut-throats, robbers and lustful wild beasts."[28] The use of #IfTheyGunnedMeDown was an attempt to expose the stamping of African Americans in the mainstream press and popular culture. This hashtag was generated out of and circulated through Black Twitter, the name for the counterpublic sphere of Black Twitter users. Feminista Jones describes it "as a collective of active, primarily African-American Twitter users who have created a virtual community that participates in continuous real-time conversations. When they work together, this collective is proving adept at bringing about a wide range of sociopolitical changes."[29] She argues for Black Twitter's origins in slavery: "African-Americans have historically relied on 'alternative' communication styles and underground means to connect and build networks. Centuries ago, newly captured African slaves were separated from those who spoke their native languages to discourage organized attempts at escape. For them, finding universal means of communication, like 'spirituals' or 'work songs,' became essential to their survival and that of future generations. We have often used grass-roots communication to organize and mobilize efforts to achieve freedom and equality."[30] Jones could also have pointed to the Black press during the Jim Crow period as venues for alternative communications that provided the truth that the mainstream media overlooked or distorted. Black Twitter works as a networked community that is not codified but that nonetheless could be mobilized for activism, both online and in public spaces.

In speaking about demonstrations against police violence, Davis states that "we may be given the opportunity to emerge from the individualism within which we are ensconced in this neoliberal era. Neoliberal ideology drives us to focus on individuals, ourselves, individual victims, individual perpetrators."[31] In essence, thinking in terms of collectivity and in terms of networks provides a counter to the imperative of individualism that undergirds neoliberalism. Decentralization then does not mean a lack of solidarity. The affordance of networks as sprawling and not containable in their totality is essential to this decentralized activism. With their constitutive decentralization, networks create connections between strangers with common concerns but not necessarily identical ones. An example would be the global women's marches that took place the day after the 2017 U.S. presidential inauguration; these marches brought together different people and multifarious concerns, including those related to the women's right to choose, immigration, race, and the environment, through resistance. In her memoir, Khan-Cullors specifically draws connections between seemingly unrelated causes such as feminism, mass incarceration, immigration, trans rights, marijuana legalization, and food politics in order to demonstrate the deep networks of structural inequality that the intersectional networks of the Black Lives Matter movement mobilize to abolish.

Not long after the February 2020 passage of the Emmett Till Antilynching Act, the United States was plunged into the global crisis caused by the COVID-19 pandemic and the inadequacies of governmental responses to it. From the beginning of the crisis within the United States, the pandemic exposed the deep networks of structural inequality that underlie the nation. Class and racial inequality have shaped the virus's effects on the country. Viral pathways seem to follow these networks of inequality, leading to disproportionate effects on poor and working-class African American and Latinx people. These effects are seen in the disproportionate rates of infection and deaths, which are the result, according to emerging accounts, of a number of factors, such as preexisting health disparities (including limited access to healthcare and insurance), jobs that lead to more viral exposure, the necessity of using public transportation, and available housing options.[32] In addition, the virus's devastating toll in prisons has affected African Americans disproportionately due to the injustices of mass incarceration. The responses to the crisis itself have created economic, health, and educational hardships for those who cannot work from home, those who cannot afford to hoard groceries and other essential products, and those who might not have access to reliable internet service for schooling. In fact, Ibram X. Kendi has suggested that "America was facing a racial pandemic within the viral pandemic."[33] At the same time, the spring of 2020 has been marked by protests and uprisings over the killings of African Americans, specifically Breonna Taylor in Kentucky, Ahmaud Arbery in Georgia, and George Floyd in Minnesota—among many, many others. These decentralized protests have been organized and amplified on social media networks. The intersection of the pandemic and the protests is not coincidental. The killings, along with the pandemic's disproportionate effects on African Americans, are part of the long history of the networks of inequality. It is too early to say how all of this will play out, but it is clear that this pandemic has laid bare what our society has chosen to prioritize and what it has chosen to devalue—choices that Jim Crow networks of periodicals, readers, and authors have long grappled with.

Over one hundred years before, in speaking about the need for the mobilization against such injustices in her 1900 pamphlet *Mob Rule in New Orleans,* Wells wrote, "Men and women of America, are you proud of this record which the Anglo-Saxon race has made for itself? Your silence seems to say that you are. Your silence encourages a continuance of this sort of horror. Only by earnest, active, united endeavor to arouse public sentiment can we hope to put a stop to these demonstrations of American barbarism."[34] The "earnest, active, united endeavor" that Wells speaks of is a network of resistance aimed at stopping racial injustices. For Wells, this endeavor is a rejection of silence in favor of collective action. In speaking about the need for this collective action, Taylor writes of the potential for solidarity between people of color and the white working class: "The common experience of oppression and exploitation creates the potential for a united struggle to better the conditions of all."[35] Taylor continues, "Solidarity is standing in unity with people even when you have not personally experienced their particular oppression."[36] What this suggests is that perceiving individuals as existing in a network allows for solidarity between strangers. In the tradition of Wells, more than a century after the publication of her words about an "earnest, active, united endeavor," Davis wrote about the transformative potential of networks: "What has kept me going has been the development of new modes of community. I don't know whether I would have survived had not movements survived, had not communities of resistance, communities of struggle. So whatever I'm doing I always feel myself directly connected to those communities and I think that this is an era where we have to encourage that sense of community particularly at a time when neoliberalism attempts to force people to think of themselves only in individual terms and not in collective terms. It is in collectivities that we find reservoirs of hope and optimism."[37] These reservoirs of hope and optimism are generated by and found in networks of resistance, both in the activism during the Jim Crow era and that of today.

NOTES

INTRODUCTION

1. Ida B. Wells, *Crusade for Justice: The Autobiography of Ida B. Wells,* ed. Alfreda M. Duster (Chicago: University of Chicago Press, 1970), 47.
2. Ida B. Wells, *Southern Horrors: Lynch Law in All Its Phases,* in *Southern Horrors and Other Writings: The Anti-Lynching Campaign of Ida B. Wells,* 1892–1900, ed. Jacqueline Jones Royster (Boston: Bedford Books, 1997), 70.
3. Ibid.
4. Sean Latham and Robert Scholes, "The Rise of Periodical Studies," *PMLA* 121, no. 2 (2006): 529.
5. See Eric Gardner, *Black Print Unbound: The Christian Recorder, African American Literature, and Periodical Culture* (Oxford: Oxford University Press, 2015); Benjamin Fagan, *The Black Newspaper and the Chosen Nation* (Athens: University of Georgia Press, 2016); and Lara Langer Cohen and Jordan Alexander Stein, ed., *Early African American Print Culture* (Philadelphia: University of Pennsylvania Press, 2012).
6. Lara Langer Cohen and Jordan Alexander Stein, "Introduction: Early African American Print Culture," in *Early African American Print Culture,* 1.
7. Ibid.
8. Fagan, *The Black Newspaper,* 7.
9. M. M. Bakhtin, "Discourse in the Novel," in *The Dialogic Imagination: Four Essays,* ed. Michael Holquist, trans. Caryl Emerson and Michael Holquist (Austin: University of Texas Press, 1981), 279.
10. See Anne Elizabeth Carroll, *Word, Image, and the New Negro: Representation and Identity in the Harlem Renaissance* (Bloomington: Indiana University Press), 2005; and Russ Castronovo, "Beauty along the Color Line: Lynching, Aesthetics, and the *Crisis,*" *PMLA* 121, no. 5 (2006): 1443–59.
11. See, for example, Frederick J. Hoffman, Charles Allen, and Carolyn F. Ulrich, *The Little Magazine: A History and a Bibliography* (Princeton: Princeton University Press, 1946); and Mark S. Morrisson, *The Public Face of Modernism: Little Magazines, Audiences, and Reception* 1905–1920 (Madison: University of Wisconsin Press, 2001).
12. Robert Scholes and Clifford Wulfman, *Modernism in the Magazines: An Introduction* (New Haven: Yale University Press, 2010), 59.
13. Ibid., 60.
14. Ibid., 61.
15. In a special issue of the *Journal of Modern Periodical Studies* titled "Visualizing Periodical Networks," guest editor J. Stephen Murphy criticizes current critical uses of networks and argues for a specific conception of them in relation to the study of

magazines and newspapers: "A network is not just any old group. The term denotes a structure of linked entities, subject to systematic analysis and visualization using a range of computational methodologies. Networks matter in all kinds of environments because they build on and shape relationships that exist between entities, affect the identities of individual nodes, and create effects made possible only as a result of the interrelated structure of the network" (vii). In making this argument, Murphy argues for the necessity of computational models grounded in network analysis software, like Gephi, in examining networks (vii). See J. Stephen Murphy, "Introduction: 'Visualizing Periodical Networks,'" *Journal of Modern Periodical Studies* 5, no. 1 (2014): iii–xv. While it is true that network analyses grounded in computational models have provided insight into the alliances and interrelated structures of literature and periodicals, it is not true that they are necessary in analyzing networks. Computational models, for the most part, are limited in capturing the bottom-up multiplicity of nodes in the networks I examine; this method cannot, by itself, provide a substantive picture of the readers in particular, or of the deliberate work that these periodicals engaged in to position themselves in relation to each other. In other words, the complexity of the individual nodes of a network is not sufficiently captured through computational approaches alone.

16. Manuel Castells, *Networks of Outrage and Hope: Social Movements in the Internet Age* (Cambridge: Polity Press), 2012.
17. See Jonathan H. Grossman, *Charles Dickens's Networks: Public Transport and the Novel* (Oxford: Oxford University Press, 2012); Richard Jean So, *Transpacific Community: America, China, and the Rise and Fall of a Cultural Network* (New York: Columbia University Press, 2016); and Patrick Jagoda, *Network Aesthetics* (Chicago: University of Chicago Press, 2016).
18. See Eric Bulson, *Little Magazine, World Form* (New York: Columbia University Press, 2017); and Wesley Beal, *Networks of Modernism: Reorganizing American Narrative* (Iowa City: Iowa University Press, 2015).
19. See M. E. J. Newman, *Networks: An Introduction* (Oxford: Oxford University Press, 2010), 3; and Alexander R. Galloway, "Networks," in *Critical Terms for Media Studies,* ed. W. J. T. Mitchell and Mark B. N. Hansen (Chicago: University of Chicago Press, 2010), 283.
20. Caroline Levine, *Forms: Whole, Rhythm, Hierarchy, Network* (Princeton: Princeton University Press, 2015), 113.
21. For an overview of ANT, including its history, see John Law, "Actor Network Theory and Material Semiotics," in *The New Blackwell Companion to Social Theory,* ed. Bryan S. Turner (Malden, MA: Wiley-Blackwell, 2009), 141–58.
22. Rita Felski, "Latour and Literary Studies," *PMLA* 130, no. 3 (2015): 738.
23. Ibid.
24. Bruno Latour, *Reassembling the Social: An Introduction to Actor-Network-Theory* (Oxford: Oxford University Press, 2005), 251.
25. Ibid., 258.

26. Rita Felski, *The Limits of Critique* (Chicago: University of Chicago Press, 2015), 147.
27. Ibid., 171.
28. Gilles Deleuze and Félix Guattari, *A Thousand Plateaus: Capitalism and Schizophrenia,* trans. Brian Massumi (Minneapolis: University of Minnesota Press, 1987), 21.
29. Ibid., 7, 21.
30. Ibid., 25.
31. Pierre Bourdieu and Loïc J. D. Wacquant, *An Invitation to Reflexive Sociology* (Chicago: University of Chicago Press, 1992), 97.
32. Donald A. Norman, *The Design of Everyday Things,* revised and expanded edition (New York: Basic Books, 2013), 11.
33. Levine, *Forms,* 6.
34. Ibid.; and Sean Latham, "Affordance and Emergence: Magazine as New Media" (paper presented during session What Is a Journal? Towards a Theory of Periodical Studies, Modern Language Association Convention, Boston, MA, January 4, 2013, Special Session 384), 1.
35. Latham, "Affordance and Emergence," 2.
36. See Jerome J. McGann, *The Textual Condition* (Princeton: Princeton University Press, 1991).
37. Leah Price, *The Anthology and the Rise of the Novel: From Richardson to George Eliot* (Cambridge: Cambridge University Press, 2000), 5.
38. Margaret Beetham, "Towards a Theory of the Periodical as a Publishing Genre," in *Investigating Victorian Journalism,* ed. Laurel Brake, Aled Jones, and Lionel Madden (London: MacMillan, 1990), 26.
39. See the Modernist Journals Project (searchable database), Brown and Tulsa Universities, ongoing, www.modjourn.org.
40. Latham, "Affordance and Emergence," 3.
41. Levine, *Forms,* 114.
42. Ibid., 115.
43. Ibid., 129.
44. George Bornstein, *Material Modernism: The Politics of the Page* (Cambridge: Cambridge University Press, 2001), 6.
45. Ibid., 7.
46. McGann, *Textual Condition,* 13.
47. Peter Brooker and Andrew Thacker, "General Introduction," in *The Oxford Critical and Cultural History of Modernist Magazines, Volume I, Britain and Ireland* 1880–1955, ed. Peter Brooker and Andrew Thacker (Oxford: Oxford University Press, 2009), 6.
48. Ibid.
49. Latham and Scholes, "Rise of Periodical Studies," 529.
50. Latour, *Reassembling the Social,* 129.
51. Jagoda, *Network Aesthetics,* 4.
52. McGann, *Textual Condition,* 116.
53. Ibid., 119.

54. Ibid., 126.
55. Roland Barthes, "The Death of the Author," in *Modern Criticism and Theory: A Reader,* ed. David Lodge (London: Longman, 1988), 172.
56. Ibid., 171.
57. Michel Foucault, "What Is an Author?," in *Modern Criticism and Theory: A Reader,* ed. David Lodge (London: Longman, 1988), 210.
58. Ibid.
59. Barthes, "Death of the Author," 171.
60. Langston Hughes, "The Negro Artist and the Racial Mountain," in *African American Literary Theory: A Reader,* ed. Winston Napier (New York: New York University Press, 2000), 27.
61. Ibid.
62. Ibid.
63. Ibid., 28.
64. Noliwe M. Rooks, *Ladies' Pages: African American Women's Magazines and the Culture that Made Them* (New Brunswick: Rutgers University Press, 2004), 3.
65. Michael North argues that "becoming modern by acting black," often through a "pattern of rebellion through racial ventriloquism," was an essential thread in works by modernist writers (8, 9): "The new voice that American culture acquired in the 1920s, the decade of jazz, stage musicals, talking pictures, and aesthetic modernism, was very largely a black one" (7). Michael North, *The Dialect of Modernism: Race, Language, and Twentieth-Century Literature* (Oxford: Oxford University Press, 1994).
66. Wells, *Southern Horrors,* 52.
67. Ibid., 69.
68. Teresa Zackodnik, *Press, Platform, Pulpit: Black Feminist Publics in the Era of Reform* (Knoxville: University of Tennessee Press, 2011), 132.
69. Wells, *Southern Horrors,* 50.
70. Jacqueline Goldsby, *A Spectacular Secret: Lynching in American Life and Literature* (Chicago: University of Chicago Press, 2006), 73–74.
71. Ida B. Wells, *A Red Record,* in *Southern Horrors and Other Writings: The Anti-Lynching Campaign of Ida B. Wells,* 1892–1900, ed. Jacqueline Jones Royster (Boston: Bedford Books, 1997), 82.
72. Zackodnik, *Press, Platform, Pulpit,* 153.
73. Wells, *Southern Horrors,* 71.
74. Ibid., 52.
75. Ibid., 53.
76. Ibid.
77. Ibid., 54.
78. Ibid., 70.
79. Ibid., 72.
80. Ibid., 70.

81. "Ida B. Wells," the Pulitzer Prizes, https://www.pulitzer.org/winners/ida-b-wells.
82. Kenneth W. Warren, *What Was African American Literature?* (Cambridge: Harvard University Press, 2011), 10–11.
83. Michael Warner, *Publics and Counterpublics* (New York: Zone Books, 2005), 119.
84. Ibid., 122.

CHAPTER ONE: MIDDLEBROW NETWORKS

1. "Editorial," *Half-Century Magazine* 1, no. 1 (August 1916): 3, reprint (New York: Negro Universities Press, 1969).
2. Psyche A. Williams-Forson, *Building Houses Out of Chicken Legs: Black Women, Food, and Power* (Chapel Hill: University of North Carolina Press, 2006), 7.
3. Patrick S. Washburn, *The African American Newspaper: Voice of Freedom* (Evanston: Northwestern University Press, 2006), 82–83.
4. Anne Elizabeth Carroll, *Word, Image, and the New Negro: Representation and Identity in the Harlem Renaissance* (Bloomington: Indiana University Press, 2005).
5. "Announcing Plans of Special Interest to the Readers of the Half-Century," *Half-Century Magazine* 3, no. 1 (July 1917): 3, *HathiTrust Digital Library.*
6. "Read It ONCE and You Will Read It ALWAYS," advertisement, *Half-Century Magazine* 3, no. 4 (October 1917): 16, *HathiTrust Digital Library.*
7. Mark Noonan, *Reading the Century Illustrated Monthly Magazine: American Literature and Culture,* 1870–1893 (Kent, OH: Kent State University Press, 2010), ix.
8. Ibid., xi, xiii.
9. Tellingly, the *Crisis* had, a couple months prior in September 1919, increased its prices to fifteen cents per issue and $1.50 for a yearly subscription. See Rachel Farebrother, "*The Crisis* (1910–34)," in *The Oxford Critical and Cultural History of Modernist Magazines, Volume II, North America* 1894–1960, ed. Peter Brooker and Andrew Thacker (Oxford: Oxford University Press, 2012), 103. The timing suggests that the *Half-Century* was well aware of the *Crisis*'s price increase and chose to follow suit.
10. Noliwe M. Rooks, *Ladies' Pages: African American Women's Magazines and the Culture that Made Them* (New Brunswick: Rutgers University Press, 2004), 70.
11. "Our Platform," *Half-Century Magazine* 6, no. 5 (May 1919): 18, *HathiTrust Digital Library.*
12. According to Farebrother, "By November 1915, with 35,000 subscriptions, Du Bois proudly proclaimed that the magazine was self-financing. Circulation peaked at 100,000 in May 1919." Rachel Farebrother, "*The Crisis* (1910–34)," 104. With regard to the *Defender,* Juliet Walker states, "By 1918 its circulation had increased to 100,000; two years later the circulation showed an almost threefold increase to 283,571, according to a circulation pamphlet distributed by the paper." Juliet E. K. Walker, "The Promised Land: The Chicago *Defender* and the Black Press in Illinois, 1862–1970,"

in *The Black Press in the Middle West,* 1865–1985, ed. Henry Lewis Suggs (Westport: Greenwood, 1996), 25.

13. "Statement of the Ownership, Management, Circulation, Etc., Required by the Act of Congress of August 24, 1912," *Half-Century Magazine* 3, no. 5 (November 1917): 17, *HathiTrust Digital Library.* By the May 1919 statement, Katherine E. Irvin (Williams's married name) is no longer listed as the "sole owner." She is listed as owner along with Asenath T. Alexander, I. B. W. Cabell, Orelia L Gougis, and Eva O. Lewis. See "Statement of the Ownership, Management, Circulation, Etc., Required by the Act of Congress of August 24, 1912," *Half-Century Magazine* 6, no. 5 (May 1919): 17, New York Public Library.
14. Robert E. Weems, Jr., "A Man in a Woman's World: Anthony Overton's Rise to Prominence in the African American Personal Care Products Industry," *Journal of African American History* 101, no. 4 (2016): 420.
15. Ibid., 424.
16. Christopher Robert Reed, *The Rise of Chicago's Black Metropolis,* 1920–1929 (Urbana: University of Illinois Press, 2011), 104.
17. Ibid.
18. James Weldon Johnson, *The Autobiography of an Ex-Colored Man,* ed. Jacqueline Goldsby (New York: W.W. Norton, 2015), 82.
19. Leona Eldridge Porter, "Domestic Surprises," *Half-Century Magazine* 2, no. 3 (March 1917): 13, reprint (New York: Negro Universities Press, 1969).
20. "Were You Ever Embarrassed?," *Half-Century Magazine* 12, no. 1 (January 1922): 14, reprint (New York: Negro Universities Press, 1969).
21. "Editorial," *Half-Century Magazine,* 1, no. 1 (August 1916): 3.
22. "Let's Chat," *Half-Century Magazine* 2, no. 3 (March 1917): 3, reprint (New York: Negro Universities Press, 1969).
23. Ethan Michaeli, *The Defender: How the Legendary Black Newspaper Changed America: From the Age of the Pullman Porters to the Age of Obama* (Boston: Houghton Mifflin Harcourt, 2016), 27.
24. "Scandal," *Half-Century Magazine* 15, no. 1 (July–August 1923): 3, reprint (New York: Negro Universities Press, 1969).
25. Abby Arthur Johnson and Ronald Maberry Johnson, *Propaganda and Aesthetics: The Literary Politics of African-American Magazines in the Twentieth Century* (Amherst: University of Massachusetts Press, 1991), 35.
26. Ann Ardis, "Making Middlebrow Culture, Making Middlebrow Literary Texts *Matter:* The *Crisis,* Easter 1912," *Modernist Cultures* 6, no. 1 (2011): 18–40.
27. "Editorial," *Half-Century Magazine,* 1, no. 1 (August 1916): 3.
28. Joan Shelley Rubin points out that "the reference to the height of the brow originally derived from phrenology and carried overtones of racial differentiation." Joan Shelley Rubin, *The Making of Middlebrow Culture* (Chapel Hill: University of Carolina Press, 1992), xii. Lawrence W. Levine observes that the terms

> "highbrow," first used in the 1880s to describe intellectual or aesthetic superiority, and "lowbrow," first used shortly after 1900 to mean someone or something neither "highly intellectual" or "aesthetically refined," were derived from the phrenological terms "highbrowed" and "lowbrowed," which were prominently featured in the nineteenth-century practice of determining racial types and intelligence by measuring cranial shapes and capacities . . . From the time of their formulation, such cultural categories as highbrow and lowbrow were hardly meant to be neutral descriptive terms; they were openly associated with and designed to preserve, nurture, and extend the cultural history and values of a particular group of peoples in a specific historical context.

Lawrence W. Levine, *Highbrow / Lowbrow: The Emergence of Cultural Hierarchy in America* (Cambridge: Harvard University Press, 1988), 221–23.

29. Rooks, *Ladies' Pages,* 83.
30. "With Our Exchanges," *Half-Century Magazine* 1, no. 1 (August 1916): 18, New York Public Library.
31. Pierre Bourdieu and Loïc J. D. Wacquant, *An Invitation to Reflexive Sociology* (Chicago: University of Chicago Press, 1992), 97.
32. Ibid., 100.
33. Melissa Sullivan and Sophie Blanch, "Introduction: The Middlebrow—Within or Without Modernism," *Modernist Cultures* 6, no. 1 (2011): 4.
34. "Let's Chat," *Half-Century Magazine,* 2, no. 3 (March 1917): 3.
35. John Guillory, "The Ordeal of Middlebrow Culture," review of *The Western Canon: The Books and School of the Ages,* by Harold Bloom, *Transition* 67 (1995): 90.
36. Johnson and Johnson, *Propaganda and Aesthetics,* 109.
37. "Who Is the Prettiest Colored Girl in the United States?," *Half-Century Magazine* 12, no. 1 (January 1922): 9, New York Public Library.
38. Kathryn M. Johnson, "East St. Louis," *Half-Century Magazine* 3, no. 4 (October 1917): 8, New York Public Library.
39. Ibid.
40. The Investigator, "Bombing Your Own Home," *Half-Century Magazine* 10, no. 2 (March–April 1921): 18, reprint (New York: Negro Universities Press, 1969).
41. Ibid.
42. "Let's Chat," *Half-Century Magazine,* 2, no. 3 (March 1917): 3.
43. "Reciprocity and Co-operation," *Half-Century Magazine* 2, no. 4 (April 1917): 3, *HathiTrust Digital Library.*
44. Nicola Humble, *The Feminine Middlebrow Novel, 1920s–1950s: Class, Domesticity, and Bohemianism* (Oxford: Oxford University Press, 2001), 11.

45. Evelyn Brooks Higginbotham, *Righteous Discontent: The Women's Movement in the Black Baptist Church,* 1880–1920 (Cambridge: Harvard University Press, 1993).
46. "Announcing Plans of Special Interest to the Readers of the Half-Century," *Half-Century Magazine* 3, no. 1 (July 1917): 3, *HathiTrust Digital Library.*
47. "East vs. West," *Chicago Defender,* October 13, 1928.
48. The Investigator, "Bombing Your Own Home," *Half-Century Magazine* 10, no. 2 (March-April 1921): 15, reprint (New York: Negro Universities Press, 1969).
49. Rubin, *Making of Middlebrow Culture,* xvii–xviii.
50. "Scandal," *Half-Century Magazine,* 15, no. 1 (July–August 1923): 3.
51. Mrs. W. M. Newman, letter to the editor, *Half-Century Magazine* 8, no. 6 (June 1920): 17, reprint (New York: Negro Universities Press, 1969).
52. E. Franklin Frazier, "La Bourgeoisie Noire," in *The New Negro: Readings on Race, Representation, and African American Culture,* 1892–1938, ed. Henry Louis Gates, Jr., and Gene Andrew Jarrett (Princeton: Princeton University Press, 2007), 137.
53. Reed, *Rise of Chicago's Black Metropolis,* 48.
54. "Can You Write?," advertisement, *Half-Century Magazine* 2, no. 2 (February 1917): 10, *HathiTrust Digital Library.*
55. "Announcing Plans of Special Interest to the Readers of the Half-Century," *Half-Century Magazine,* 3, no. 1 (July 1917): 3, *HathiTrust Digital Library.*
56. Maureen Honey points out that the *Ladies' Home Journal* and *Woman's Home Companion* were two of "the five top leaders in advertising revenue in 1920" (89). "It was," she states, "the decision in the early teens to include a large amount of fiction that propelled the circulation of these and other industry giants into the millions and that constituted their core marketing strategy throughout the postwar period" (88–90). She continues, "Periodicals originally designed as fashion or household service magazines in the late nineteenth century shifted their emphasis, gradually including more fiction and hiring top book illustrators as well as best-selling authors" (90). See Maureen Honey, "Feminist New Woman Fiction in Periodicals of the 1920s," in *Middlebrow Moderns: Popular American Women Writers of the* 1920s, ed. Lisa Botshon and Meredith Goldsmith (Boston: Northeastern University Press, 2003), 87–109. The *Half-Century* is part of this trend via Johnson's celebrity and overall inclusion of fiction. Jaime Harker discusses the politics of the middlebrow *Woman's Home Companion, whose* editor, Gertrude Lane, "incorporated an unusual emphasis on politics, particularly Progressive politics, into her magazine. She encouraged middle-class women to be politically active citizens" (35). Harker also describes the magazine as "not coincidentally, a leading publisher of fiction in the twenties and thirties" (35). Writers like Willa Cather, Ellen Glasgow, Sherwood Anderson, and F. Scott Fitzgerald were published in its pages. See Jaime Harker, *America the Middlebrow: Women's Novels, Progressivism, and Middlebrow Authorship between the Wars* (Amherst: University of Massachusetts Press, 2007).

57. Helen Damon-Moore, *Magazines for the Millions: Gender and Commerce in the Ladies' Home Journal and the Saturday Evening Post,* 1880–1910 (Albany: State University of New York Press, 1994), 13.
58. Jennifer Scanlon, *Inarticulate Longings:* The Ladies' Home Journal, *Gender, and the Promises of Consumer Culture* (New York: Routledge, 1995), 5.
59. Ibid.
60. Damon-Moore, *Magazines for the Millions,* 107.
61. "Read More," *Half-Century Magazine* 12, no. 4 (April 1922): 3, reprint (New York: Negro Universities Press, 1969).
62. Ibid.
63. "Notice," *Half-Century Magazine* 2, no. 2 (February 1917): 3, *HathiTrust Digital Library.*
64. "What Do Your Children Read?," *Half-Century Magazine* 13, no. 1 (July–August 1922): 3, reprint (New York: Negro Universities Press, 1969).
65. Ibid., 22. At the same time, there is an interesting letter in "The People's Forum" of this July–August 1922 issue. The author, Mrs. M., writes,

> I am proud of the girl of today—glad that she is not like the girl of yesterday. Of course there were good and bad girls then just as there are now, but when I think how strict my parents were with me I am forced to say that I am glad the girl of today is not living under the same restriction the girls of my class were forced to live . . . The girl of today thinks and acts to please herself and does far better in life than the one that was raised in a band box. It is a sad thing for a girl to grow up with no knowledge of men and the ways of the world.

See Mrs. M., letter to the editor, *Half-Century Magazine* 3, no. 1 (July–August 1922): 21, reprint (New York: Negro Universities Press, 1969). This letter suggests the presence of other discourses, both within the pages of the magazine and outside.
66. "Why Don't You Get Acquainted with Your Race?," advertisement, *Half-Century Magazine* 12, no. 5 (May–June 1922): 15, reprint (New York: Negro Universities Press, 1969).
67. "Our Program," *Half-Century Magazine* 6, no. 3 (March 1919): 3, *HathiTrust Digital Library.*
68. Evelyn Eastman, "Bab Prepares Herself," *Half-Century Magazine* 8, no. 4 (April 1920): 5, reprint (New York: Negro Universities Press, 1969).
69. Ibid.
70. Ibid.
71. Ibid.
72. Margaret Lyndon, "Serving the Dinner," *Half-Century Magazine* 8, no. 2 (February 1920): 10, reprint (New York: Negro Universities Press, 1969); and Mary Black, "The

Duties of the Hostess," *Half-Century Magazine* 12, no. 2 (February 1922): 17, reprint (New York: Negro Universities Press, 1969).

73. Advertisement for Universal Metal Polish, *Half-Century Magazine* 12, no. 1 (January 1922): 21, reprint (New York: Negro Universities Press, 1969).
74. Ellen Gruber Garvey, *The Adman in the Parlor: Magazines and the Gendering of Consumer Culture, 1880s to 1910s* (Oxford: Oxford University Press, 1996), 8.
75. Ibid., 15.
76. Jane Jones, "The Awakening of Jim Gray," *Half-Century Magazine* 12, no. 2 (February 1922): 5, reprint (New York: Negro Universities Press, 1969).
77. Ibid., 8.
78. Ibid., 17.
79. Ibid., 5.
80. Ibid.
81. Ibid.
82. Ibid., 17.
83. "Betrayers of the Race," *Half-Century Magazine* 8, no. 2 (February 1920): 3, reprint (New York: Negro Universities Press, 1969).
84. Ibid.
85. Garvey, *Adman in the Parlor,* 11.
86. Margaret Beetham, *A Magazine of Her Own?: Domesticity and Desire in the Woman's Magazine, 1800–1914* (London: Routledge, 1996), 2.
87. Scanlon, *Inarticulate Longings,* 220.
88. Ibid.
89. Ibid., 170.
90. Leona Gray, "Mammy Sue," *Half-Century Magazine* 9, no. 3 (October 1920): 5 and 12, reprint (New York: Negro Universities Press, 1969).
91. W. Edward Davenport, "Identification for Two," installment, *Half-Century Magazine* 9, no. 3 (October 1920): 6, 12, and 14, reprint (New York: Negro Universities Press, 1969).
92. James Weldon Johnson, *The Autobiography of an Ex-Colored Man,* installment, *Half-Century Magazine* 9, no. 3 (October 1920): 4, 14, and 15, reprint (New York: Negro Universities Press, 1969).
93. "Can You Write?," advertisement, *Half-Century Magazine* 2, no. 2 (February 1917): 10, *HathiTrust Digital Library.*
94. See *Half-Century Magazine* 9, no. 3 (October 1920): 2, 7, 16, 18, reprint (New York: Negro Universities Press, 1969).
95. In the 2015 Norton Critical Edition of the 1912 novel, Jacqueline Goldsby examines the novel's reprinting by the New American Library in a 1948 mass market edition. Jacqueline Goldsby, "Introduction: 'Giving the Country Something New and Unknown': James Weldon Johnson's *The Autobiography of an Ex-Colored Man,*" in *The Autobiography of an Ex-Colored Man,* by James Weldon Johnson (New York: W. W. Norton & Company, 2015), ix–lix.

96. "On the Road to Tomorrow," *Half-Century Magazine* 7, no. 1 (July 1919): 3, *HathiTrust Digital Library;* and Howard A. Phelps, "Persons of Note," *Half-Century Magazine* 7, no. 3 (September 1919): 9, *HathiTrust Digital Library.*
97. Goldsby, "Introduction," xlv.
98. Goldsby, "Keeping the 'Secret of Authorship': A Critical Look at the 1912 Publication of James Weldon Johnson's *Autobiography of an Ex-Colored Man,*" in *Print Culture in a Diverse America,* ed. James P. Danky and Wayne A. Wiegand (Urbana: University of Illinois Press, 1998), 263.
99. Ibid., 271n63.
100. Matthew J. Bruccoli, "Introduction," in *The Great Gatsby,* by F. Scott Fitzgerald (Cambridge: University of Cambridge Press, 1991), xx–xxin24.
101. Goldsby, "Introduction," xiv.
102. Virginia Woolf, "Middlebrow," in *The Death of the Moth and Other Essays* (San Diego: Harcourt Brace and Company, 1942), 180. Woolf ends her essay with the following line: "If any human being, man, woman, dog, cat or half-crushed worm dares call me 'middlebrow' I will take my pen and stab him, dead" (186).
103. Goldsby, "Introduction," xxiv, xxvi. Scholars like those in Lisa Botshon and Meredith Goldsmith's edited collection *Middlebrow Moderns* challenge modernism's self-defined separation from the middlebrow. See Lisa Botshon and Meredith Goldsmith, ed., *Middlebrow Moderns: Popular American Women Writers of the* 1920s (Boston: Northeastern University Press, 2003).
104. Indeed, Goldsby at first analyzed this novel in the context of realism in her book *A Spectacular Secret,* but she then aligned it with modernism in the Norton; this very critical response displays the instability and contradictions of the middle. She explains her discussion of the novel's oscillation between realism and modernism in a footnote: The Norton critical edition introduction "builds upon but differs from the analysis of [*The Autobiography of an Ex-Colored Man*] that I offer in *A Spectacular Secret: Lynching in American Life and Literature* (Chicago: University of Chicago Press, 2006), chap. 4. There, I argue that the novel's experimental energies are vested in challenging the norms of literary realism as adequate to the task of depicting the violence of lynching. Here, I place emphasis on the modernist innovations that [*The Autobiography of an Ex-Colored Man*'s] defiance of realism made possible." Goldsby, "Introduction," xiv.
105. Johnson, *The Autobiography of an Ex-Colored Man,* 97.
106. Ibid., 99–100.
107. I will discuss shame's relationship to respectability during this period more deeply in the next chapter.
108. W. E. B. Du Bois, "On Being Ashamed of Oneself: An Essay on Race Pride," in *The Oxford W. E. B. Du Bois Reader,* ed. Eric J. Sundquist (Oxford: Oxford University Press, 1996), 73.
109. Johnson, *Autobiography of an Ex-Colored Man,* 31.

110. Ibid., 99. This kinship is echoed again when the narrator tells his white beloved that he is Black: "I felt her hand grow cold, and when I looked up she was gazing at me with a wild, fixed stare as though I was some object she had never seen. Under the strange light in her eyes I felt that I was growing black and thick-featured and crimp-haired." Ibid., 106.
111. Ibid., 110.
112. Johnson, Autobiography of an Ex-Colored Man, 100.
113. "The Confessions of an Ex-White Actress," *Half-Century Magazine* 7, no. 1 (July 1919): 16, New York Public Library.
114. William H. Scott, "The Color Line," *Half Century Magazine* 4, no. 6 (June 1918): 5, New York Public Library.
115. Ibid.
116. William Louis Board, "The Black Brute," *Half-Century Magazine* 1, no. 4 (November 1916): 4, New York Public Library.
117. Ibid., 16.
118. Johnson, *Autobiography of an Ex-Colored Man*, 98.
119. See, for example, Robert E. Fleming, "Irony as a Key to Johnson's *The Autobiography of an Ex-Colored Man*," *American Literature: A Journal of Literary History, Criticism, and Bibliography* 43, no. 1 (March 1971): 83–96; and Stephen M. Ross, "Audience and Irony in Johnson's *The Autobiography of an Ex-Colored Man*," *CLA Journal* 18, no. 2 (1974): 198–210. See also Roxanna Pisiak, "Irony and Subversion in James Weldon Johnson's *The Autobiography of an Ex-Colored Man*," *Studies in American Fiction* 21, no. 1 (Spring 1993): 83–96.
120. Johnson, Autobiography of an Ex-Colored Man, 110.
121. "General Race News," *Half-Century Magazine* 9, no. 3 (October 1920): 8, reprint (New York: Negro Universities Press, 1969).
122. "Get Behind the N. A. A. C. P.," *Half-Century Magazine* 7, no. 1 (July 1919): 3, New York Public Library.
123. Goldsby, *A Spectacular Secret*, 212.

CHAPTER TWO: AFFECTIVE NETWORKS

1. Zora Neale Hurston, "How It Feels to Be Colored Me," in *I Love Myself When I Am Laughing . . . and Then Again When I Am Looking Mean and Impressive: A Zora Neale Hurston Reader,* ed. Alice Walker (New York: Feminist Press, 1979), 155.
2. W. E. B. Du Bois, "On Being Ashamed of Oneself: An Essay on Race Pride," in *The Oxford W. E. B. Du Bois Reader,* ed. Eric J. Sundquist (Oxford: Oxford University Press, 1996), 73.
3. Ibid., 72.
4. Eve Kosofsky Sedgwick, "Queer Performativity: Henry James's *The Art of the Novel,*" *GLQ* 1, no. 1 (1993): 13.

5. Ibid., 12.
6. Shawn Michelle Smith, *Photography on the Color Line: W. E. B. Du Bois, Race, and Visual Culture* (Durham: Duke University Press, 2004), 2.
7. W. E. B. Du Bois, *The Souls of Black Folk,* ed. Henry Louis Gates Jr. and Terri Hume Oliver (New York: Norton, 1999), 11.
8. Bernard Williams, *Shame and Necessity* (Berkeley: University of California Press, 1993), 82.
9. Ralph Ellison, introduction, *Invisible Man* (New York: Vintage, 1990), xv. See Elizabeth Abel, *Signs of the Times: The Visual Politics of Jim Crow* (Berkeley: University of California Press, 2010); Anne Elizabeth Carroll, *Word, Image, and the New Negro: Representation and Identity in the Harlem Renaissance* (Bloomington: Indiana University Press, 2005); Caroline Goeser, *Picturing the New Negro: Harlem Renaissance Print Culture and Modern Black Identity* (Lawrence: University of Kansas Press, 2007); W. J. T. Mitchell, *Seeing Through Race* (Cambridge: Harvard University Press, 2012); Martha Jane Nadell, *Enter the New Negroes: Images of Race in American Culture* (Cambridge: Harvard University Press, 2004); Smith, *Photography on the Color-Line;* and Miriam Thaggert, *Images of Black Modernism: Verbal and Visual Strategies of the Harlem Renaissance* (Amherst: University of Massachusetts Press, 2010).
10. Carroll, *Word, Image, and the New Negro,* 12.
11. Thaggert, *Images of Black Modernism,* 2.
12. W. E. B. Du Bois, "Criteria of Negro Art," in *African American Literary Theory: A Reader,* ed. Winston Napier (New York: New York University Press, 2000), 22.
13. Jean-Paul Sartre, *Being and Nothingness: A Phenomenological Essay on Ontology,* trans. Hazel E. Barnes (New York: Washington Square, 1956), 302.
14. Richard Wright, "The Ethics of Living Jim Crow: An Autobiographical Sketch," in *Early Works,* ed. Arnold Rampersad (New York: Library of America, 1991), 233.
15. Frantz Fanon, *Black Skin, White Masks,* trans. Charles Lam Markmann (New York: Grove Press, 1967), 138.
16. Ibid., 138n24.
17. Nella Larsen, *Quicksand,* in *Quicksand and Passing,* ed. Deborah E. McDowell (New Brunswick: Rutgers University Press, 1998), 88.
18. See, for example, Geneviève Fabre and Michel Feith, "'Temples for Tomorrow': Introductory Essay," in *Temples for Tomorrow: Looking Back at the Harlem Renaissance,* ed. Fabre and Feith (Bloomington: Indiana University Press, 2001).
19. Arnold Rampersad, "Racial Doubt and Racial Shame in the Harlem Renaissance," in *Temples for Tomorrow,* 31–32.
20. Larsen, *Quicksand,* 83 and 89.
21. Ibid., 89.
22. Variants of the word "shame" occur at least twenty-two times in the novel.
23. Larsen, *Quicksand,* 83.

24. Ibid., 82–83.
25. Ibid., 83.
26. Ibid., 59.
27. Ibid., 88.
28. Ibid., 44.
29. Ibid., 1.
30. Ibid., 43.
31. Ibid., 44.
32. Ibid., 48.
33. Frank Luther Mott, *A History of American Magazines* 1885–1905, vol. IV (Cambridge: Harvard University Press, 1957), 521.
34. "Table of Contents," *Forum* 83, no. 1 (January 1930): iii.
35. Mott, *History of American Magazines,* 512.
36. "Are Outlines Good or Bad?," *Forum* 83, no. 4 (April 1930): xlv.
37. "Our Rostrum," *Forum* 83, no. 5 (May 1930): xxxvi–xxxvii.
38. John D. Leslie, letter to the editor, *Forum* 83, no. 3 (March 1930): xlv.
39. "Editor's Note [to John D. Leslie]," *Forum* 83, no. 3 (March 1930): xlv.
40. J. H. O'Neill, letter to the editor, *Forum* 83, no. 3 (March 1930): xlv.
41. Nella Larsen, "Sanctuary," *Forum* 83, no. 1 (January 1930): 15–18.
42. Marion Boyd, letter to the editor, *Forum* 83, no. 4 (April 1930): xli.
43. Sheila Kaye-Smith, "Mrs. Adis," *Century Magazine* 103, no. 3 (January 1922): 321–26, *HathiTrust Digital Library.*
44. "Editor's Note [to Marion Boyd]," *Forum* 83, no. 4 (April 1930): xli.
45. Nella Larsen, letter to the editor, *Forum* 83, no. 4 (April 1930): xli.
46. Larsen, "Sanctuary," 16.
47. Kaye-Smith, "Mrs. Adis," 326; and Larsen, "Sanctuary," 18.
48. Patrick S. Washburn, *The African American Newspaper: Voice of Freedom* (Evanston: Northwestern University Press, 2006), 83.
49. Ethan Michaeli, *The Defender: How the Legendary Black Newspaper Changed America: From the Age of the Pullman Porters to the Age of Obama* (Boston: Houghton Mifflin Harcourt, 2016), 37.
50. Juliet E. K. Walker, "The Promised Land: The Chicago *Defender* and the Black Press in Illinois, 1862–1970," in *The Black Press in the Middle West,* 1865–1985, ed. Henry Lewis Suggs (Westport, CT: Greenwood, 1996), 25.
51. Ibid.
52. Washburn, *African American Newspaper,* 83.
53. Michele Mitchell, *Righteous Propagation: African Americans and the Politics of Racial Destiny after Reconstruction* (Chapel Hill: University of North Carolina Press, 2004), 13.
54. Kevin K. Gaines, *Uplifting the Race: Black Leadership, Politics, and Culture in the Twentieth Century* (Chapel Hill: University of North Carolina Press, 1996);

James R. Grossman, *Land of Hope: Chicago, Black Southerners, and the Great Migration* (Chicago: University of Chicago Press, 1989); Evelyn Brooks Higginbotham, *Righteous Discontent: The Women's Movement in the Black Baptist Church, 1880–1920* (Cambridge, MA: Harvard University Press, 1993); Anne Meis Knupfer, *Toward a Tenderer Humanity and a Nobler Womanhood: African American Women's Clubs in Turn-of-the-Century Chicago* (New York: New York University Press, 1996); and Jacqueline Najuma Stewart, *Migrating to the Movies: Cinema and Black Urban Modernity* (Berkeley: University of California Press, 2005).

55. Higginbotham has argued that turn-of-the-century African Americans, particularly those of the middle class, constructed a "politics of respectability [that] emphasized reform of individual behavior and attitudes both as a goal in itself and as a strategy for reform of the entire structural system of American race relations." *Righteous Discontent*, 187.

56. See, for example, Rasmus Kleis Neilsen, "Participation through Letters to the Editor: Circulation, Considerations, and Genres in the Letters Institution," *Journalism* 11, no. 1 (2010): 21–35. The genre of the correspondence column also seems to be an object of study in English-language studies. See Monique Mémet, "Letters to the Editor: A Multifaceted Genre," *European Journal of English Studies* 9, no. 1 (April 2005): 75–90; or Anne Magnet and Didet Carnet, "Letters to the Editor: Still Vigorous after All These Years? A Presentation of the Discursive and Linguistic Features of the Genre," *English for Specific Purposes* 25 (2006): 173–99.

57. Teresa Zackodnik, "Indigenous and Black Geographies in Letters to the Editor," *Common-place: The Journal of Early American Life* 15, no. 2 (Winter 2015), http://www.common-place-archives.org/vol-15/no-02/zackodnik/; Barbara Green, "Complaints of Everyday Life: Feminist Periodical Culture and Correspondence Columns in *The Woman Worker, Women Folk* and *The Freewoman*," *Modernism/modernity* 19, no. 3 (September 2012): 461–85; and Janet Galligani Casey, "Farm Women, Letters to the Editor, and the Limits of Autobiography Theory," *Journal of Modern Literature* 28, no. 1 (Fall 2004): 89–106.

58. For scholarship that focuses on the readers, see for example, Elizabeth McHenry, *Forgotten Readers: Recovering the Lost History of African American Literary Societies* (Durham: Duke University Press, 2002); Shawn Anthony Christian, *The Harlem Renaissance and the Idea of a New Negro Reader* (Amherst: University of Massachusetts Press, 2016); and Eric Gardner, *Black Print Unbound: The Christian Recorder, African American Literature, and Periodical Culture* (Oxford: Oxford University Press, 2015), particularly chapter four. Notably, in chapter six, Gardner devotes substantive space to the letters in the *Christian Recorder*. The correspondence published in the periodical "highlighted the tensions between the paper's goals of building a united community and offering public spaces for individual and individualized African American voices" (167).

59. Green, "Complaints of Everyday Life," 462.

60. Robert Scholes and Clifford Wulfman, *Modernism in the Magazines: An Introduction* (New Haven: Yale University Press, 2010), 145.
61. Ibid.
62. Ibid., 146.
63. Zackodnik, "Indigenous and Black Geographies," n.p.
64. Casey, "Farm Women, Letters to the Editor," 89
65. Teresa Zackodnik, "Recirculation and Feminist Black Internationalism in Jessie Fauset's 'The Looking Glass' and Amy Jacques Garvey's 'Our Women and What They Think,'" *Modernism/modernity* 19, no. 3 (September 2012): 449.
66. Michael Warner, *Publics and Counterpublics* (New York: Zone Books, 2005), 95.
67. Casey, "Farm Women, Letters to the Editor," 89 and 90.
68. Green, "Complaints of Everyday Life," 464.
69. Mrs. James, "'Down-Homers' in Chicago," letter to the editor, *Chicago Defender,* July 30, 1927, *ProQuest Black Historical Newspapers.*
70. Williams, *Shame and Necessity,* 220.
71. "Overalls Make Parkway Look Like Root St., and Bunions Also Get Plenty of Air," editorial, *Chicago Defender,* July 23, 1927.
72. Ibid.
73. Lauren Berlant, *The Female Complaint: The Unfinished Business of Sentimentality in American Culture* (Durham: Duke University Press, 2008), vii.
74. Ibid., viii.
75. Ibid., 7.
76. Ibid.
77. Michel Foucault, *Discipline and Punish: The Birth of the Prison,* trans. Alan Sheridan (New York: Vintage, 1977), 202.
78. Starnes S. Peak Jr., "Drive Out the Clowns," letter to the editor, *Chicago Defender,* August 13, 1927, *ProQuest Black Historical Newspapers.*
79. O. B., "Race Behavior," letter to the editor, *Chicago Defender,* May 28, 1927, *ProQuest Black Historical Newspapers.*
80. Silvan Tomkins, "Shame-Humiliation and Contempt-Disgust," in *Shame and Its Sisters: A Silvan Tomkins Reader,* ed. Eve Kosofsky Sedgwick and Adam Frank (Durham, NC: Duke University Press, 1995), 156.
81. Jürgen Habermas, *The Structural Transformation of the Public Sphere: An Inquiry into a Category of Bourgeois Society,* trans. Thomas Burger and Frederick Lawrence (Cambridge: MIT Press, 1989), 43.
82. Warner, *Publics and Counterpublics,* 56.
83. Kathryn Bond Stockton, *Beautiful Bottom, Beautiful Shame: Where "Black" Meets "Queer"* (Durham: Duke University Press, 2006), 27.
84. Langston Hughes, "The Negro Artist and the Racial Mountain," in *African American Literary Theory: A Reader,* ed. Winston Napier (New York: New York University Press, 2000), 30.

85. Du Bois, "On Being Ashamed," 76.
86. Ibid., 73.
87. Du Bois, "The Browsing Reader," *Crisis* 35, no. 6 (June 1928): 202.
88. Ibid.
89. Ibid.
90. Ibid.
91. Claude McKay, "Correspondence with Claude McKay: *Home to Harlem,*" letter to W. E. B. Du Bois, June 18, 1928, *The Correspondence of W. E. B. Du Bois: Volume I, Selections* 1877–1934, ed. Herbert Aptheker (Amherst: University of Massachusetts Press, 1973), 374.
92. Hughes, "Negro Artist and the Racial Mountain," 28.
93. Ibid., 30.
94. Ibid.
95. Hazel V. Carby, *Reconstructing Womanhood: The Emergence of the Afro-American Woman Novelist* (Oxford: Oxford University Press, 1987), 174.
96. Ann duCille, *The Coupling Convention: Sex, Text, and Tradition in Black Women's Fiction* (Oxford: Oxford University Press, 1993), 87.
97. Thaggert, *Images of Black Modernism,* 71.
98. Ibid., 85.
99. Claudia Tate, "Desire and Death in *Quicksand,* by Nella Larsen," *American Literary History* 7, no. 2 (1995): 234–36.
100. Sianne Ngai, *Ugly Feelings* (Cambridge: Harvard University Press, 2005), 201.
101. Ibid., 207–208.
102. Larsen, *Quicksand,* 2.
103. Ibid., 29.
104. Ibid., 34, 39, 91, 94, 119, and 129.
105. Ibid., 7.
106. Ibid., 125.
107. Ibid., 119.
108. The representation of dialect in this scene is notably not aural due to the constitutive characteristic of the written text, but the use of apostrophes to indicate Sary's dialect renders it visual, as Daylanne English notes. See Daylanne K. English, *Unnatural Selections: Eugenics in American Modernism and the Harlem Renaissance* (Chapel Hill: University of North Carolina Press, 2004). The omission of certain letters is highlighted by the apostrophe, pointing to Sary's lack of education and status; dialect becomes a visible marker of difference in the novel. English contends that this scene upholds a split between Sary, "the southern rural African American woman," and Helga, "the modern, New Negro woman": "Sary functions almost as Helga's contemporary ancestor; she resides in a still agrarian, premigration African American history. In other words, Sary's incomplete diction—with the apostrophe as signifier—discloses her necessarily inadequate subjectivity in any authentically

modern setting" (134). However, the fact that earlier in the story, the novel displays a critique of Helga's patronizing uplift ambitions in the South—in addition to exposing the problems with romanticizing the folk—reveals Larsen's double-edged critique of both the folk and the elite.

109. Larsen, *Quicksand*, 75.
110. Ibid., 7.
111. Ibid., 83.
112. Williams, *Shame and Necessity*, 102.
113. Sartre, *Being and Nothingness*, 302.
114. Berlant, *Cruel Optimism* (Durham: Duke University Press, 2011), 1.

CHAPTER THREE: READERLY NETWORKS

1. Albert Murray to Ralph Ellison, April 19, 1956, *Trading Twelves: The Selected Letters of Ralph Ellison and Albert Murray*, ed. Albert Murray and John F. Callahan (New York: The Modern Library, 2000), 125.
2. William Faulkner, "A Letter to the North," *Life* 40, no. 10 (March 5, 1956): 52.
3. Ralph Ellison to Albert Murray, March 16, 1956, *Trading Twelves*, 117.
4. "Cover," *Ebony* 11, no. 11 (September 1956): 13. For more on *Ebony*'s depiction of Black women, see Adam Green, *Selling the Race: Culture, Community and Black Chicago, 1940–1955* (Chicago: University of Chicago Press, 2007), chap. 4; and Brenna Wynn Greer, *Represented: The Black Imagemakers Who Reimagined African American Citizenship* (Philadelphia: University of Pennsylvania Press, 2019), chap. 4.
5. "Backstage," *Ebony* 11, no. 11 (September 1956): 14.
6. William Faulkner to Harold Ober, June 23, 1956, *Selected Letters of William Faulkner*, ed. Joseph Blotner (New York: Random House, 1977), 401.
7. Julian Murphet and Stefan Solomon, ed., *William Faulkner in the Media Ecology* (Baton Rouge: Louisiana State University Press, 2015); and John T. Matthews, ed., *William Faulkner in Context* (New York: Cambridge University Press, 2015).
8. Jay Watson, Jaime Harker, and James G. Thomas Jr., ed., *Faulkner and Print Culture: Faulkner and Yoknapatawpha, 2015* (Jackson: University Press of Mississippi, 2017).
9. Jaime Harker and Jay Watson, "Introduction," in *Faulkner and Print Culture*, xvii.
10. William Faulkner, "If I Were a Negro," *Ebony* 11, no. 11 (September 1956): 70–73.
11. The *Negro Digest* was published from 1942 to 1951, by John H. Johnson, the founder of *Ebony* and *Jet*. It was modeled after *Reader's Digest* but aimed specifically at Black readers.
12. Faulkner, "A Letter to the North," 51–52.
13. Faulkner, "If I Were a Negro," 70. In response to Du Bois's challenge, Faulkner sent a telegram saying, "I DO NOT BELIEVE THERE IS A DEBATABLE POINT BETWEEN US. WE BOTH AGREE IN ADVANCE THAT THE POSITION YOU WILL TAKE IS RIGHT MORALLY LEGALLY AND ETHICALLY. IF IT IS NOT EVIDENT TO YOU THAT THE POSITION I TAKE IN ASKING FOR

MODERATION AND PATIENCE IS RIGHT PRACTICALLY THEN WE WILL BOTH WASTE OUR BREATH IN DEBATE." See William Faulkner, telegram to W. E. B. Du Bois published in the *New York Times,* April 17, 1956, *Selected Letters of William Faulkner,* 398.

14. James B. Meriwether and Michael Millgate, introductory notes to "Interview with Russell Howe," *Lion in the Garden: Interviews with William Faulkner,* 1926–1962, ed. James B. Meriwether and Michael Millgate (New York: Random House, 1968), 257.
15. William Faulkner, "Interview with Russell Howe," *Lion in the Garden,* 260–61.
16. Catherine Gunther Kodat, "Unsteady State: Faulkner and the Cold War," in *William Faulkner in Context,* ed. John T. Matthews (New York: Cambridge University Press, 2015), 161–62.
17. William Faulkner, "To the Editor of the *Reporter,*" April 19, 1956, *Essays, Speeches and Public Letters,* ed. James B. Meriwether (New York: The Modern Library, 2004), 225.
18. Meriwether and Millgate, introductory notes to "Interview with Russell Howe," 257.
19. Louis Daniel Brodsky, "Faulkner and the Racial Crisis, 1956," *Southern Review* 24, no. 4 (Autumn 1988): 796.
20. Ibid., 798.
21. Charles D. Peavy, *Go Slow Now: Faulkner and the Race Question* (Eugene: University of Oregon, 1971), 13.
22. Ibid., 69.
23. James Baldwin, "Faulkner and Desegregation," *Partisan Review* 23, no. 4 (Fall 1956): 570–71, Howard Gotlieb Archival Research Center at Boston University.
24. Ralph Ellison, "The World and the Jug," *Shadow and Act* (New York: Vintage International, 1995), 140.
25. George Hutchinson, "Tracking Faulkner in the Paths of Black Modernism," in *Faulkner and the Black Literatures of the Americas: Faulkner and Yoknapatawpha,* 2013 (Jackson: University Press of Mississippi, 2016), 65.
26. Ibid., 66 and 65.
27. W. E. B. Du Bois, *The Souls of Black Folk,* ed. Henry Louis Gates Jr. and Terri Hume Oliver (New York: Norton, 1999), 5.
28. Kodat, "Unsteady State," 163.
29. Lawrence H. Schwartz, *Creating Faulkner's Reputation: The Politics of Modern Literary Criticism* (Knoxville: University of Tennessee Press, 1988), 9.
30. Kodat, "Unsteady State," 157.
31. Murray to Ellison, April 19, 1956, *Trading Twelves,* 125.
32. Robert Coughlan, "Private World of William Faulkner," *Life* 35, no. 13 (September 28, 1953): 118–36, https://books.google.com/books?id=7UcEAAAAMBAJ&pg=PA118&source=gbs_toc_r&cad=2#v=onepage&q&f=false; and Robert Coughlan, "The Man Behind the Faulkner Myth," *Life* 35, no. 14 (October 5, 1953): 55–68, https://books.google.com/books?id=AUgEAAAAMBAJ&pg=PA55&source=gbs_toc_r&cad=2#v=onepage&q&f=false.

33. William Faulkner to Phillip E. Mullen, [October 7, 1953], *Selected Letters of William Faulkner,* 354.
34. Donald Wetzel, letter to the editor, *Life* 35, no. 17 (October 26, 1953): 19, https://books.google.com/books?id=p0YEAAAAMBAJ&pg=PA22&source=gbs_toc_r&cad=2#v=onepage&q&f=false.
35. John H. Snow, letter to the editor, *Life* 35, no. 16 (October 19, 1953): 15, https://books.google.com/books?id=HkgEAAAAMBAJ&pg=PA18&source=gbs_toc_r&cad=2#v=onepage&q&f=false.
36. Betty Ann Calvert, letter to the editor, *Life* 35, no. 17 (October 26, 1953): 16, https://books.google.com/books?id=p0YEAAAAMBAJ&pg=PA22&source=gbs_toc_r&cad=2#v=onepage&q&f=false.
37. William Faulkner, "On Privacy (The American Dream: What Happened to It?)," in *Essay, Speeches and Public Letters,* 72.
38. Richard Gray, "On Privacy: William Faulkner and the Human Subject," in *Faulkner and Ideology: Faulkner and Yoknapatawpha,* 1992, ed. Donald M. Kartiganer and Ann J. Abadie (Jackson: University of Mississippi Press, 1995), 55.
39. Faulkner, "On Privacy," 62.
40. Kodat, "Unsteady State," 158.
41. Robert Jackson, "Skin and Structure: William Faulkner's Media Surfaces," in *William Faulkner in the Media Ecology,* ed. Julian Murphet and Stefan Solomon (Baton Rouge: Louisiana State University Press, 2015), 165.
42. Ibid., 155.
43. Maren Stange, "'Photographs Taken in Everyday Life': *Ebony*'s Photojournalistic Discourse," in *The Black Press: New Literary and Historical Essays,* ed. Todd Vogel (New Brunswick: Rutgers University Press, 2001), 207.
44. Greer, *Represented,* 150.
45. Harker and Watson, "Introduction," xii.
46. For *Life*'s circulation figures, see Loudon Wainwright, *The Great American Magazine: An Inside History of* Life (New York: Alfred A. Knopf, 1986), 179. For *Ebony*'s figures, see Megan E. Williams, "'Meet the Real Lena Horne': Representations of Lena Horne in *Ebony* Magazine, 1945–1949," *Journal of American Studies* 43, no. 1 (2009): 120.
47. Faulkner, "A Letter to the North," 51.
48. Ibid., 52.
49. Ibid.
50. Borden Deal, letter to the editor, *Life* 40, no. 13 (March 26, 1956): 19, https://books.google.com/books?id=wFQEAAAAMBAJ&pg=PA20&source=gbs_toc_r&cad=2#v=onepage&q&f=false.
51. M. A. Harris, letter to the editor, *Life* 40, no. 13 (March 26, 1956): 19, https://books.google.com/books?id=wFQEAAAAMBAJ&pg=PA20&source=gbs_toc_r&cad=2#v=onepage&q&f=false.

52. Lewis Herring, letter to the editor, *Life* 40, no. 13 (March 26, 1956): 19, https://books.google.com/books?id=wFQEAAAAMBAJ&pg=PA20&source=gbs_toc_r&cad=2#v=onepage&q&f=false; and Leslie H. Engram, *Life* 40, no. 13 (March 26, 1956): 19, https://books.google.com/books?id=wFQEAAAAMBAJ&pg=PA20&source=gbs_toc_r&cad=2#v=onepage&q&f=false.
53. Murray to Ellison, April 19, 1956, *Trading Twelves*, 125.
54. William Faulkner, letter to the editor, *Life* 40, no. 13 (March 26, 1956): 19, https://books.google.com/books?id=wFQEAAAAMBAJ&pg=PA20&source=gbs_toc_r&cad=2#v=onepage&q&f=false.
55. "No Sign of Peace for Autherine," *Life* 40, no. 11 (March 12, 1956): 40, https://books.google.com/books?id=-1YEAAAAMBAJ&pg=PA40&source=gbs_toc_r&cad=2#v=onepage&q&f=false.
56. "Go Slow Now," *Life* 40, no. 11 (March 12, 1956): 37, https://books.google.com/books?id=-1YEAAAAMBAJ&pg=PA37&source=gbs_toc_r&cad=2#v=onepage&q&f=false.
57. Faulkner, "If I Were a Negro," 72.
58. Peavy, *Go Slow Now*, 92.
59. William Faulkner, *Faulkner in the University*, ed. Frederick L. Gwynn and Joseph L. Blotner (Charlottesville: University Press of Virginia, 1995), 211.
60. Faulkner, "If I Were a Negro," 71.
61. William Faulkner, "Address upon Receiving the Nobel Prize for Literature," *Essays, Speeches and Public Letters*, 120.
62. Faulkner, "If I Were a Negro," 72.
63. William Faulkner, *Absalom, Absalom!* (New York: Vintage International, 1990), 155.
64. Michael North, *The Dialect of Modernism: Race, Language, and Twentieth-Century Literature* (Oxford: Oxford University Press, 1994), 81.
65. Donald Kartiganer, "'So I, Who Had Never Had a War . . .': William Faulkner, War, and the Modern Imagination," *Modern Fiction Studies* 44.3 (1998): 632.
66. Thadious M. Davis, *Faulkner's "Negro": Art and the Southern Context* (Baton Rouge: Louisiana State University Press, 1983), 64.
67. William Faulkner to Allan Morrison, June 23, 1956, *Selected Letters of William Faulkner*, 400–401.
68. "Letters to the Editor," *Ebony* 12, no. 1 (November 1956): 6–10.
69. "Letters to the Editor," *Ebony* 12, no. 2 (December 1956): 10.
70. Donald C. Wilson, letter to the editor, *Ebony* 12, no. 1 (November 1956): 6.
71. Wanda Pittman, letter to the editor, *Ebony* 12, no. 1 (November 1956): 8.
72. Henry Louis Gates Jr., *The Signifying Monkey: A Theory of African-American Literary Criticism* (Oxford: Oxford University Press, 1988), xxiv.
73. Wanda Pittman, letter to the editor, *Ebony* 12, no. 1 (November 1956): 8.
74. Ibid.

75. Mrs. Corinne Poole Tane, letter to the editor, *Ebony* 12, no. 1 (November 1956): 8.
76. Ibid., 10.
77. Janet Galligani Casey, "Farm Women, Letters to the Editor, and the Limits of Autobiography Theory," *Journal of Modern Literature* 28, no. 1 (Fall 2004): 91.
78. Jerome J. McGann, *The Textual Condition* (Princeton: Princeton University Press, 1991), 124.
79. Ibid.
80. Ralph Ellison, "Twentieth-Century Fiction and the Black Mask of Humanity," in *Shadow and Act* (New York: Vintage International, 1995), 43–44.
81. Lynne Warren, "'Women in Conference': Reading the Correspondence Columns in *Woman* 1890–1910," in *Nineteenth-Century Media and the Construction of Identities*, ed. Laurel Brake, Bill Bell, and David Finkelstein (Basingstoke: Palgrave, 2000), 122.
82. Ibid., 123.
83. James Wald, "Periodicals and Periodicity," in *A Companion to the History of the Book*, ed. Simon Eliot and Jonathan Rose (Malden, MA: Blackwell Publishing, 2007), 430.
84. Bridget Griffen-Foley, "From *Tit-Bits* to *Big Brother*: A Century of Audience Participation in the Media," *Media, Culture & Society* 26, no. 4 (2004): 533.
85. Ibid., 544.
86. Warren, "'Women in Conference,'" 133–34.
87. Ibid., 123.
88. Noliwe M. Rooks, *Ladies' Pages: African American Women's Magazines and the Culture that Made Them* (New Brunswick: Rutgers University Press, 2004), 134.
89. "How to Handle Beautiful Women," *Ebony* 11, no. 11 (September 1956): 74–81. The article asks, "How do you handle a woman who has everything—looks, charm, sex appeal—and knows it?" Accompanied by a photo spread of these beautiful women—many of whom are in swimwear—the article provides the tips of "experts, who handle thousands of stunning women every year" (74). Preceding Faulkner's essay is a "photo-editorial" titled "Nobody Loves Them," about the need to accept Black rural Southern migrants in the urban North (68–69). Rooks's claim, in other words, is somewhat overstated; the magazine was a site of political discussions, along with positive depictions of African Americans. In fact, these two threads cannot be untangled from one another.
90. Rooks, *Ladies' Pages*, 134.
91. William Faulkner, *The Sound and the Fury* (New York: W. W. Norton & Company, 1994).
92. Faulkner, "On Privacy," 72.
93. Mrs. Clementine B. Spencer, letter to the editor, *Ebony* 12, no. 1 (November 1956): 8.
94. Faulkner, "If I Were a Negro," 72.
95. *Ebony* 11, no. 12 (October 1956). Faulkner wrote about Emmett Till in his essay "On Fear: Deep South in Labor: Mississippi," published in *Harper's* in June 1956.
96. Frances Stonor Saunders, *The Cultural Cold War: The CIA and the World of Arts and Letters* (New York: The New Press, 1999), 160.

97. *Partisan Review* 23, no. 4 (Fall 1956), Howard Gotlieb Archival Research Center at Boston University.
98. Baldwin, "Faulkner and Desegregation," 568.
99. Ibid.
100. Tyler Williams, "How Faulkner Means Everything He Says: An Essay on James Baldwin's Politics of Intentionality," *CR: The New Centennial Review* 15, no. 3 (Winter 2015): 50–51.
101. *Partisan Review* 24, no. 3 (Summer 1957), Howard Gotlieb Archival Research Center at Boston University and *Partisan Review* 22, no. 3 (Summer 1955), Howard Gotlieb Archival Research Center at Boston University.
102. *Partisan Review* 18, no. 5 (September–October 1951), Howard Gotlieb Archival Research Center at Boston University.
103. "Contributors," *Partisan Review* 23, no. 4 (Fall 1956): 434, Howard Gotlieb Archival Research Center at Boston University.
104. Calvin Israel, "The Last Gentleman," *Partisan Review* 35, no. 2 (Spring 1968): 315–19, Howard Gotlieb Archival Research Center at Boston University.
105. Ibid., 318.
106. Ibid., 319.
107. Ellison, "Twentieth-Century Fiction," 24.

CHAPTER FOUR: GLOBAL NETWORKS

1. The media attention included a *New York Times* article and an article by the editors of the Norton edition in the *Chronicle of Higher Education*. See Felicia R. Lee, "Scholars Say Chronicler of Black Life Passed for White," *New York Times*, December 26, 2010; and also Rudolph P. Byrd and Henry Louis Gates, Jr., "Jean Toomer's Conflicted Racial Identity," *Chronicle of Higher Education*, February 6, 2011. The more recent Penguin Classics edition, published in 2019, makes a point of stating that it "restores [Toomer's] note of thanks to the magazines in which his pieces first appeared." See George Hutchinson, "A Note on the Text," *Cane*, by Jean Toomer (New York: Penguin Books, 2019), xxxv.
2. Jean Toomer Papers, Box 25, Folder 607, James Weldon Johnson Collection, Beinecke Rare Book and Manuscript Library, Yale University.
3. See, for example, Rudolph P. Byrd and Henry Louis Gates Jr., introduction, *Cane*, by Jean Toomer, 2nd edition (New York: W. W. Norton, 2011), xix–lxx. There are exceptions, however. Mark Whalan writes, "The range of little magazines and other outlets to which he sent pieces of *Cane* . . . is evidence of the scope of the audience that Toomer felt he could address." See Mark Whalan, *Race, Manhood, and Modernism in America: The Short Story Cycles of Sherwood Anderson and Jean Toomer* (Knoxville: University of Tennessee Press, 2007), 219. John Young uses a materialist-semiotic approach, grounded in Bruno Latour's actor-network theory, to discuss *Cane*'s pre-book publication life in the *Double Dealer* magazine. See John K. Young, "The Roots of

Cane: Jean Toomer in *The Double Dealer* and Modernist Networks," in *Race, Ethnicity and Publishing in America,* ed. Cécile Cottenet (London: Palgrave Macmillan, 2014), 171–93. Barbara Foley also discusses Toomer's persistence in publishing his work in the *Liberator,* "the premier postwar radical cultural journal," as evidence for his interest in leftist politics. See Barbara Foley, *Jean Toomer: Race, Repression, and Revolution* (Urbana: University of Illinois Press, 2014), 36. For a different approach, see Jennifer J. Sorensen, *Modernist Experiments in Genre, Media, and Transatlantic Print Culture* (Oxford: Routledge, 2017). In chapter four, Sorensen focuses not on Toomer's engagement with magazines but on his use of the bibliographic codes of *Cane* in relation to its marketing. She reads "Toomer's aesthetic explorations in *Cane* as experiments with the particular format of the material printed book" (107). She compellingly argues for "the centrality of the printed book to Toomer's project" (130), but my claim is that the printed book can only fully be understood by mapping out the magazine network in which it existed and from which it sprang.

4. There are numerous scholarly works that take part in and examine the global turn in modernist studies (and literary studies more generally). See, for example, Mark Wollaeger, ed., with Matt Eatough, *The Oxford Handbook of Global Modernisms* (Oxford: Oxford University Press, 2012); Laura Doyle and Laura Winkiel, ed., *Geomodernisms: Race, Modernism, Modernity* (Bloomington: Indiana University Press, 2005); and Susan Stanford Friedman, *Planetary Modernisms: Provocations on Modernity Across Time* (New York: Columbia University Press, 2015). For a focus on periodicals, see, in particular, Eric Bulson, *Little Magazine, World Form* (New York: Columbia University Press, 2017).
5. It is included in the more recent Penguin Classics edition. See the opening to Jean Toomer, *Cane* (New York: Penguin Books, 2019).
6. Jean Toomer, *Cane,* 2nd edition (New York: W. W. Norton, 2011), 63.
7. Caroline Levine, *Forms: Whole, Rhythm, Hierarchy, Network* (Princeton: Princeton University Press, 2015), 122.
8. Robert Scholes and Clifford Wulfman, *Modernism in the Magazines: An Introduction* (New Haven: Yale University Press, 2010), 48.
9. James Wald, "Periodicals and Periodicity," in *A Companion to the History of the Book,* ed. Simon Eliot and Jonathan Rose (Malden, MA: Blackwell Publishing, 2007), 422.
10. M. M. Bakhtin, "Forms of Time and of the Chronotope in the Novel: Notes Toward a Historical Poetics," in *The Dialogic Imagination: Four Essays,* ed. Michael Holquist, trans. Caryl Emerson and Michael Holquist (Austin: University of Texas Press, 1981), 84.
11. Cary Nelson, *Repression and Recovery: Modern American Poetry and the Politics of Cultural Memory,* 1910–1945 (Madison: University of Wisconsin Press, 1991), 219.
12. Rachel Farebrother, *The Collage Aesthetic in the Harlem Renaissance* (Farnham, UK: Ashgate, 2009), 83.
13. Sean Latham and Robert Scholes, "The Rise of Periodical Studies," *PMLA* 121, no. 2 (2006): 529.

14. Wesley Beal, *Networks of Modernism: Reorganizing American Narrative* (Iowa City: Iowa University Press, 2015), 55, 59.
15. Sorensen, *Modernist Experiments,* chap. three.
16. Young, "The Roots of *Cane,*" 177.
17. Charles Scruggs and Lee VanDemarr, *Jean Toomer and the Terrors of American History* (Philadelphia: University of Pennsylvania Press, 1998), 109.
18. See Karen Jackson Ford, who argues that *Cane* ends with Kabnis's failure and with "the failure of poetry"; in essence, "the loss of poetry is *Cane*'s formal equivalent to the loss of an idealized time and culture." Karen Jackson Ford, *Split-Gut Song: Jean Toomer and the Poetics of Modernity* (Tuscaloosa: University of Alabama Press, 2005), 143. Robert Jones states that *Cane* "ends on a note of alienation rather than of union, which implies the narrator's loss of empathetic union with African-American consciousness." See Robert B. Jones, *Jean Toomer and the Prison-House of Thought: A Phenomenology of Spirit* (Amherst: University of Massachusetts Press, 1993), 57. Toomer himself writes, "The folk-spirit was walking in to die on the modern desert. That spirit was so beautiful. Its death was so tragic. Just this seemed to sum life for me. And this was the feeling I put into *Cane. Cane* was a swan-song. It was a song of an end." See Jean Toomer, "The *Cane* Years," *The Wayward and the Seeking: A Collection of Writings by Jean Toomer,* ed. Darwin T. Turner (Washington, DC: Howard University Press, 1980), 123.
19. Bulson, *Little Magazine, World Form,* 1.
20. Frederick Hoffman, Charles Allen, and Carolyn F. Ulrich, *The Little Magazine: A History and a Bibliography* (Princeton: Princeton University Press, 1946), 4.
21. Ibid., 2.
22. For the *Double Dealer* figures, see Craig Monk, "Negotiating the Margins of the American South: *The Double Dealer* (1921–9)," in *The Oxford Critical and Cultural History of Modernist Magazines, Volume II, North America* 1894–1960, ed. Peter Brooker and Andrew Thacker (Oxford: Oxford University Press, 2012), 525. For the *Little Review,* see Alan Golding, "*The Little Review* (1914–29)," in *Oxford Critical and Cultural History,* 70. The circulation figures for *Broom* are taken from Peter Nicholls, "Destinations: *Broom* (1921–4) and *Secession* (1922–4)," in *Oxford Critical and Cultural History,* 643.
23. Farebrother, "*The Crisis* (1910–34)," in *Oxford Critical and Cultural History,* 104.
24. "New Orleans and the *Double Dealer,*" *Double Dealer* 1, no. 4 (1921): 126, reprint (New York: Kraus Reprint Corporation, 1966).
25. "Southern Letters," *Double Dealer* 1, no. 6 (1921): 214, reprint (New York: Kraus Reprint Corporation, 1966).
26. Ibid.
27. John McClure to Jean Toomer, April 14, 1922, Jean Toomer Papers, Box 2, Folder 46, James Weldon Johnson Collection, Beinecke Rare Book and Manuscript Library, Yale University.
28. "Southern Letters," 214; and Toomer, "*Cane* Years," 123.

29. John McClure, "Jean Toomer," review of *Cane* by Toomer, *Double Dealer* 6, no. 32 (1924): 27, reprint (New York: Kraus Reprint Corporation, 1966).
30. Tom Lutz, *Cosmopolitan Vistas: American Regionalism and Literary Value* (Ithaca: Cornell University Press, 2004), 15.
31. "A National Magazine from the South," *Double Dealer* 2, no. 7 (1921): 2, reprint (New York: Kraus Reprint Corporation, 1966).
32. *Double Dealer* 4, no. 21 (1922).
33. Monk, "Negotiating the Margins," 525–26.
34. Pierre Loving, "Towards Walt Whitman," *Double Dealer* 4, no. 21 (1922): 139. Toomer himself read Whitman and would eventually write an unpublished long poem called *The Blue Meridian* (1936) in the style of *Song of Myself.* In Toomer's "Box Seat," a short narrative piece in *Cane,* Dan Moore thinks about a man born into slavery who lives long enough to see "the first Oldsmobile." He reflects on what this former slave must have witnessed: "He saw Grant and Lincoln. He saw Walt—old man, did you see Walt Whitman? Did you see Walt Whitman! Strange force that drew me to him. And I went up to see" (Toomer, *Cane,* 65). For Dan, Whitman is associated with figures of the Emancipation, suggesting that Dan is particularly interested in Whitman as a force for social change, which is also where Toomer's interest lies.
35. John N. Duvall, "Regionalism in American Modernism," in *The Cambridge Companion to American Modernism,* ed. Walter Kalaidjian (Cambridge: Cambridge University Press, 2005), 242.
36. John McClure to Jean Toomer, July 5, 1922, Jean Toomer Papers, Box 2, Folder 46, James Weldon Johnson Collection, Beinecke Rare Book and Manuscript Library, Yale University.
37. Scholes and Wulfman, *Modernism in the Magazines,* 43.
38. Golding, "*The Little Review* (1914–29)," 61.
39. *Little Review* 9, no. 1 (1922), *Modernist Journals Project.*
40. Toomer, *Cane,* 41 and 19.
41. Golding, "*The Little Review* (1914–29)," 62.
42. Wai Chee Dimock, *Through Other Continents: American Literature Across Deep Time* (Princeton: Princeton University Press, 2006), 3–4.
43. Jean Toomer, "Karintha," *Broom: An International Magazine for the Arts* 5, no. 3 (1923): 83–85, reprint (New York: Kraus Reprint, 1967).
44. Ibid., 83.
45. Bulson, *Little Magazine, World Form,* 155.
46. McClure to Toomer, July 5, 1922.
47. See Matthew Josephson, "Great American Novels," review of *The Great American Novel* by William Carlos Williams and *Cane* by Toomer, *Broom* 5, no. 3 (October 1923): 178–80, *Blue Mountain Project* and William Carlos Williams, *The Great American Novel* (Copenhagen: Green Integer, 2003), 31.

48. For a discussion of the affiliations and disaffiliations between Williams and Toomer, see Michael North, *The Dialect of Modernism: Race, Language, and Twentieth-Century Literature* (New York and Oxford: Oxford University Press, 1994), 147–74.
49. J. T. [Jean Toomer], review of *Faint Perfume* by Zona Gale, *Broom* 5, no. 3 (October 1923): 180–81, *Blue Mountain Project.*
50. Jean Toomer, "Song of the Son," *Crisis: A Record of the Darker Races* 23, no. 6 (1922): 261, *Modernist Journals Project.*
51. Langston Hughes, "The Great Surgeon," *Crisis: A Record of the Darker Races* 25, no. 2 (December 1922): 58–60, *Modernist Journals Project.*
52. Anne Elizabeth Carroll and Russ Castronovo have written about the inextricable relationship between politics and art in the *Crisis,* but their readings deal with the workings of the magazine and do not focus on reading the individual work of art itself through the lens of periodical studies. See Anne Elizabeth Carroll, *Word, Image, and the New Negro: Representation and Identity in the Harlem Renaissance* (Bloomington: Indiana University Press, 2005); and Russ Castronovo, "Beauty along the Color Line: Lynching, Aesthetics, and the *Crisis,*" *PMLA* 121, no. 5 (2006): 1443–59. Placing the art—in this case, the poem—back into the original context provides another way of reading it.
53. For more on the *Crisis*'s role during the Harlem Renaissance, see, for example, George Hutchinson, *The Harlem Renaissance in Black and White* (Cambridge: Belknap Press of Harvard University Press, 1995), 137–69. See also Carroll, *Word, Image, and the New Negro,* especially 20–54 and 89–121.
54. Robert W. Bagnall, "Lex Talionis," *Crisis: A Record of the Darker Races* 23, no. 6 (1922): 254–59, *Modernist Journals Project.*
55. Carroll, *Word, Image, and the New Negro,* 27–28.
56. For more on this short story, see Eurie Dahn, "Forgotten Manuscripts: 'Lex Talionis: A Story' By Robert W. Bagnall," *African American Review* 51, no. 4 (Winter 2018): 279–87.
57. Jessie Fauset, "Benjamin Brawley's 'Social History of the American Negro,'" *Crisis: A Record of the Darker Races* 23, no. 6 (1922): 260, *Modernist Journals Project.*
58. Toomer, *Cane,* 90.
59. Barbara Foley, *Jean Toomer: Race, Repression, and Revolution* (Urbana: University of Illinois Press, 2014), 61.
60. Ibid., 160.
61. Walter White, "The Work of a Mob," *Crisis: A Record of the Darker Races* 16, no. 5 (1918): 222, *Modernist Journals Project.*
62. In a September 5, 1923, letter to his publisher, Horace Liveright, about the marketing of his book, Toomer wrote, "My racial composition and my position in the world are realities which I alone may determine . . . Feature Negro if you wish, but do not expect me to feature it in advertisements for you. For myself, I have sufficiently featured Negro in *Cane.* Whatever statements I give will inevitably come from a

synthetic human and art point of view; not from a racial one." See Jean Toomer, "To Horace Liveright, September 5, 1923," *The Letters of Jean Toomer, 1919–1924*, ed. Mark Whalan (Knoxville: University of Tennessee Press, 2006), 171.

63. Jessie Fauset to Jean Toomer, February 17, 1922, Jean Toomer Papers, Box 1, Folder 37, James Weldon Johnson Collection, Beinecke Rare Book and Manuscript Library, Yale University.
64. Jean Toomer, "Banking Coal," *Crisis: A Record of the Darker Races* 24, no. 2 (1922): 65, *Modernist Journals Project*.
65. Scholes and Wulfman, *Modernism in the Magazines*, 45.
66. Carroll, *Word, Image, and the New Negro*, 116.
67. For another discussion of the history of the word "magazine," see Scholes and Wulfman, *Modernism in the Magazines*, 45–46.
68. Dimock, *Through Other Continents*, 4.
69. Toomer, *Cane*, 14.
70. Ibid.
71. Ibid., 20, 14.
72. Ibid., 19.
73. Peter Brooker and Andrew Thacker, "General Introduction," in *The Oxford Critical and Cultural History of Modernist Magazines, Volume I, Britain and Ireland 1880–1955*, ed. Peter Brooker and Andrew Thacker (Oxford: Oxford University Press, 2009), 17.
74. In *Jean Toomer: Race, Repression, and Revolution*, Foley provides further insight into Toomer's radical politics in her analysis of his publication record in the *Liberator* and *New York Call* (although no pieces from the *Call* were published in *Cane*).
75. Max Eastman, editorial, *Liberator* 1, no. 1 (March 1918): 3, the Tamiment Library and Robert F. Wagner Labor Archives at the New York University Library.
76. Ibid.
77. Toomer, *Cane*, 29.
78. In his introduction to the recent Penguin Classics edition of Toomer's book, Hutchinson emphasizes that "[t]he 'cane' of the book is that of sorghum, a plant brought from Africa during the slave trade. Throughout the southeastern United States, the cane stalks of sorghum were crushed for their sap, which was then boiled to make molasses, the chief sweetener in southern homes. Sorghum molasses, moreover, was a key ingredient for moonshine whiskey in the early twentieth century. Yet in the 1920s and 1930s it was being replaced by cane sugar as new roads integrated the southern countryside into larger national and international economic networks, networks that helped carry moonshine north via 'bootleggers in silken shirts,' to quote from the opening of the second section of Toomer's book." See George Hutchinson, "Introduction," *Cane*, by Jean Toomer (New York: Penguin Books, 2019), xv–xvi. Some commenters have seen the "cane" of the book to be sugar cane, and the poem, "Conversion," with its reference to rum, as an

indication that *Cane*'s title is capacious enough to refer both to sorghum cane and sugar cane.

79. Paul Gilroy, *The Black Atlantic: Modernity and Double Consciousness* (Cambridge: Harvard University Press, 1993), 4.
80. Jean Toomer, "The Gurdjieff Experience," in *The Wayward and the Seeking: A Collection of Writings by Jean Toomer,* ed. Darwin T. Turner (Washington, DC: Howard University Press, 1980), 132.
81. Ibid.
82. Kenneth W. Warren, *What Was African American Literature?* (Cambridge: Harvard University Press, 2011), 42.
83. Alain Locke, ed., *The New Negro* (New York: Atheneum, 1992), vii.
84. Langston Hughes, "The Negro Artist and the Racial Mountain," in *African American Literary Theory: A Reader,* ed. Winston Napier (New York: New York University Press, 2000), 30.
85. Langston Hughes, "The Negro Speaks of Rivers," *The New Negro,* ed. Alain Locke (New York: Atheneum, 1992), 141.
86. Ibid., lines 10–11, 4, and 8.
87. Locke, ed., *The New Negro,* vii.
88. Countée Cullen, "Heritage," *Survey Graphic* 6, no. 6 (March 1925): 674, reprint (Baltimore: Black Classic Press, 1980). Larsen uses the version from Cullen's poetry collection *Color;* the ninth line of the poem in that version is "Spicy grove, cinnamon tree," not "Spicy grove and banyan tree," as it is in *Survey Graphic.* See the epigraph in Nella Larsen, *Passing,* in *Quicksand and Passing,* ed. Deborah E. McDowell (New Brunswick: Rutgers University Press, 1998), 140. For a discussion of the difference between the *Color* version of the poem and the versions used by Locke in *Survey Graphic* and *The New Negro,* see James Kelley, "Blossoming in Strange New Forms: Male Homosexuality and the Harlem Renaissance," *Soundings: An Interdisciplinary Journal* 80, no. 4 (Winter 1997): 507–13. Kelley notes that Locke, as editor of the anthology, was most likely responsible for the differences.
89. Cullen, "Heritage," 675.
90. Ibid.
91. Toomer, *Cane,* 14.
92. Ibid., 115.
93. Toomer, "*Cane* Years," 123.
94. Toomer, *Cane,* 5.
95. Ibid., 6, 26, 83, 90, and 110.
96. Scruggs and VanDemarr, *Jean Toomer and the Terrors of American History,* 203.
97. Carroll, *Word, Image, and the New Negro,* 27.
98. Jean Toomer, "The Americans," in *A Jean Toomer Reader: Selected Unpublished Writings,* ed. Fredrik L. Rusch (New York: Oxford University Press, 1993), 107.

CONCLUSION: MEDIA NETWORKS AND ACTIVISM

1. See, for example, Campbell Robertson's coverage of the memorial in the *New York Times*. Campbell Robertson, "A Lynching Memorial Is Opening. The Country Has Never Seen Anything Like It," *New York Times*, April 25, 2018. Just a few months later, in December, the Senate unanimously passed the Justice for Victims of Lynching Act of 2018, a bill that, like the Dyer Anti-Lynching Bill, proposes making lynching a federal crime.
2. Barbara Foley, *Jean Toomer: Race, Repression, and Revolution* (Urbana: University of Illinois Press, 2014), 61–62.
3. Brian Lyman, "'There Will Be Lynchings': How the *Advertiser* Failed Victims of Racial Terror," *Montgomery Advertiser*, April 20, 2018 (updated April 27, 2018); and Brian Lyman, "Our Shame: The Sins of Our Past Laid Bare for All to See," *Montgomery Advertiser*, April 26, 2018.
4. Claudia Grisales, "'It's About Time': House Approves Historic Bill Making Lynching a Federal Crime," National Public Radio, February 26, 2020.
5. Jacqueline Goldsby, *A Spectacular Secret: Lynching in American Life and Literature* (Chicago: University of Chicago Press, 2006), 15.
6. Kenneth W. Warren, *What Was African American Literature?* (Cambridge: Harvard University Press, 2011), 9.
7. Ibid., 22.
8. Ida B. Wells (Wells-Barnett), *Southern Horrors: Lynch Law in All Its Phases*, in *Southern Horrors and Other Writings: The Anti-Lynching Campaign of Ida B. Wells, 1892–1900*, ed. Jacqueline Jones Royster (Boston: Bedford Books, 1997), 70.
9. Lyman, "Our Shame," *Montgomery Advertiser*.
10. Bridget Griffen-Foley, "From *Tit-Bits* to *Big Brother*: A Century of Audience Participation in the Media," *Media, Culture & Society* 26, no. 4 (2004): 533.
11. Keeanga-Yamahtta Taylor, *From #BlackLivesMatter to Black Liberation* (Chicago: Haymarket Books, 2016), 151–52.
12. Alicia Garza, "A Herstory of the #BlackLivesMatter Movement," *Feminist Wire*, October 7, 2014, https://thefeministwire.com/2014/10/blacklivesmatter-2/.
13. Taylor, *From #BlackLivesMatter to Black Liberation*, 105.
14. Ibid., 106.
15. Patrick Jagoda, *Network Aesthetics* (Chicago: University of Chicago Press, 2016), 81.
16. Ibid.
17. Ibid.
18. Ibid.
19. Angela Y. Davis, *Freedom Is a Constant Struggle: Ferguson, Palestine, and the Foundations of a Movement*, ed. Frank Barat (Chicago: Haymarket Books, 2016), 17–18.
20. Patrisse Khan-Cullors and asha bandele, *When They Call You a Terrorist: A Black Lives Matter Memoir* (New York: St. Martin's Press, 2017), 205.

21. "Herstory," *Black Lives Matter Global Network,* https://blacklivesmatter.com/herstory/.
22. See "About," *Black Lives Matter Global Network,* https://blacklivesmatter.com/about/. Like the *Half-Century,* the website integrates consumerism with a concern with Black representation, as it includes the ability to buy merchandise with the website's logo.
23. Davis, *Freedom Is a Constant Struggle,* 85.
24. Taylor points out the problems with this kind of activism: "#BLM has reinvigorated the Occupy method of protest, which believes decentralized and 'leaderless' actions are more democratic, essentially allowing its followers to act on what they want to do without the restraint of others weighing in. But at a time when many people are trying to find an entry point into anti-police activism and desire to be involved, this particular method of organizing can be difficult to penetrate. In some ways, this decentralized organizing can actually narrow opportunities for the democratic involvement of many in favor of the tightly knit workings of those already in the know." Taylor, *From #BlackLivesMatter to Black Liberation,* 176.
25. Taylor, *From #BlackLivesMatter to Black Liberation,* 168.
26. Ralph Ellison, *Invisible Man* (New York: Vintage, 1990), 581.
27. For an account of this instance of hashtag activism, see Tanzina Vega, "Shooting Spurs Hashtag Effort on Stereotypes," *New York Times,* August 12, 2014.
28. Wells, *Southern Horrors,* 71.
29. Feminista Jones, "Is Twitter the Underground Railroad of Activism?," *Salon.com,* July 17, 2013, https://www.salon.com/2013/07/17/how_twitter_fuels_black_activism/.
30. Ibid.
31. Davis, *Freedom Is a Constant Struggle,* 137.
32. Some of these emerging accounts include Oliver Laughland and Lauren Zanolli, "Why Is Coronavirus Taking Such a Deadly Toll on Black Americans?," *Guardian*, April 25, 2020; and Kenya Evelyn, "'It's a Racial Justice Issue': Black Americans Are Dying in Greater Numbers from Covid-19," *Guardian*, April 8, 2020. See also John Eligon, Audra D. S. Burch, Dionne Searcey, and Richard A. Oppel Jr., "Black Americans Face Alarming Rates of Coronavirus Infections in Some States," *New York Times*, April 7, 2020.
33. Ibram X. Kendi, "Stop Blaming Black People for Dying of the Coronavirus," *Atlantic*, April 14, 2020.
34. Ida B. Wells, *Mob Rule in New Orleans,* in *Southern Horrors and Other Writings: The Anti-Lynching Campaign of Ida B. Wells,* 1892–1900, ed. Jacqueline Jones Royster (Boston: Bedford Books, 1997), 206.
35. Taylor, *From #BlackLivesMatter to Black Liberation,* 214
36. Ibid., 215.
37. Davis, *Freedom Is a Constant Struggle,* 49.

INDEX

Page references in *italics* refer to figures.